Locating Social Justice in Higher Education Research

Also available from Bloomsbury

Academic Identities in Higher Education, Linda Evans and Jon Nixon
Aspirations, Education and Social Justice, Caroline Sarojini Hart
Assessment for Social Justice, Jan McArthur
Rethinking Knowledge within Higher Education, Jan McArthur

Locating Social Justice in Higher Education Research

Edited by
Jan McArthur and Paul Ashwin

BLOOMSBURY ACADEMIC
LONDON • NEW YORK • OXFORD • NEW DELHI • SYDNEY

Bloomsbury Academic
An imprint of Bloomsbury Publishing Plc
50 Bedford Square, London, WC1B 3DP, UK
1385 Broadway, 1 New York, NY 10018, USA
29 Earlsfort Terrace, Dublin 2, Ireland

www.bloomsbury.com, BLOOMSBURY and the Diana logo are trademarks of Bloomsbury Publishing Plc

First published 2020
This paperback edition published in 2021

© Jan McArthur and Paul Ashwin and contributors, 2020

Jan McArthur and Paul Ashwin have asserted their right under the Copyright, Designs and Patents Act, 1988, to be identified as Authors of this work.

Cover image: © johnason/iStock

All rights reserved. No part of this publication may be reproduced or transmitted in any form or by any means, electronic or mechanical, including photocopying, recording, or any information storage or retrieval system, without prior permission in writing from the publishers.

No responsibility for loss caused to any individual or organization acting on or refraining from action as a result of the material in this publication can be accepted by Bloomsbury or the author.

A catalogue record for this book is available from the British Library.

A catalog record for this book is available from the Library of Congress.

ISBN: HB: 978-1-3500-8675-3
PB: 978-1-3502-0969-5
ePDF: 978-1-3500-8676-0
ePUB: 978-1-3500-8677-7

Typeset by Deanta Global Publishing Services, Chennai

Contents

Acknowledgements vii
Author Biographies viii

Introduction: Locating Social Justice in Higher Education Research
Jan McArthur and Paul Ashwin 1

Part One Locating Social Justice in Higher Education Research and Policies

1 Bridging Near and Far Perspectives in Socially Just Higher Education Research *Jan McArthur* 23
2 New Public Management and Social Justice in Higher Education *Teresa Carvalho* 38
3 Researching Social Justice in Higher Education from Both Insider and Outsider Perspectives *Vicki Trowler* 53
4 Understanding Social Justice through the Lens of Research Impact across the Academy *Sharon McCulloch and Karin Tusting* 70

Part Two Locating Social Justice in Higher Education Pedagogies

5 Higher Education Research to Investigate Epistemic In/Justice *Monica McLean* 89
6 The Promise of Community-Based Research for Greater Social Justice through Higher Education *Carolin Kreber* 104
7 Twitter and Social Media as Critical Media Pedagogy 'Tools' in Higher Education *Natasa Lackovic* 119

Part Three Locating Social Justice in the Preparation of Graduates to Contribute to Societies

8 Engaging the Normative with the Analytical in Higher Education Research *Jennifer M. Case* 139
9 Developing Socially Responsible Graduates through Global Citizenship Programme *Sarah Goodier, Carren Duffy and Suki Goodman* 151

10 Developing Critical Citizens by Changing the Higher Education
    Curriculum *Langutani M. Masehela*   169
11 Human Flourishing and Child Protection in Teacher
    Education *Angela Fenton*   182

Part Four Conclusions

12 What Is Different about Socially Just Higher Education
    Research? *Paul Ashwin and Jan McArthur*   201

Index   215

Acknowledgements

The inspiration for this book was a Higher Education Close-up Conference (HECU8) held at Lancaster University, UK, in July 2016. Therefore, we hold a debt of thanks to all of those involved in this engaging and enjoyable conference. We would like to thank all of the participants who contributed to such thoughtful and stimulating conversations before, during and after the conference. Particular thanks goes to Alice Jesmont, whose exceptional care and organization ensured we had a collegial space in which to exchange and develop ideas. Thanks also goes to other members of the Department of Educational Research at Lancaster University who contributed to the conference in many ways – all of them greatly appreciated.

Author Biographies

Paul Ashwin is Professor of Higher Education, Lancaster University, UK. Paul's research focuses on teaching, learning and curriculum practices in higher education and how they are shaped by higher education policies. He is the lead author of *Reflective Teaching in Higher Education* (2015, Bloomsbury), which is designed for all of those working in higher education who are interested in further developing research-informed approaches to university teaching. Paul is a researcher in the ESRC- and HEFCE-funded 'Centre for Global Higher Education', a coordinating editor for the international journal *Higher Education* and co-editor of the Bloomsbury book series 'Understanding Student Experiences of Higher Education'.

Teresa Carvalho is Associate Professor at the University of Aveiro, Portugal, and Senior Researcher at CIPES (Center for Research in Higher Education Policies). She is a member of the ESA (European Sociological Association) Executive Committee and of the editorial team of the journal *Professions and Professionalism*. She develops research in public reforms and has a special interest in issues related with the role of professionals in formulating and implementing public policies. She has published her work in these areas in reference journals in the field of higher education and has also co-edited, with other colleagues, five international books.

Jennifer M. Case is Professor and Head of the Department of Engineering Education at Virginia Tech in the United States. Prior to her appointment in this post, she was a professor in the Department of Chemical Engineering at the University of Cape Town, where she retains an honorary appointment. She completed her postgraduate studies in the UK, Australia and South Africa. With more than two decades of undergraduate teaching and curriculum reform work, she is also a renowned researcher in engineering education and higher education. Her work, especially on the student experience of learning, as well as on topics around teaching and curriculum, has been widely published. She was the founding president of the South African Society for Engineering Education (SASEE). She is a coordinating editor for the international journal *Higher Education* and a co-editor for the Routledge/SRHE series Research into Higher Education.

Carren Duffy is Head of Section in Organisational Psychology, School of Management Studies, University of Cape Town, South Africa. She has supervised and graduated over fourteen Programme Evaluation Masters students. She holds a PhD in Programme Evaluation. Her PhD research focused on Organizational Learning and Training Evaluation in South Africa. Her evaluation interests lie in the areas of training evaluation, as well as programme theory. She has worked collaboratively on a few evaluation projects, investigating the design, implementation and immediate short-term outcomes of development programmes implemented in higher education institutions.

Angela Fenton has a Bachelor of Education with Honours from the University of Leeds, UK, and a Masters of Early Childhood Education from James Cook University (JCU) in Queensland, Australia. In her Doctoral thesis, Angela explored child protection and pre-service education using a strengths-based approach. Alongside her studies, Angela worked in early childhood classrooms and services for over twenty years as a teacher, director and training project officer. Angela has worked in inclusion roles with children with disabilities and was the state manager for the Indigenous Children's Services Unit in Queensland. She has taught in the UK and in Australia. In the tertiary sector of education, Angela has taught early childhood education in the TAFE and university sector for over ten years (at JCU previously and now for the ninth year with Charles Sturt University, NSW). Angela is passionate about teaching and researching in all sectors of education and values an interdisciplinary approach to collaborative learning.

Sarah Goodier is a Monitoring, Evaluation and Learning (MEL) consultant who works to provide evaluation support to a variety of funded projects, including in the Higher Education and International Development sectors. She has previously worked as a MEL specialist and an evaluation adviser at the Institute of Development Studies (UK) and the University of Cape Town (South Africa), respectively. She has a passion for data, science and research communication, and education. Sarah holds an MSc in Molecular and Cell Biology and an MPhil (Commerce) in Programme Evaluation.

Suki Goodman is Professor and Head of Department in the School of Management Studies, University of Cape Town, South Africa. Her research foci include organizational and individual learning, work–school enrichment and conflict and training and programme evaluation.

Carolin Kreber is Professor of Education and Dean, School of Professional Studies (Education and Health Sciences) at Cape Breton University in Nova Scotia, Canada. Prior to moving to CBU, she spent ten years as professor and chair of Teaching and Learning in higher education at Edinburgh University. Over the past two decades, she has published widely on issues related to higher education pedagogy, most recently *Educating for Civic-Mindedness* (authored book, 2017); 'The idea of a decent profession' (article, *Studies in Higher Education*, 2017) and "Cultivating authentic professional identities through transformative higher education: An application of Mezirow's comprehensive theory of adult learning" (chapter, in E. Kostara, A. Gavrielatos, and D. Loads (eds), *Transformative Learning Theory and Praxis; New Perspectives and Possibilities*, forthcoming).

Natasa Lackovic is Director of the Centre for Higher Education Research and Evaluation (CHERE) at Lancaster University. She is also a member of the Centre for Social Justice and Wellbeing, and the Centre for Technology Enhanced Learning. Her research interest broadly explores educational futures via new approaches to knowledge, research and pedagogy, including multimodality, visual and digital artefacts in education, semiotics, critical theory and media pedagogy. Natasa is also Director of Lancaster University's comics and graphic novels research, pedagogy and outreach network 'ReOPeN', which explores the role of illustration and image-based communication in pedagogy, research, engagement and outreach. She is interested in research topics such as art forms as mediators of communication (e.g. photographs, comics, videos); semiotic theory of learning and multimodal pedagogy; student and staff well-being and empowerment, education for sustainability, geo-social justice, peace and compassion; and new paradigms of student employment futures.

Langutani M. Masehela is a senior educational development practitioner and Head of the Academic Development Unit in the Centre for Higher Education Teaching and Learning at the University of Venda, South Africa. Langutani holds a Master's degree in Applied Linguistics from the University of Johannesburg and a PhD in Higher Education Studies from Rhodes University. After completing her PhD, she enrolled for a Postgraduate Diploma in Higher Education (for Academic Developers) with the same institution, Rhodes University. Her research interests are quality assurance in higher education teaching and learning, and student academic development in the higher education sector. The focus of her PhD study was to explore the conditions that constrain or enable academics from implementing quality assurance policies at the University of Venda.

Her current portfolio requires her to manage academic development programmes and projects for both academics and students at the University of Venda.

Jan McArthur is Senior Lecturer in Education and Social Justice in the Department of Educational Research, Lancaster University, UK. Her research focuses on the nature and purposes of higher education and how these relate to practices of teaching, learning and assessment. She has a particular interest in critical theory and in her published work explores the ideas of Theodor Adorno, Max Horkheimer and Axel Honneth, applying these to higher education. She has previously published a book exploring how Adorno's critical theory can inform our understanding of, and engagement with, knowledge in higher education for the purposes of greater social justice: *Rethinking Knowledge in Higher Education*. Her most recent book uses Honneth's conceptualization of mutual recognition to rethink the nature of assessment in higher education, where one is committed to greater social justice: *Assessment for Social Justice*.

Sharon McCulloch is Senior Lecturer at the University of Central Lancashire, UK, and Associate Lecturer at Lancaster University, UK. Her research interests lie in academic literacies as they pertain to both students and professional writers in higher education. She has published articles on student writing, specifically on voice and engagement with source material, and on professional writing, including the role of networked learning and the effects of research evaluation on academics' writing practices. She co-runs the British Association for Applied Linguistics special interest group on Professional, Academic and Work-Based Literacies.

Monica McLean is Professor of Higher Education in the School of Education at the University of Nottingham, UK. Her main area of expertise is university curriculum and pedagogy and their relationship to social justice. Research projects, both funded by the ESRC, have investigated the relevance of the capability approach to university-based professional education for the public good in South Africa and that of quality and inequality in social science departments in universities of different reputation in the UK. She is currently a co-investigator for an ESRC/DfID-funded project focused on raising the learning outcomes of rural and township youth in South Africa. Her books are *Pedagogy and the University: Critical Theory and Practice* (2008), *Professional Education, Capabilities and the Public Good* (2013) and *Quality in Undergraduate Education: How Powerful Knowledge Disrupts Inequalities* (2017).

Vicki Trowler has been unable to escape the gravitational pull of universities and has spent her entire adult life studying at, working at or researching higher education, in South Africa and the UK. Vicki has an MEd in Higher Education Studies from the University of the Western Cape, South Africa, and a PhD from the University of Edinburgh, UK. With research interests in social justice, alterity in higher education, engaging students, 'imagined communities' and student becoming, social media, differential outcomes and student geographies, she is currently a postdoctoral researcher at the University of Huddersfield, UK, seeking to understand the world of higher education in order to change it.

Karin Tusting is Professor of Linguistics and English Language at the Department of Linguistics and English Language, Lancaster University, UK. Her research interests are workplace writing, bureaucracy, accountability and identity. She has published in the areas of adult literacy, communities of practice, academic writing and linguistic ethnography. Her most recent book is *Academics Writing: The Dynamics of Knowledge Creation*, written with Sharon McCulloch, Ibrar Bhatt, David Barton and Mary Hamilton.

Introduction:
Locating Social Justice in Higher Education Research

Jan McArthur and Paul Ashwin

The title of this book alludes to an important metaphorical aspect running through it as we consider social justice and higher education research. The idea of 'locating' serves many purposes, including the philosophical, spatial, temporal and methodological ones. Locating also provides a dynamic dimension – a sense of an ongoing mission rather than simply an account of current practice. In this way, the varied contributions to this book offer glimpses of diverse elements of what it means to locate social justice within higher education research. These in turn offer insights into a number of key questions that unite our interests. What do we do differently when social justice is at the fore of what and how we research? Our position is that the research process itself is enhanced when informed by a commitment to social justice (Griffiths, 1998; McArthur, 2012). Should social justice inform all higher education research, or is it a specialist enclave? We see the answer to this lying in our understanding of the nature and purposes of higher education, for if they revolve around making a positive contribution to the social whole, then clearly social justice permeates all. If we see the purposes of higher education as extending far beyond only those who study or work within it (McArthur, 2013), then social justice is a core concern, and the aim of this book is to demonstrate its multiple locations within higher education practice and research.

Potentially this could mean that social justice can be located in any or all higher education research. But we do not want a conceptualization that is so nebulous that it loses meaning. The distinction to be made is that while social justice could inform any area of higher education research, it clearly does not always do so. While it seems unlikely that anyone would claim that their research is against social justice, there are those who argue that educational research should not have the explicit political agenda that, we argue, comes with the commitment to social justice (see, for example, Hammersley, 1995, 2000). It can sometimes seem that those who seek to unite social justice and education lie outside the mainstream of research and teaching (McLean, 2006). We offer a different perspective, and one that locates social justice front and centre in the practices of higher education, and our research of it.

Thus, locating social justice in higher education research also means that we locate such research in the social realm, encompassing the political, economic and cultural. While each of the contributions to this book focus on a different aspect of higher education, their focus is always, necessarily, outward looking because of the role played by social justice. Therefore, these contributions highlight an inherently two-way relationship between social justice and higher education research. We suggest that what this book offers is a range of insights into how this two-way relationship plays out, as well as the implications of this for those of us who both research in higher education and stand committed to greater social justice within and through higher education.

More than anything else, what binds this book together is our shared commitment to social justice. This is unashamedly passionate, radical research based on a belief that the current organization of society is unjust and that our role as higher education researchers is to contribute to the move towards greater social justice (McLean, 2006). As the subtitle of Morwenna Griffiths's fabulous book on social justice and educational research states, this is research that *gets off the fence* (Griffiths, 1998). What follows from this is that our location of social justice within higher education research is always about more than simply social justice as a research topic. In Chapter 3, Vicki Trowler explains that it is possible to have different positions about the relationship between research *into* and research *for* social justice. This is certainly true, and while it dismays us to acknowledge this, it is possible to do research with social justice as a topic but to lack the commitment to social justice itself. However, this is not true of this book. Each author, in their own way, reveals a passionate commitment to move social justice forward. Our chapters are not written as isolated pieces of research: they are intended to contribute to an ongoing discussion about how we can and should do things differently in higher education (and society) and the role of research in doing this.

The chapters in this book are a mixture of accounts *about* researching higher education and social justice and accounts *of* researching higher education and social justice. This mixture is deliberate as we seek to constantly be moving between theories and ideas and the realities of practice. Therefore, more than just being an edited book, this is a collaborative endeavour, and it stands as a collaboration not just between the authors, but between all of them and the reader. Those chapters which engage more with theory or philosophy provide lenses through which to understand better the chapters which deal with different examples of practice, while these chapters provide the examples which bring the theoretical insights to life. One thing we believe is clear in the range of contributions is that theory needs to speak with practice, as practice does with theory – and it is through that dialogue that we can further our understandings of social justice. Having contributions which are both examples of social justice research and explorations of what it means to locate social justice in higher education research enables us to continue this mediation between theory and practice.

Social justice brings with it a joint, mutually reinforcing embrace of both diversity and shared humanity. This has two important dimensions in this book. First, as indicated in the preceding paragraph, the authors of this book share a commitment to social justice and our own humanity, but we also make rather different contributions and we would like to celebrate this diversity. Secondly, what is true for this book is true for the social context in which it resides. Griffiths (2003) poses what she describes as an 'exhilarating' question: 'How is it possible to understand difference and diversity within a single humanity?' (p. 7). Indeed, she puts these dual aspects as central to her own understanding of social justice. A feature of the book, therefore, is the parallel unravelling of shared perspectives balanced with different approaches, foci and contexts. For us, the numerous dialogues that can, and hopefully will, sprout up between these differences are central to what we offer the reader.

Another unifying aspect of the book is the idea of 'close-up' research, and this is referred to in several places. This reflects, in part, the origins of this book in a conference held at Lancaster University, UK, in July 2016. This conference, held biannually, is known as the Higher Education Close-Up (HECU) conference and champions the close-up, in-depth, theoretically informed and qualitative research into this sector. But as McArthur argues in Chapter 1, we should not dichotomize close-up research with some other notion of far away. Even as close-up researchers, we are keen to situate our work in a broader social context and to make use of the important work of scholars in different traditions.

It is important to note that this book does not claim to offer an exhaustive exploration of all of the important issues relating to social justice and higher education research. It is particularly important to be clear that the chapters in the book do not offer in-depth analyses of the intersections between age, disabilities, ethnicities, genders, sexualities and social class in higher education. This is incredibly important work that is being taken forward by others (e.g. see Waller, Ingram and Ward, 2017; Arday and Mizra, 2018; Howell, 2018; Ngabaza et al., 2018; Walker, 2018) but is not the central focus of this book. Similarly, this book is not a research methods text, intended to outline the processes of researching social justice in higher education, although some chapters give helpful insights into the research approaches of the authors. In the general education sphere, there are already two excellent texts that offer guidance into research methods for social justice, and these are Morwenna Griffiths's *Educational Research for Social Justice* (Griffiths, 1998) and the recent book by Atkins and Duckworth, *Research Methods for Social Justice and Equity in Education* (Atkins & Duckworth, 2019). We would wholeheartedly recommend both as providing practical and philosophical insights into researching education and social justice. This book is complementary to these texts and offers something different with a specific focus on higher education.

Our focus on higher education shapes the encounters we explore in a number of ways. To give three examples, first, issues of power between the researcher and subject are arguably sometimes more diffuse and harder to capture in higher education than in school education. Second, the knowledge that students engage with at degree level often has a closer relationship to research than in other areas of education, and teachers in higher education often have identities as researchers or professional practitioners that they see as more important than their identities as teachers. Third, the role that policy makers envisage for higher education is very often different than for other areas of education. These differences between higher education and other kinds of education mean that issues of social justice tend to take a particular form in higher education.

As Griffiths (1998) has argued, having a commitment to social justice can actually improve research, rather than being seen as an impediment or distortion. Indeed, the contributions in this book share a perspective that our research is enhanced by a commitment to social justice. We would argue that such a commitment helps to make visible the partial or easily missed aspects of academic and social life. It renders more clearly the suffering and injustices that mainstream views may miss or wish to not acknowledge. This is why we can make a claim that higher education research with a social justice focus offers powerful insights into the academy and its place in society.

We now turn to consider in greater depth the different ways in which this book seeks to locate social justice in higher education research. Broadly, we consider these in terms of the philosophical, spatial, temporal and methodological dimensions, although clearly these aspects interrelate with one another.

Philosophical Perspectives – Meanings of Social Justice

Social justice is clearly a contested term, and the contributors in this book seek not to resolve this contestation but rather to make a contribution to its healthy continuance. There is no need to agree on a uniform definition, as such a stance would constrain thought and work against celebrating diversity. But we do, of course, need some provisional stability in terms of how we understand the broad area of social justice. In this section, we outline the unifying qualities of the ways in which social justice is understood in this book and the basis on which our shared dialogues can take place.

Social justice is a difficult term to pin down. It has a long antecedence which has witnessed a number of changes over time. We can begin our efforts to locate social justice as far back as Plato and Aristotle. What is really interesting in terms of the themes of this book is that Plato's influential discussion of social justice in *The Republic* clearly links education and social justice together (Griffiths, 2003). With Aristotle we then have the innate connection between social justice and political life. Then we can work through the Enlightenment tradition of Hume and Kant. And the most influential account in the modern era, with Rawls's *A Theory of Justice* (Rawls, 1971). But these are not the names that feature in this book and those which do point to a particular understanding of social justice. Thus, the theorists drawn on here include Sen and Nussbaum and the capabilities approach, Adorno's critical theory, Honneth as a third-generation critical theorist and Fricker's philosophical concept of epistemic justice.

In a moment we will explain what unites these different approaches to social justice, but first it is important to say something about why a conceptualization of social justice matters. What is meant here is not the 'buzzword' (Atkins & Duckworth, 2019; Jones, 2006) use of social justice which increasingly permeates policy statements or political speeches. Griffiths (2003) warns of the danger of social justice becoming such a general term that it loses potency and simply slides over the 'difficult, political practical issues' (p. 41).

We do not use social justice as a 'feel-good' term but as a rigorous theoretical concept that illuminates our understandings of the social world. Therefore, different theories may illuminate different aspects, such as, for example, if we compare the work of Honneth and Fricker, Honneth foregrounds mutual recognition as the foundation on which all social justice is nurtured, and his work has a clearly relational character to it. Fricker's work is different to Honneth, but in a way that is complementary as she focuses on a specific form of justice – the epistemic – in a way that is also relational as it refers to how different people are enabled to engage with knowledge.

We want to celebrate these different theoretical perspectives, but we also believe that they coalesce around some common themes in the understandings of social justice they suggest. McArthur (2013) has outlined four aspects of social justice which she argues are fundamental to a critical, transformative approach, and these are helpful in understanding what unites the contributions in this book. She argues that a *critical* understanding of social justice is one with clear radical intent, and we suggest the four aspects identified reflect the understandings of social justice in this book.

First, social justice is understood as a multifaceted term, 'which defies easy or simple definitions' (p. 24). Certainly, the understandings of social justice running through this book are nuanced and complex. They can, as in Lackovic's chapter, involve bringing diverse bodies of literature together to address modern social justice issues. Indeed, such complexity and the lack of an easy definition are very much at the heart of both critical theory and the capabilities approach. A key reason why social justice must be understood in a multifaceted way lies in ensuring recognition of the complex intersectionalities that make up human experience and the social world. It can be argued that social justice was once seen in a more one-dimensional way as, for example, related to social class or gender in isolation. Indeed Griffiths (2003) argues that when we finally looked beyond associating social justice solely with social class in the 1970s and 1980s and focused on race and gender, we did so at the expense of social class. Over time, however, a myriad of intersectionalities has come to be embraced by what we mean by social justice. Now our understandings roam across the diverse characteristics that make up both individual and social experience. Indeed, Nancy Fraser (1997) refers to the 'unsurpassable gain' made by debate moving from individual differences to 'multiple intersecting differences'; however, such a gain does not void the need to continue the debate about equality and difference: 'We need, in other words, to reconnect the problematic of cultural difference with the problematic of social equality' (p. 187).

Secondly, there exists a belief that social justice is about both process and outcomes. This view rejects both the process domination of certain procedural or social contract approaches to social justice and a focus on outcomes alone which does not recognize the ways in which those outcomes are shaped by the processes that bring them about. This is something explored explicitly by both Sen and Nussbaum and their work on the capabilities approach. Sometimes the capabilities approach is referred to as an 'outcomes-based' understanding of social justice, and the reason for this is clear in the emphasis upon the lived realities of people's lives, and also in comparison with traditional procedural approaches to social justice. But Sen (2010) makes clear that procedures are important, but they are simply not ends in themselves. In her critique of Rawls, Nussbaum (2006) also makes this point about procedure and outcome. Similarly, in her distinction between testimonial epistemic injustice and hermeneutical epistemic injustice, Fricker (2007) demonstrates the importance of how knowledge is engaged with and the outcomes of that engagement in terms of social justice.

Thirdly, social justice is understood as being 'grounded in relationships between people, and achieved through those relationships' (p. 24). Fricker's understanding of epistemic injustice, for example, makes this clear in the ways in which access to knowledge is not a technical skill but a social relation mediated by human interactions. Similarly, at the heart of Honneth's critical theory is the idea of mutual recognition, and as such social justice is rooted in the relationships between people. In this book, we see this theme played out in many ways. For example, it features in Vicki Trowler's examination of insider/outsider research, Jenni Case's reflections on higher education in South Africa and Angela Fenton's analysis of research into incorporating child protection into initial teaching education.

Finally, the theoretical influences informing this book share an 'an imperfect understanding of social justice, such that our goal is to aspire to more justice and less injustice rather than some perfect state of "social justice"' (p. 24). Sen (2010) leads the way for many of us in making the case that justice need not be perfect. Importantly, this is a feature of both the more theoretical and the more empirical contributions in this book. For the latter, this imperfection is easy to see in the messy nature of the social world, and the implication of this is an urgency to move forward with progressive social change, not just debate on the sidelines. This is what Sen meant: we don't need to wait to have a perfect notion of social justice when much injustice is simply fundamentally apparent and in need of change. However, in keeping with the critical nature of his thought, Sen is clearly not eschewing the theoretical and philosophical exploration of social justice. What he is doing is emphasizing the folly of perfecting a definition of an idea that Adorno would describe as a necessarily imperfect concept, in the sense that trying to tie social justice down to a perfect definition necessarily loses so much of what we actually mean by social justice: the concept will always be more complex and messy than any definition of it.

There is a further dimension of social justice which we can add to the four characteristics outlined by McArthur and which is central to the themes of this book. This is the idea that a theory of social justice should be useful for action. Here we return to the interrelationship between theory and practice that runs through this book. All of these critical approaches to social justice go beyond simply illuminating what 'is' and offer insights into what could be, and how we get from here to there. In this way, this book is about changing the location of higher education: of movement towards greater social justice.

Locations of Social Justice and Injustice

We explore social justice in higher education research in a number of national settings and in different institutional contexts while being aware that what we offer here is just a glimpse of the international diversity that exists. But we believe that the insights we provide in this book can be taken and recontextualized, debated and engaged with by people in other contexts. Our authors are spread over four continents, and the book includes contributions from South Africa, the United States, Canada, Portugal, UK and Australia. There are commonalities across these locations, as well as differences between them. Some are former colonial powers and other former colonies, and such histories have shaped both society and higher education. In addition, each national community has its own diversity and often many parts. How one recognizes these locales can itself be a social justice issue subject to considerable debate. For example, with the rise of calls for Scottish independence and for the unification of Ireland, the description 'UK' is itself highly politicized.

In terms of national settings, a particular feature of the book is a number of contributions from South Africa or written by South Africans. This is partly a coincidence, but it illuminates some important issues concerning social justice and higher education because in South Africa we see in sharp relief the issues around what it means to locate higher education itself in a social justice context. We can see the challenges in realizing social justice in ways that are both inclusive and diverse. The stark realities of injustice are also close in space and time for South Africa as the country deals with the enduring legacy of multiple injustices from both the apartheid era and colonialism. South African higher education is located in a society in which social justice is a key part of civic discourse, and it has unique pressures to change. As such, these South African perspectives add rich insights into the theme of this book.

Another coincidence that is worthy of mention is that all the authors of this book are women, with the exception of one of the editors/authors. This is something we celebrate but which also gives us pause to reflect on what the implications might be. In part, we suggest, the situation it reflects is demographic as education is a field with a high proportion of women. Nonetheless, with historical forces at play, women's voices are not necessarily those most heard – or loudest – in this research community. In many of the countries that feature in this book, the problem of a gender pay gap is still evident, as are entrenched disparities in promotion opportunities, research funding and other forms of career advancement. Indeed, in Chapter 2, Teresa Carvalho explicitly considers the impact of neoliberal management approaches to women's career experiences and trajectories. In the rest of the book where gender may not be an explicit focus, it nevertheless informs all that we do and intersects with issues of social class, race, marginalization and separation.

We have already outlined how the location of this book in the literal sense ranges over different national contexts. But there are other ways of understanding place and the location of ourselves and our research. Many of the chapters in this book have a self-conscious sense of the idea of location. In Chapter 1, Jan McArthur explores the social justice implications of conceptions of being near or far and considers the distortions and hostile relationships that can arise from perceived distance and separation. This idea of near and far is taken up in another way by Sarah Goodier, Carren Duffy and Suki Goodman (Chapter 9) who draw our attention to the global sphere and the concept of global citizenship, its implications and the relationship between the local and global. Within nations, there can also be fundamental local differences. In South Africa, for example, the distinction between urban and rural is important, and in Chapter 10, Langutani Masehela provides insights into a historically disadvantaged rural university.

There are, therefore, numerous ways of thinking about location, including Vicki Trowler's (Chapter 3) analysis of insider–outsider research and what it can mean to be an insider. Indeed, she demonstrates the multiple levels on which the idea of insider research can play out and raises important issues about how to do such research in just ways. Place is important in Sharon McCulloch and Karin Tusting's Chapter 4 in the sense of the location of higher education within society. How is research different if one explicitly looks to locate it within broader society? In relation to a different kind of place, Natasa Lackovic (Chapter 7) takes us into the virtual realm and the domain of social media, while Carolin Kreber (Chapter 6) focuses on community-based research and what it offers for higher education and social justice bringing in students as research partners. The aim for Kreber is to focus on the public space that is critical for freedom and social justice. Teresa Carvalho (Chapter 2) considers the whole higher education landscape and how it is shaped by neoliberal management practices.

In one way or another, all chapters consider how we place ourselves in the social world to which we belong, because that is the essence of how we understand – and live – a commitment to social justice. These are not research projects that objectify and distance the research participants from ourselves as researchers. We are also, arguably, emotionally close-up in the sense of caring deeply about what we research and write about.

This highlights the social justice implications of a sense of place. Part of this also has to consider our place as researchers in relation to those whom we research. Later we will consider this in terms of methodology, but there is a broader point to be made here about perspective and about the different ways in which we are positioned in higher education compared with those who may be the focus of research. The challenge for social justice researchers again comes back to the theme of similarity and difference. We need a heightened sensitivity to how we may be positioned differently to our research subjects, but also how they may be positioned differently to one another even though they may appear to be studying the same discipline or at the same university or belong to the same social group. A social justice perspective takes particular care to avoid what is known as 'othering', in other words the imposition of an identity on someone else on the basis of real or assumed differences between them and ourselves.

But the other thing to be watchful of is the idea of identity appropriation. Here Vicki Trowler (Chapter 3) draws our attention to the dangers of appropriating the experiences of the subaltern – the marginalized in higher education and society. Sometimes, it might be more socially just *not* to research a particular group or phenomenon and to give way instead so that such a group can research themselves, for their own good. In making this observation, Trowler highlights the relative privilege among many of those who work and research in higher education. For example, should people who are white and/or not South African build careers studying the experiences of black academics in South Africa? The answer is not simple and brings us back to the issue McArthur raises about harmful separations. White academics in the global north do experience privilege in comparison, for example, to black academics in the global south. But we also have a shared humanity and with that a shared commitment to social justice. Retreating into our silos is not the answer – but locating the right approach requires sensitivity, reflectivity and self-awareness.

It could, therefore, be argued that social justice research in higher education has a particularly collaborative character. Not simply in the sense that there might be two or more researchers or research teams, but in the broader sense that we cannot do it justice working in isolation, or from just one perspective or location. A good example of this was a recent Economic and Social Research Council, UK, and National Research Foundation, South Africa, funded project between South Africa and the UK. Known as the 'Pathways to personal and public good: understanding access to, student experiences of, and outcomes from South African undergraduate higher education', this project was a collaboration between higher education researchers in South Africa and the UK, with a particular emphasis on encouraging and developing newer researchers. It aimed to give people from varied backgrounds the skills and experience to research their own practice and to understand that in relation to others. (For more on this project see the edited book, Ashwin & Case, 2018.)

Locating Moments of Social Justice and Injustice

Locating social justice in different temporal moments raises another series of issues and challenges. On a macro level, we need to consider the systems of higher education which dominate today across our national areas and beyond. Clearly there are two trends here worth highlighting. The first is internationalization. More than ever before, higher education providers look to position themselves in a global scene, offer their provision across national borders and seek the esteem and prestige that come with global rankings. The second trend which shapes higher education today at the macro level is the relationship between the sector and economic interests. Clearly, these two factors are mutually reinforcing.

Higher education has always had an economic role, right from the origins of the university in elite artisan guilds (Kivinen & Poikus, 2006). But over time, we have seen different phases characterized by different relationships between economic and social purposes and also differing understandings of what counts as an economic role. A sense of privileging certain parts of society arguably runs through the history of the university, from its origins. Even the much feted Humboltian tradition was linked to the development of people to support the functioning of the prevailing civil society. Today, what characterizes higher education in relation to an economic role is twofold. First, universities are positioning themselves as competitive economic actors in an international market. Universities are increasingly run along business lines, and marketization, placing the university as a distinctive player in a competitive setting, is the norm. Moves to make higher education more financially robust and accountable could potentially be done in the name of greater social justice but not if undertaken solely in a profit-driven mindset. Here such moves undermine social justice, distorting the particular functions of higher education, namely the generation of, and engagement with, complex, contested and dynamic forms of knowledge (McArthur, 2013). Secondly, if we consider the economic role of the university looking outward to society, then it has again become more narrow in its conceptualization and outlook. What counts as 'the economy', albeit often implicitly, is taken to mean the interests of government, large business and the economically powerful (McArthur, 2011). This is the social justice issue – the selective narrowness of the link between higher education and economic interests, and this issue is explored by Carvalho in Chapter 2.

This book is therefore situated in a time of higher education that is hugely problematic from a social justice perspective and arguably hostile to affording genuine, progressive social change. While this perspective may seem based in a Western setting and the context of the global north, we would argue the pressures of marketization and commodification are necessarily international ones and they will, perhaps in different ways, impact on higher education in diverse settings. The key social justice issue, which is to promote an understanding of economic and social well-being that includes all members of society, including the poor and the marginalized, is a universal one.

One striking aspect of higher education today is the differentiation within the sector, often along lines of historically advantaged and disadvantaged institutions. Attempts to provide a competitive marketplace of higher education, such as in the UK, arguably increase this differentiation. However, as Monica McLean (Chapter 5) illustrates, there are some considerable myths around this differentiation. Here, she draws on her work with Paul Ashwin and Andrea Abbas (2018) and looks at experiences of sociology students in very different UK universities. Their work makes it clear that relative (usually historically endowed) prestige does not translate into qualitatively different engagement with knowledge or greater levels of personal transformation. However, while the prestige and history of a university tell us nothing about the quality of the education that it offers, many employers, students, government ministers judge the quality of a degree by these very factors. Given that more prestigious universities tend to admit a higher proportion of privileged students, this distortion has profound implications for the role of higher education in promoting social justice.

Our chapters based in the South African context also reveal the experience of historically advantaged and disadvantaged institutions and that the current higher education sector is still rife with these divisions and resultant injustices.

Indeed, this is one of the reasons why South Africa is so illuminating from a social justice perspective, because the stark levels of inequality allow us to see so clearly how entrenched historically imbued privilege can be. Jenni Case (Chapter 8) provides some rich insights here with her perspective on post-apartheid higher education in South Africa. Indeed, she argues that social justice has only relatively recently been located within South African higher education, although we can see from the contributions to this book that it is now a major concern.

Monica McLean (Chapter 5) introduces a further temporal dimension as she outlines the three phases in which injustice can occur within higher education, here focusing on the experiences of students. These three phases include coming into higher education (access), being at university (participation) and leaving university for life beyond (outcomes). In so doing, McLean demonstrates that we have to go beyond simple associations of social justice in higher education with access alone – a point also made by Carolin Kreber (Chapter 6). McLean highlights the dynamic nature of the student experience, and this is something we as researchers committed to social justice need to take particular care with. We must be alert that we never research static phenomenon but rather processes of personal and intellectual development and change. This is not to prejudge whether students experience this positively or negatively; as a student who fails to flourish at university can still be changed by the experience.

The Methodological Challenges of Locating Social Justice

A question which underpins and unites the varied contributions to this book revolves around what it means to locate social justice in higher education research? What should we do differently? What should we take care to avoid? The implication is, therefore, that to locate social justice within higher education research is to necessarily influence the manner and processes of that research. Remembering here, that what unites this book is the fact that these are not simply accounts about social justice, but contributions aimed to actively further social justice.

Atkins and Duckworth (2019) argue that social justice research must clearly demonstrate that social justice is at the heart of both its purpose and its process. It is therefore worth spending a little time on the issue of methodology and the role it plays in social justice research, for Atkins and Duckworth also argue that power should play a central role in methodological debates. This is demonstrated in Chapter 3 as Vicki Trowler reflects on her own position as a researcher and her relationship with those she is researching. This sense of self-awareness (and potentially even self-criticism) as a researcher seems central to social justice research. Research in higher education is different from secondary or primary education. Our students are adults, at university to develop increasingly independent, autonomous lives. The power relationships between academics and students, while still manifestly present, are different. This raises different issues for social justice research. It also raises possibilities, such as those in Carolin Kreber's exploration of community-based research (Chapter 6).

Similarly, as Griffiths (1998) argues, any epistemology is linked to power relations. Griffiths argues that even the use of technical, and sometimes intimidating, terms such as 'epistemology' has significant social justice implications. Most importantly, it relates to whether or not we see, and accept, a divide where some sorts of knowledge are for an elite only, and other sorts of knowledge (and terminology) for the great masses. This position has strong resonance with Monica McLean's (Chapter 5) discussion of epistemic injustice and the work of Miranda Fricker. Indeed, from the perspective of decolonization, we also need to consider the extent to which Western epistemological paradigms have dominated and distorted our knowledge of the social world.

We mentioned earlier in this chapter that some writers, such as Hammersley (1995, 2000), argue against the politicization of research. However, our position is that social justice requires a normative commitment and that this makes any claims to neutrality in our research simply invalid. Certainly, we reject the association of neutrality with rigour and argue that the critical forms of reflexivity, which are a feature of the contributions to this book, carry with them a necessary form of research robustness.

Overview of This Book

Part One – Locating Social Justice in Higher Education Research and Policies

Chapter 1 is based on the critical theory of the Frankfurt School, and particularly early critical theorist Theodor Adorno. In this chapter, Jan McArthur uses Adorno's understanding of a critical form of dialecticism to critique many common dichotomies, such as the divide between qualitative and quantitative approaches, in higher education and in higher education research. She calls these 'perilous dichotomies' because they risk distorting the nuanced complexity of the social world and as such promote rather than ameliorate social injustice. In their place, she offers Adorno's negative dialectics as a way to better understand the research challenges that face higher education. But more than this, McArthur argues that the understanding of social justice that emerges from Adorno's critical theory offers a path to understanding which can improve the, always imperfect, processes of research. On this basis, we research differently with a social justice commitment because our perspectives on phenomena such as student–teacher relationships or the purposes of higher education are shaped by this dialecticism.

Chapter 2 focuses on the implications of neoliberalism, and particularly new public management (NPM) to higher education, through the lens of social justice. Teresa Carvalho explores the ways in which these forces have shaped higher education as a workplace and the social justice ramifications of this. She particularly highlights issues of gender and age to demonstrate the ways in which neoliberal reform has led to a divided workforce with a privileged elite, on the one hand, and many subjected to stressful and difficult work practices with few opportunities, on the other.

As already touched upon, Chapter 3 by Vicki Trowler considers issues of power which surface when researching for, or about, social justice in higher education. Trowler questions the political choice made to focus research on particular, relatively marginalized groups such as women or second-language speakers. The problem identified by Trowler lies in the appropriation of the experiences of others, even when we think they may be similar to us. Thus, Trowler problematizes the very notion of insider or outsider research and demonstrates, through a series of different research projects, the fluidity of these concepts and the need for vigilance in how one positions oneself against one's research subject, particularly when researching in the name of social justice.

Chapter 4 by Sharon McCulloch and Karin Tusting is important for the ways in which it locates social justice research in another location – and this is the public assessment of research excellence, such as through the UK Research Excellence Framework (REF). This is a third space for research in one way, beyond the realm of the researchers themselves and distinct from broader society. But it is also a contested space and, arguably, a dangerous one for academics. Indeed, the challenges of positioning research as both 'REFable' and linked to social impact are discussed. In this chapter, the authors draw a link to a further location – academic writing – and consider how social justice is located in the ways in which academics go about their writing. They also consider disciplinary spaces – and that the researcher's location within different disciplines can have an impact upon how research is oriented with social justice. Here they consider the extent to which research should exist beyond the university and be explicitly aimed towards the furtherance of social justice.

Part Two – Locating Social Justice in Higher Education Pedagogies

In Chapter 5, Monica McLean locates social justice within the framework of Fricker's concept of epistemic in/justice as she considers what it means for different students to participate in higher education. Here social justice, or injustice, is located in the nature of knowledge itself and which forms of knowledge are privileged in society. In drawing on Bourdieu (among others) to understand the different experiences of working-class and middle-class students, McLean uses concepts such as field and habitus to convey the barriers working-class students face locating themselves within higher education.

Chapter 6 by Carolin Kreber turns our gaze to who is actually involved in research into higher education. She argues that community-based research is both a powerful pedagogy and an expression of professional practice which has strong social justice associations. Drawing on Nussbaum's capabilities approach, Kreber considers the ways in which certain capabilities can be promoted through community-based research. She brings this together with Hannah Arendt's notion of action to demonstrate how participation in community-based research can prepare our graduates (future professionals) to make a contribution to the social whole of benefit to everyone, not simply any elite.

In Chapter 7, Natasa Lackovic takes our location beyond the physical bricks and mortar of the university and into the realm of social media to consider the opportunities for justice afforded by engagement with social media, particularly Twitter. McArthur's theme of dichotomization is also taken up by Lackovic in her discussion of the non-neutrality of social media and the implications of implied 'whiteness' or 'blackness' leading, respectively, to positive or negative associations. Lackovic argues that the 'othering' of different groups rests on these types of dichotomies to establish differences. What Lackovic offers is a reinterpretation of critical pedagogy relevant to a world in which social media plays a major part, and which therefore has to be key to broader understandings of social justice.

Part Three – Locating Social Justice in the Preparation of Graduates to Contribute to Societies

In Chapter 8, Jenni Case offers a warning against the dominance of notions of social justice grounded in the contexts of powerful Western countries such as the United States and the United Kingdom. Using South Africa as her example, Case considers the role of the university in society and particularly its important function in producing new knowledge and a highly educated citizenry who can contribute to progressive social change. She draws on key postcolonial authors to demonstrate the dangers of overly ideological approaches to higher education. Case then considers the ways in which scholars of education can respond to these challenges. She calls for research that is both close-up and is located carefully in an historical and social context.

Chapter 9 by Sarah Goodier, Carren Duffy and Suki Goodman also highlights the idea of perspective introduced by McArthur as they argue for the interconnections between global issues and local communities. Goodier et al position global citizenship as central to our understanding of social justice. What Goodier et al demonstrate is that even when our focus is global, local context matters, as in their discussion of global citizenship education in South Africa. The authors therefore continue the theme found in other chapters, of seeking to locate what happens within higher education within broader society. Through a critical review of the literature on global citizenship across different countries, the authors are able to locate the unique South African experience and to shed light on the factors which can promote success and thereby contribute to social justice.

In Chapter 10, Langutani Masehela provides another rich insight from the South African context. Where Case asks the questions about what social justice role higher education should have, Masehela offers a distinctive answer in terms of the role of the curriculum in preparing students for social participation, including employment. Here, her focus, like Kreber's in Chapter 6, is on what comes of students once they leave higher education? How do we know how higher education has helped prepare them for life beyond? And is this preparation attuned to social justice? Using Sen's capabilities approach, Masehela explores how the curriculum can be rethought, reimagined, to support this social justice role. While highlighting a range of different subjectivities that impact students' experiences, Masehela's work has a particular focus on rural-based universities that attract students from low economic backgrounds, whose earlier generations may have possessed less formal education.

With Angela Fenton in Chapter 11, we move to a specific aspect of teacher education, that of child protection. After Masehela's overarching argument for the importance of nurturing good citizens through teaching education, Fenton offers a specific example of what is involved and of the social justice challenges. In both cases, Fenton and Masehela's, what is foregrounded is the university's responsibility to prepare not only future citizens but also citizens committed to social justice. Fenton discusses a timely and important issue in considering how best to prepare trainee teachers to deal with the complex issues of child protection.

Part Four – Conclusions

Finally, Chapter 12 acts as a conclusion to the book, reflecting on the major themes and questions arising from the chapters as a whole. In this chapter, we focus on considering what the chapters tell us about what we do differently when social justice is at the fore of what and how we research. We draw on Bernstein's (2000) notion of the 'pedagogic device' to explore how issues of social justice are implicated in the production of knowledge through higher education research, the transformation of knowledge into higher education curricula and who students become through their engagement with this knowledge. We conclude by considering the additional commitments that are required when we seek to locate social justice in higher education.

* * *

This book is testament to the shared commitment of all its authors to furthering social justice within and through higher education and the place of research in doing this. The beauty of an edited book lies in the diverse perspectives it brings together. We would position this book as a celebration of both difference and shared humanity. As the reader works through the book, different perspectives will become evident, but so too will shared conversations. We hope this book provides some intellectual stimulation that helps these shared conversations to develop and grow.

References

Arday, J., & Mirza, H. S. (Eds.). (2018). *Dismantling Race in Higher Education: Racism, Whiteness and Decolonising the Academy*. Cham, Switzerland: Palgrave Macmillan.

Ashwin, P., & Case, J. (Eds.). (2018). *Higher Education Pathways: South African Undergraduate Education and the Public Good*. Cape Town: African Minds.

Atkins, L., & Duckworth, V. (2019). *Research Methods for Social Justice and Equity in Education*. London: Bloomsbury.

Bernstein, B. (2000). *Pedagogy, Symbolic Control and Identity: Theory, Research and Critique*. Revised Edition. Oxford: Rowman and Littlefield Publishers.

Fraser, N. (1997). *Justice Interruptus*. New York: Routledge.
Fricker, M. (2007). *Epistemic Injustice*. Oxford: Oxford University Press.
Griffiths, M. (1998). *Educational Research for Social Justice*. Buckingham: Open University Press.
Griffiths, M. (2003). *Action for Social Justice in Education*. Maidenhead: Open University Press.
Hammersley, M. (1995). *The Politics of Social Research*. London: Sage.
Hammersley, M. (2000). *Taking Sides in Social Research*. London: Routledge.
Howell, C. (2018). Participation of students with disabilities in South African higher education: Contesting the uncontested. In N. Singal, P. Lynch, & S. T. Johansson (Eds.), *Education and Disability in the Global South: New Perspectives from Africa and Asia*, 127–143. London: Bloomsbury.
Jones, C. (2006). Falling between the Cracks: What diversity means for black women in higher education. *Policy Futures in Education*, 4(2), 145–159.
Kivinen, O., & Poikus, P. (2006). Privileges of *Universitas Magistrorum et Scolarium* and their justification in charters of foundation from the 13th to the 21st centuries. *Higher Education*, 52(2), 185–213.
McArthur, J. (2011). Reconsidering the social and economic purposes of higher education. *Higher Education Research & Development*, 30(6), 737–749.
McArthur, J. (2012). Virtuous mess and wicked clarity: Struggle in Higher Education Research. *Higher Education Research & Development*, 31(3), 419–430.
McArthur, J. (2013). *Rethinking Knowledge in Higher Education: Adorno and Social Justice*. London: Bloomsbury.
McLean, M. (2006). *Pedagogy and the University*. London and New York, NY: Continuum.
McLean, M., Abbas, A., & Ashwin, P. (2018). *Quality in Undergraduate Education: How Powerful Knowledge Disrupts Inequality*. London: Bloomsbury.
Ngabaza, S., Shefer, T., & Clowes, L. (2018). Students' narratives on gender and sexuality in the project of social justice and belonging in higher education. *South African Journal of Higher Education*, 32(3), 139–153.
Nussbaum, M. C. (2006). *Frontiers of Justice*. Cambridge, MA: Belknap Press of Harvard University Press.
Rawls, J. (1971). *A Theory of Justice*. Cambridge, MA: Belknap Press of Harvard University Press.
Sen, A. (2010). *The Idea of Justice*. London: Penguin.
Walker, M. (2018). Aspirations and equality in higher education: Gender in a South African University. *Cambridge Journal of Education*, 48(1), 123–139.
Waller, R., Ingram, N., & Ward, M. R. (Eds.). (2017). *Higher Education and Social Inequalities: University Admissions, Experiences, and Outcomes*. London: Routledge.

Part One

Locating Social Justice in Higher Education Research and Policies

1

Bridging Near and Far Perspectives in Socially Just Higher Education Research

Jan McArthur

Introduction

Perspective is a social justice issue. The astronomer and popular science writer Carl Sagan draws our attention to perspectives when he describes the earth and its position in the universe:

> The Earth is a very small stage in a vast cosmic arena. Think of the endless cruelties visited by the inhabitants of one corner of this pixel on the scarcely distinguishable inhabitants of some other corner, how frequent their misunderstandings, how eager they are to kill one another, how fervent their hatreds. Think of the rivers of blood spilled by all those generals and emperors so that, in glory and triumph, they could become the momentary masters of a fraction of a dot. (Sagan, 1994, p. 6)

A commitment to social justice requires an appreciation of alternative perspectives and the interplays between these vantage points. Social justice requires a recognition that we are bound by commonalities that are both large and minute and similarly distinguished by diverse and eccentric differences: an overemphasis on one or the other leads to distortions and pathologies and in their name grave social injustices.

As the earlier quote suggests, we can gain perspective and thus greater understanding through knowing the difference between close and far; the enormity of the cosmos evokes an intimacy within life on earth we might otherwise miss. However, we can also be mistaken – and through such mistakes distort what there is to know and act in unjust ways. This is the case with Sagan's generals and emperors; they hold a distorted sense of distance that enables them to deny mutual recognition of each other's shared humanity, and thus to justify their own acts of terror. This is a story still familiar today. To deny or misrepresent recognition to another is to do injustice.

In this chapter, I argue that bridging these perspectives of near and far is both a central purpose for higher education research committed to social justice, and made possible by the mediating role that a commitment to social justice brings. In particular, I draw on the critical theory of the Frankfurt School to inform both my understanding of social justice and its location in higher education research. My argument is in two parts. First, I discuss the problem of dichotomization of the social world in our approaches to research and how this can reduce our ability to see and comprehend issues and understandings core to social justice research. Next, I outline how research undertaken in the spirit of critical theory's dialectics can avoid such problems and take us further in our goal towards both greater social justice and deepening our understandings of higher education. Finally, I consider several areas of higher education research and the relative roles of dichotomization and dialectics in understanding these areas. In particular, I consider how we understand student identity and our conceptualizations of the purposes of higher education. I argue that the mediating role of a critical theory approach to social justice, which encourages a radical dialecticism, can enhance the research we do by ensuring a more diverse, inclusive and robust understanding of the phenomena we research. Most important is a commitment that justice should never just be a topic of research. Social justice embraces the motivation, means, approach and focus of our research. Social justice must exist in our philosophies, relationships and demeanour as we research. To research social justice within higher education is to embody the principles of social justice in our actions and thoughts, our relationships and dispositions and our methods and methodologies. There is, therefore, no dichotomization of what we research and how we research; each informs the other and each is as important as the other.

Perilous Dichotomies

I begin my argument by emphasizing that a commitment to social justice when researching higher education demands that we avoid imposing artificial distance or harmful separations as these represent misdirections of our perceptions of the world in which we live. In addition, they consequently can lead to greater injustice as they misrepresent the experiences of diverse groups and individuals within higher education and society. I argue that social justice, understood from a critical theory perspective, illuminates the need to breach these separations and, indeed, shines light on how that can be done, and I elaborate on this way forward in the next section when I consider dialectics and the research process.

The distances and separations I refer to are represented by a number of common dichotomies to be found in the research methods literature and the higher education literature. Key among these are qualitative and quantitative, individual and social, conceptual and empirical, structure and agency and theory and practice. The problem with these enduring dichotomies is that they ghettoize, distort and put a veil over the richness of what can be known. They can also impair understandings of power relations and their impact, especially those nurtured by artificial separations. Seen through the lens of a critical theory approach to social justice, such dichotomies are revealed as fictions. In this section, I consider the dichotomies that apply to *how* we research. Then, in the final section of this chapter, I consider some examples of dichotomization of *what* we research and the associated benefits of a more dialectical approach.

Arguably the most common dichotomy in social science research is the qualitative–quantitative divide. Sometimes, qualitative and quantitative are used almost as synonyms for the close-up and the large scale. Similarly, the conflation of quantitative and positivism and qualitative and interpretivism severely hampers the social justice project. The term 'mixed methods' also often only serves to reinforce the dichotomy, affirming that there is some inherent difference here that must be revered and canonized. Qualitative researchers have done themselves no favours by perpetuating stereotypes of the quantitative 'other'. I still read far too many papers that begin their methodology along the lines 'because I am not a positivist I am going to do small-scale, qualitative research' and therefore pity anyone who does quantitative research for they then bear the mark of the positivist!

We are wrong to decree that positivists monopolize numbers: social justice is located in quantitative research, and furthered through it, every bit as much as in qualitative. All we are talking about here are numbers and words. Neither binds us to particular world views; neither absolves us of responsibility for thinking through the nature and implications of our own research dispositions and actions. Dichotomization is a form of *othering* – a form of epistemological power through false separation. It is also a form of not taking responsibility and is thus anathema to a social justice commitment. For example, I might be concerned about the plight of individual students from working-class backgrounds; thus, I position myself as a close-up, qualitative researcher. But this makes no sense, for the individual and the group cannot be sheared apart for analytical purposes. This serves to truncate identity, and hence works against social justice.

I suggest that it is necessary to openly embrace a range of approaches to researching higher education in order to ensure we fulfil the promise of social justice. This need not mean that each of us individually does a little bit of everything, but rather that we all *engage* with diverse and varied forms of research when we seek to understand our social world. We have to understand that social justice is a communal research project, in which we all play different contributing parts. Close-up research is clearly key to revealing and understanding the minutiae of commonalities and differences that so eluded Sagan's generals and emperors, and which I fear continue to elude many of their current day counterparts – political leaders, captains of industry, the rich and the powerful. However, it cannot do this alone or in isolation. As close-up researchers, we need to consider our relationships with large-scale, survey work, for example. In Britain, research such as that undertaken by Charles Booth and Seebhom Rowntree in the nineteenth and twentieth centuries laid bare the extent of poverty and also demonstrated the fallacious nature of assertions at the time that poverty was somehow a lifestyle choice: it changed social opinion and public policy. Even so, such research can only provide one facet of the experience. Other forms of research and historical analysis – such as E. P. Thompson's later, *The Making of the English Working Class* (1963) – provide the complementary close-up insights. The raw pain of losing a child, the endless fatigue of working for scraps – all these are there in the work of Booth and Rowntree but are illuminated in different ways by Thompson. Both works draw our attention to power imbalances and injustices in society, albeit in different ways. Thus, a commitment to social justice research requires a methodological openness and the capacity to locate our own work within often multiple narratives of other contrasting and complementary work.

The distinction between theory and practice is another common dichotomy and one which undermines our ability to truly understand the social world and to appreciate injustice within it. The problem that arises if we artificially separate theory and practice is that we leave theory inert and practice unguided. Adorno's critical theory is helpful here for understanding that there is no simple dichotomy between theory and practice (Adorno, 2008). For Adorno, 'thinking itself is always a form of behaviour' (Adorno, 2000, p. 4, 2008, p. 53) and to think about reality is itself a practical act. He describes thinking as 'a doing, theory a form of praxis' (Adorno, 2005, p. 261). Theory and practice 'are neither immediately one nor absolutely different, ... their relation is one of discontinuity. No continuous path leads from praxis to theory. ... But theory is part of the nexus of society and at the same time is autonomous. Nevertheless praxis does not proceed independently of theory, nor theory independently of praxis' (Adorno, 2005, p. 276).

Moreover, because thought can more easily escape what already 'is', that is more easily step outside the prevailing mainstream, then for Adorno thinking can be a more powerful form of resistance than action alone (Tettlebaum, 2008). To separate thinking from doing is surely to perpetuate the greatest of injustices. Such distance allows licence to behave without thought – to pretend away the myriad of complex social factors that bind us together. It enables us to act like warmongering generals and emperors.

Indeed, Adorno illuminates that what binds these two concepts together is indeed social justice:

> Theory that bears no relation to any conceivable practice either degenerates into an empty, complacent and irrelevant game, or, what is even worse, it becomes a mere component of culture, in other words, a piece of dead scholarship, a matter of complete indifference to us as living minds and active, living human beings. (Adorno, 2000, p. 6)

The essence of bringing practice and theory together in this way is that practice is actually strengthened by not dominating theory. This has interesting implications for higher education research and for the apparent privileging of data. From an Adornean perspective, the privileging of data or empirical research – a sense that this is what research is 'really' about – is self-defeating as it leads to only a partial understanding of such data. The purposes of social justice are served only by the rigorous interplay of theory and practice, conceptual and empirical. Moreover, from a social justice perspective, what conceptual research offers is an opportunity to think beyond what currently exists, to step outside the prevailing status quo and to imagine society differently. Without this act of imagination, social change is limited.

Critical Theory and Dialectics

Adorno's position on theory and practice is a classic example of his general intellectual approach known as dialectics. Indeed, dialectics is at the heart of critical theory and, I suggest, it offers a rich opportunity for thinking about how we avoid the perilous dichotomies that can threaten our research and our work towards greater social justice. Such an understanding of dialectics is more than simply a methodological issue but a moral one as well. It is through their commitment to dialectics that Adorno and the Frankfurt School offer a robust alternative to the status quo. This does not mean Adorno provides a rigid timetable or map for social revolution. Indeed, Adorno is rather scathing of those who expect a 'recipe' for how to achieve this (Adorno, 2017/1958, p. 25). He states: 'Dialectical thought refuses to provide intellectual recipes' (Adorno, 2017/1958, p. 194). Adorno and his colleagues offer a complex alternative to orthodox methodological scripture, providing a foundation for a way of thought (and action) grounded in resistance, which pushes back and opens revolutionary alternatives.

This notion of dialectics, of moving between and constructing understanding through different perspectives, offers much in our quest to avoid the stagnation which accrues from artificial separation. At its heart is the sense that meaning comes from neither extreme, not from the part or the whole, nor the subject or object, but from a radical mediation. The term 'radical' is important here. Dialectics for critical theory is not about a smooth compromise between positions. In particular, it does not follow the neat formula of thesis, antithesis and synthesis that is sometimes associated with the term. Indeed, Adorno refers to the 'particularly dubious use of dialectic' whereupon 'this triadic schema is manipulated to produce the opposite of truth'. In contrast, he argues, 'to think dialectically is precisely to think through rupture' (Adorno, 2017/1958, p. 50). It is the visceral tensions and fractious inconsistencies that come to the fore in Adorno's approach to dialectics and which offer so much to understanding issues of social justice. It requires not simply an appearance of challenge or disagreement, but a genuine commitment to swimming against the tide of mainstream social structures and the status quo (Adorno, 2005).

In an early lecture outlining the work of the Frankfurt School, Horkheimer explained its purpose in the following way:

> Its ultimate aim is the philosophical interpretation of the vicissitudes of human fate – the fate of humans not as mere individuals, however, but as members of a community. (Horkheimer, 1993/1931, p. 1)

We research the social world because we are a part of it. Thus, distance in the form of strident objectivity or carefully constructed barriers between self and research runs counter to a focus on social justice. What is needed, therefore, are multiple perspectives and movement between them to avoid any distortions from a rigidly fixed position. Moreover, the commitment to a dialectical method also reflects the importance of open rather than closed philosophical systems. The search for understanding in the social world thus has an 'essentially open-ended, probing, unfinished quality' (Jay, 1996, p. 41).

Brookfield (2003) observes that critical theory rests on 'a deep conviction that society is organized unfairly' (p. 141). The view from where we are now is one of injustice. For some critics, this is where critical theory stops: it affords a view only of that which it critiques and offers little more. But this misunderstands the foundations of critical theory. Critical theory evokes a complex, dialectical relationship between past, present and future, as well as between theory and practice, which represents a radical path for those of us committed to social justice in our research. But it is a path that requires a little work to be done. Social justice, from a critical theory perspective, cannot be understood through superficial manifestations of social relationships and actions, but must be seen in the light of hidden forces and potentially distorted relations. Thus, critical theory rejects the false dichotomization of the social world and places stress on the intricate web of interactions that makes up human experience, both those easily seen and those more obscure.

Such a dialectical approach ensures that rather than accepting dichotomies, one brings these concepts together in a robust engagement the outcome of which is neither simple nor easy. Indeed, it is a form of virtuous mess (McArthur, 2012) which requires an epistemological perspective that releases the unseen and the easily distorted and refuses to privilege that which is orderly and most easily seen. Quite understandably social science research is often about looking for patterns and trends in the data. Indeed, identifying such phenomena plays important social justice roles, as it did in that groundbreaking research of Booth and Rowntree. But this does not mean that we only value the regular and that which is easy to audit and measure. Adorno is vehement in his attack on the imposition of the traditional scientific method of research to understanding the human world. The dialectical approach seriously problematizes method for researchers. Many of the accepted laws or received tenets of respectable research approaches are undermined. Rather than truth being reached through the systematic approach of categorizing and ordering data, dialectics suggest that what matters is the tireless questioning and dissembling of order. Adorno argues that dialectical thinking 'involves a concrete sense of its opposition to the need for security' (Adorno, 2017/1958, p. 51). But this does not mean that Adorno's critical theory espouses an aimless approach, nor one without rigour: 'The vital nerve of the dialectic is precisely to resolve all that is rigid, reified, ossified' (Adorno, 2017/1958, p. 51).

Thus, at the heart of this dialectics is the notion of movement. Understanding is not reached by tying meaning down in rigid concepts or fixed definitions, but through an ongoing process of questioning, enquiry and challenge. Before explaining more about the conceptual movement Adorno sees at the heart of dialectics, it is worth pointing out that a key feature of his approach rests on such dialectics fitting with neither the absolutism of grand theories and traditional scientific knowledge nor the relativism of postmodernist approaches. Meaning cannot be isolated to a discrete, bounded and contained single entity but is formed by *constellations* of elements that are dynamic and act together for meaning-making.

To appreciate Adorno's approach to dialectics, one must understand the significance of the idea of 'non-identity'. Adorno argues that there is an inevitable and insurmountable gap between thought and being. As we seek to understand aspects of our social world, there is always an elusive element – that non-identity – which cannot be captured and tied down neatly in a concept, let alone definition. This is why thought is always, necessarily, unable to fully complete itself. In the face of this inevitability, dialectics requires ongoing mediation and movement. But to be clear again, this does not mean that concepts become random, but rather that the making of meaning – and its sharing through research – is complex and ongoing. Adorno entreats that we must forgo the traditional research orthodoxy that we should careful pin down the concepts we use:

> Defining the relevant concepts 'cleanly' by means of a certain number of specific features; and one is expected to demonstrate this theoretical cleanliness by not confusing these concepts through the introduction of other differently defined concepts – in other words, by not allowing our concepts to move. (Adorno, 2017/1958, p. 7)

It is helpful here to think of an example pertinent to social justice research in higher education. If we consider the experiences of non-traditional students and the important research conducted to understand their experience of higher education, an orthodox research method would require that we define this term very carefully and pin down exactly what is or is not counted as non-traditional. But however one goes about doing this, there will always be aspects of who these non-traditional students are, which elude such definition. To put it simply, no two non-traditional students are the same: and nor are two traditional students. This may seem obvious, but the implications are profound. There are strong social justice implications if we essentialize identity in this way, defining it down to a common core and losing individual non-identity. Instead, we need to allow the concept of non-traditional to 'move' between manifestations. These series of movements form the constellation of our understanding and allow for a more radical outcome.

Movement of the concept enables the, in many ways helpful, term 'non-traditional' to shift between different iterations and experiences of what it means. And it is in the constellation of these different experiences that we get closest to truth. However, at all times, we need to be aware of the dangers of rigidly tying meaning down. Critical theory dialectics, and especially Adorno's negative dialectics, renounces all attempts to fix meaning in rigid ways. But it is not relativist. Indeed, here is another dichotomy shown to be inadequate, artificial and misleading. While not occupying a relativist position, the critical theory dialectician does necessarily occupy a position without easy stability or comfortable security. In relation to firm definitions, Adorno warns against 'the belief that, once we have firmly and cleanly defined a certain concept, we are thereby absolved of all further worries and stand on absolutely secure ground' (Adorno, 2017/1958, p. 194). In contrast to the neat orderliness of traditional Cartesian scientific thought, Adorno describes the labyrinthine quality of knowledge understood through the practice of dialectics.

Dialectics also explains more subtle aspects of critical theory and, perhaps, some of the most misunderstood features. For example, the critical theorists of the Frankfurt School have often been described as unremittingly pessimistic. The philosopher Lukács referred to them as abiding in 'The Grand Hotel Abyss' (Jeffries, 2016), while Brookfield (2005) refers to being struck by 'a pessimistic fit of the vapors' upon initial reading of Horkheimer or Adorno: 'The situation they describe seems one of unrelieved hopelessness' (p. 75). But the real position is more nuanced, and can best be described as expressing 'an unavoidable note of sadness, but without succumbing to resignation' (Jay, 1996, p. 47). This tenuous and finely balanced state is generated by their dialectical approach, which keeps thought active and moving around when it could so easily lapse into a cul-de-sac of despair. Indeed, another dichotomy to challenge is perhaps that between optimism and pessimism. Critical theory cannot allow the unfettered celebration of possible futures, when built on the injustices of the past, but this does not mean we should not strive for change.

Jay (1996) argues that it is the refusal of the Frankfurt School to 'succumb to the temptation' of either a purely metaphysical or rigidly empirical approach that gave it its 'cutting edge' (p. 48). As such, it could both understand the current world in which it was based and envisage a life beyond simply that which had already been experienced. Fraser (2003) suggests this is the defining feature of critical theory: having 'a foothold in the social world that simultaneously points beyond it' (p. 202). But there is nuance upon nuance here in the work of the Frankfurt School. This becomes evident in Horkheimer's seminal essay from 1937, in which he outlines the difference between traditional and critical theory. Horkheimer makes a simple but striking statement:

> Critical theory maintains: it need not be so … and the necessary conditions for such change already exist. (Horkheimer, 1995)

Here, the movement that is inherent in the dialectical approach becomes clear. There is no simple dichotomy between present and future. Rather, the future lies implicated in the present (and the past). But it is neither fixed nor predetermined, but open to radical change. It was vital to Horkheimer and Adorno that their thought never rested in a single moment or place. To do so would signify either paralysis or apathy. This is thought that roams tirelessly and relentlessly looking for meaning. Moreover, as Adorno explains, we must not have only one way of understanding the relationship between past, present and future: a true dialectics is 'the attempt to see the new in the old instead of simply the old in the new' (Jay, 1996, p. 69). Indeed, Richter (2007) uses the idea of a 'paleonomy' in his discussion of the Frankfurt School to explain this process: 'The paleonomic gesture requires us to stand inside and outside a tradition at the same time, perpetuating the tradition while breaking with it, and breaking with the tradition while perpetuating it' (p. 1).

Moreover, what I am suggesting is that the refusal to dichotomize the past with the future – the dual commitment to critique and social change – is grounded in the dialectical approach to theory and practice, as introduced in the previous section. The two pairings are inherently linked, and this has implications for us as social justice researchers. Theory offers a portal into a different future, as well as an understanding of our past practices.

Understanding Higher Education: The Implications of Critical Theory Dialectics

I have already touched on one of the dichotomies frequently associated with higher education, this being the distinction between traditional and non-traditional students. Using Adorno's understanding of non-identity, a richer understanding emerges of students who may fall into either category and who are not made up of simply one characteristic or another, but a whole constellation of characteristics that shape who they are, how they experience higher education and, by implication, how we should approach them in our research. Another dichotomization of student identity rests on the idea of the student as a consumer, generally regarded in fairly negative terms and posited against the more positive idea of the student as a critical learner. Some academics are highly disparaging of the emergence of a so-called consumer culture in which higher education takes the form of a vending machine into which students pay their money and therefore expect a degree to fall into the tray below. But if we eschew this dichotomization and instead look at how different elements of student identity work together dialectically, then we may reach different conclusions. There is, for example, a social justice argument to be made that students should get good value for money from higher education. It is surely unjust to force an identity divide on students that they either have a love of learning or care about the tuition and student experience they get in return for fees. In many countries in which students pay high fees (and the UK has some of the highest fees), we require a nuanced and multifaceted approach to be able to understand student motivation and behaviour. But if we force a rigid dichotomization between having a love of learning and being conscious of the fees one is paying, then we are likely to lose or repress the most interesting and important data about the student experience. This demonstrates the ways in which a social justice commitment *improves* the research process because it gets us closer to the complex web of human experiences.

Even the seemingly obvious distinction between student and teacher can be challenged through a social justice lens. Here, I have been influenced by Rowland's (2005) notion of pedagogical love and the ways in which both students and academics are involved in learning about their discipline, and both need that commitment to wanting to know more. If we understand both these identities in terms of constellations of features, then there are multiple points of overlap between student and teacher, particularly in higher education. Indeed, sociocultural understandings of learning have been central to the argument that students are *legitimate peripheral participants* (Lave & Wenger, 1991) in the disciplinary worlds of academics, and thus share aspects of identity while being qualitatively different at the same time.

This is a good example to demonstrate that dialecticism does not mean a melting or conceptual averaging of two positions (as in the traditional notion of thesis, antithesis and synthesis) but rather a more complex, compound form of understanding that does not seek to iron everything out. Thus, the solution to the dichotomy of student and teacher is not to deny differences and adopt an extreme notion of student-centredness such that the teaching role is utterly diminished. Rather, it is to appreciate that the student–teacher relationship is shaped by what all parties bring to their shared activities and in turn shapes future identities. We need more higher education research that brings together student and academic perceptions, values and experiences and that allows for understanding and celebration of the complex ways in which they interrelate.

Thus, researching higher education, from a social justice perspective informed by critical theory, suggests we consider the multivariate aspects of student identity and allow for both intersections and differences between student groups and between students and academics. Any research approach that rests on essentializing identity, particularly in order to make certain research metrics easier, risks both missing the true nature of what is going on and perpetuating injustices by privileging easily seen information over complex forms of knowledge.

So far, I've considered problems of dichotomization in terms of how we understand student identity in higher education and suggested that a critical theory approach of working through a dialectical understanding of different aspects is both more socially just and likely to be more productive as a research approach. I now turn to the same argument to the example of the identity of the university itself and, in this way, consideration of the purposes of the university. Here again, there are common, but unhelpful, dichotomies. The first is between the social and the economic purposes of higher education, and this clearly mirrors the above discussion of student identity. Here, the traditional distinction made is between a pursuit of the love of learning as a good in its own right and higher education as a mechanism for training the professional workforce. Recognition of an economic role for higher education is feared by some because it seeks to trespass across a more wholesome social purpose. But the dichotomy is false, and what we need instead is to have richer understandings of the social and the economic, as would arise through a dialectical approach, to appreciate their interplay and mutuality. As I've argued elsewhere (McArthur, 2011), higher education that works towards greater social justice must have both social and economic purposes and understand each of these in diverse ways rather than, for example, simply from the perspective of employers or business.

Finally, I want to introduce a dichotomy I've not previously discussed but which is at the heart of critical theory. This is between the individual and the social. Only a dialectical approach that appreciates the socially situated nature of individual experience and the myriad of individual experiences that make up the social can reasonably, and justly, understand higher education. Here, it is useful to invoke the work of the third-generation critical theorist Axel Honneth, who explains social justice in terms of

> that which allows the individual member of our society to realize his or her own life's objectives, in cooperation with others, and with the greatest possible autonomy. (Honneth, 2010, p. 13)

The implications of this resonate with earlier observations on a dialectical approach to student identity and to the purposes of higher education. We can reduce higher education to neither individual students' experiences nor an overarching social role – but must appreciate the interplay between the two. Thus, if we consider the purposes of higher education research being to further our knowledge and understanding of higher education, then the mediating role of social justice is to ensure that the constituent parts of higher education are understood in their full complexity and interrelations. This can also work to ensure that we do not simply research higher education and social justice, but that we research justly.

Conclusion

In looking to locate social justice within close-up higher education research care is needed to appreciate the many ways in which social justice must actively inhabit multiple moments, diverse roles and challenging perspectives within the research task. There can be no greater injustice than to consider social justice as simply another topic of research: an interesting and perhaps vaguely honourable area of data to be mined and processed into academic papers and promotion applications. To locate social justice within close-up higher education research is to recognize its pervasiveness combined with its human tangibility. Social justice can neither be confined to only certain bits of the undertaking nor be dismissed as so nebulous as to be immune to efforts to locate, and thus to reflect upon and critique. A deep and rich appreciation of all that a commitment to social justice brings to our activities as researchers can help to mediate some aspects of research that otherwise seem dislocated or unreasonably dichotomized. Higher education becomes a more complex place to research – one that requires sometimes messy understandings to do it justice. Those of us who study and work within higher education are not just subjects of research but have our own complex identities which research should celebrate. A commitment to social justice is a powerful tool to enable us to research both near and far, to understand difference and to accept the implications of a dialectical approach. Social justice can and should drive higher education research, not just wait patiently for polite attention or misplaced flattery; social justice should not just be considered a feel-good lens, but rather be understood as central to making sense of all we do.

References

Adorno, T. W. (2000). *Problems of Moral Philosophy*. Cambridge: Polity.
Adorno, T. W. (2005). *Critical Models*. New York, NY: Columbia University Press.
Adorno, T. W. (2008). *Lectures on Negative Dialectics*. Cambridge: Polity.
Adorno, T. W. (2017/1958). *An Introduction to Dialectics*. Cambridge: Polity.
Brookfield, S. (2003). Putting the critical back into critical pedagogy: A commentary on the path of dissent. *Journal of Transformative Education*, 1(2), 141–149.
Brookfield, S. (2005). *The Power of Critical Theory for Adult Learning and Teaching*. Maidenhead: Open University Press.
Fraser, N. (2003). Distorted beyond all recognition: A rejoinder to Axel Honneth. In N. Fraser & A. Honneth (Eds.), *Redistribution or Recognition: A Political-Philosophical Exchange*, 198–236. London: Verso.
Honneth, A. (2010). The political identity of the Green Movement in Germany: Social-philosophical reflections. *Critical Horizons*, 11(1), 5–18.
Horkheimer, M. (1993/1931). The present situation of social philosophy and the tasks of an institute for social research. In G. F. Hunter, M. S. Kramer & J. T. Torpey (Eds.), *Between Philosophy and Social Science: Selected Early Writings*, 1–14. Cambridge, MA: The MIT Press.
Horkheimer, M. (1995). *Critical Theory: Selected Essays*. New York: Continuum.
Jay, M. (1996). *The Dialectical Imagination*. Berkeley and Los Angeles, CA: University of California Press.
Jeffries, S. (2016). *Grand Hotel Abyss: The Lives of the Frankfurt School*. London: Verso.
Lave, J., & Wenger, E. (1991). *Situated Learning*. Cambridge: Cambridge University Press.
McArthur, J. (2011). Reconsidering the social and economic purposes of higher education. *Higher Education Research & Development*, 30(6), 737–749.
McArthur, J. (2012). Virtuous mess and wicked clarity: Struggle in Higher Education Research. *Higher Education Research & Development*, 31(3), 419–430.
Richter, G. (2007). *Thought Images: Frankfurt School Writers' Reflections from Damaged Life*. Stanford CA: Stanford University Press.
Rowland, S. (2005). Intellectual love and the link between teaching and research. In R. Barnett (Ed.), *Reshaping the University*, 92–101. Maidenhead: Open University Press.
Sagan, C. (1994), *Pale Blue Dot*. London: Random House.

Tettlebaum, M. (2008). Political philosophy. In D. Cook (Ed.), *Theodor Adorno: Key Concepts*, 131–146. Stocksfield: Acumen.

Thompson, E. P. (1963). *The Making of the English Working Class*. London: Penguin.

2

New Public Management and Social Justice in Higher Education

Teresa Carvalho

Introduction

Reforms in higher education have become common in the last decades almost all over the world. Attempts to change higher education find legitimacy in political discourses which suggest that the higher education system, and its institutions, do not reform themselves as fast as the changes that occur in their environment. In addition to this, traditional governance models are said to be dominated by traditional academic structures and practices, aligned with guild-like interests, thus creating 'irrationalities' and 'inefficiencies' in both the system and its institutions. Finally, these discourses suggest that institutions need to be rational and efficient and that they can only achieve these values if they are submitted to market competition.

Market competition has been introduced with NPM and managerialism that was used in the Anglo-Saxon countries for the conservative and neoliberal purpose of transforming the welfare state. Since NPM and managerialism value competition, metrics and financial profit rather than collective interests, cooperation or community, it may call into question the relevance of social justice as a value in higher education.

Social justice, however, is a concept relevant to higher education both in political discussions and in research, although there is still a lack of consensus concerning its meaning. Based on the literature, one can say that two main perspectives prevail: one endogenous – emphasizing internal differences – and the other exogenous – translating the contribution of higher education to turn societies towards greater equality.

Although there is a vast literature on NPM and managerialism in higher education, the impact of these reforms is less studied. Aiming to contribute to the knowledge in this area, this chapter intends to reflect on the extent to which NPM reforms in higher education can be considered as socially just. The chapter starts by reflecting on NPM/managerialism reforms in higher education, followed by a reflection on the specificities of the concept of social justice. It then examines the effects of NPM-driven reforms on social justice in higher education.

NPM and Managerial Reforms in Higher Education

NPM is not grounded on a single fundamental theory, but it is a concept rooted in neoliberalism, entrepreneurialism and managerialism and is presented as an instrument to provide practical solutions to operational problems confronting public organizations in general and higher education in particular (Gow & Dufour, 2000; Carvalho & Santiago, 2010). NPM is a conception of public sector governance that is in fundamental contrast to European traditions of administration by calling for an end to the principles of (Weberian) bureaucracy and Habermas's ideas of knowledge as human interest and that it should, hence, be a public good to society (Habermas, 1975). It is strongly rooted in neoliberal values of market, management and performativity (Ball, 2016) and in individual values, as well as in the core idea that by creating competition and simultaneously more freedom for managers to take decisions, public organizations will be more focused in their central goals and more efficient (Dunn & Miller, 2007). Furthermore, it is sustained in the assumption that it will bring the needed innovation to a system and to institutions which are assumed to be conservative regarding their culture, activities and forms of organization.

The higher education sector in Europe, as well as other geographical contexts, experienced substantial transformations under this ideology introducing corporate values and practices novel to the traditional concepts of higher education organization (Hüther & Krücken, 2018).

Submitted to NPM-driven reforms, higher education institutions (HEIs) can be argued to be moving away from traditional public-value-oriented principles of collegial and value-oriented higher education management (public value orientation) towards a marketized, competition- and performance-oriented view on higher education (NPM). This paradigm shift is based the three main policy technologies identified by Stephen Ball: Market, Management (or managerialism) and Performance (or performativity) (Ball, 2003, 2016).

The short-term oriented criteria of economic productivity has been assuming a dominant role in the culture of HEIs. Within these reforms, HEIs are conceptualized as organizational or corporate actors, having as a main purpose the provision of higher education as formalized degree programmes, incorporating public, semi-public and private organizations (Carvalho & Santiago, 2010). NPM reforms promoted changes in the institutions' organizational model, attempting to turn them from collegial to top-down models and to also impose an ethos transformation – from a public to enterprise ethos. The intention is that HEIs start to be ruled by emphasizing the importance of performance and income generation. Neoliberalists consider that the consumer perspective should prevail as the fact that HEIs are only operating in a free market based on competition and individual choice; they have a stimulus to be more efficient (Shepherd, 2018).

The impact of these reforms has been highly scrutinized in the literature and has also been the object of political debate. Among the several criticisms made of the paradigm shift promoted by these reforms is the idea that their principles are in conflict with higher education goals. HEIs are assumed to be aiming to make profit for survival in a competitive market like any for-profit company that produces any kind of consumer good, while their goals are still institutionalized as being the provision, the generation, transmission and dissemination of knowledge resulting from a creative and free environment. The attempts to deinstitutionalize higher education main goals result in questioning also the notion of social justice in higher education.

Social Justice in Higher Education

Although considerable social research has been developed about higher education's role in relation to social equity and the issue has been simultaneously driving heated political discussions, the concept still lacks a precise meaning with significant differences found in the ways the concept is conceptualized in the literature. Jan McArthur expresses this complexity when saying that the concept is 'complex and multi-faceted, as encompassing different contexts and perspectives and as formed by our being and learning together in the social world' (2013, p. 24). McArthur concludes that social justice is both a concept and a piece of knowledge that integrates four main aspects: is complex and multifaceted, includes both processes and outcomes, is based on the relationship between people and incorporates the desire to aspire to more social justice in society (McArthur, 2013). (For more on this, see the discussion in the Introduction chapter.)

The relevance of social justice to higher education is defined in an apparently simple question by Zajda and his colleagues as: 'How can we contribute to the creation of a more equitable, respectful, and just society for everyone?' (Zajda et al., 2006, p. 13). This contribution to achieve a fair and just society can be interpreted as an exogenous meaning of social justice, that is to say, the focus is on what higher education can do for the achievement of justice and social justice in society as a whole. Nevertheless, the literature tends to focus more on endogenous aspects of social justice. In fact, the main concern in the literature has been with equity and social justice within higher education with the most frequent reflections being based on the analysis of the social composition of higher education's staff and student populations and on the way access is more or less socially representative. Brennan and Naidoo (2008) argue that this perspective aligns the representation of social justice with the one that is dominant in other large organizations and in this context restricts HEIs' view and assessment of social justice into these aspects.

More recent literature highlights that the specific nature of higher education or its main functions in society should incorporate a wider concept, which includes the way higher education can contribute to achieve a fair and just society (Calhoun, 2006; Zajda et al., 2006; McArthur, 2013). It is acknowledged that contemporaneous societies are becoming more unjust (McArthur, 2013; Piketty & Saez, 2014). This chapter intends to contribute to the discussion on the effects of NPM and managerialism policies in higher education both to endogenous and to exogenous dimensions of social justice. More specifically, this chapter intends to reflect on the way transformations imposed by NPM may have impact both on the shape of academic profession and on those who benefit from higher education.

NPM in Higher Education – A Socially Just Reform?

The debate on the impact of NPM and managerialism on social justice in higher education is placed not only under the context of the most recent developments of increasing social inequalities but also in its relation to the notions of social justice within HEIs – the endogenous effect – and to whole society – the exogenous effects.

NPM and managerialism reforms, being sustained by a neoliberal ideology, question the purpose of higher education. The dominant values of market, competition, individual choice, responsibility and efficiency influence the conceptualization of HEIs' missions and ultimate goals, or the actors' perceptions about them, and, as such, guide the behaviour and strategies of the different social actors involved in decision-making (Santiago & Carvalho, 2004).

Since the emergence of the Modern University, with the Humboldtian revolution, the main goals of higher education have been institutionalized as the disinterested pursuit of knowledge on a disciplinary basis, the adoption of the relationship between research and teaching and the intervention over the student's personal development. With the new political and social environment of the welfare state along with the Keynesian economic principles and the pressures from middle and popular classes to a broad movement of social democratization, these goals started to be recovered and re-contextualized (Scott, 1995). If, in an initial phase, this re-conceptualization was related to the need to train professionals in public services and other social and economic sectors, in a second phase, which started in the 1970s, a focus was made on the democratization of higher education, stressing the need to shift higher education from an elite to a mass higher education system (Scott, 1995, 2000). At this time, a hegemonic perspective was evidenced that incorporates social justice in the goals of higher education, assumed simultaneously as the widening of access to higher education to less privileged groups and the need for higher education to be a guarantee of the existence of an increased possibility to support social mobility.

These dominant conceptions about higher education roles in society started to be questioned in the 1980s. The university lost its knowledge-creation monopoly, and both political discourses and the economic environment started pressuring HEIs to produce more transferable and applicable knowledge. Although this was not totally new to higher education, what seems to be relevant is contributed to a reversal of higher education's priorities (Scott, 1995; Amaral et al., 2003) with the economic dimension becoming more important (Santiago & Carvalho, 2004). The economic relevance of higher education is particularly evidenced in knowledge production and dissemination but is also present in teaching roles.

Actually, 'research was put at the centre of the debate on the relationship between university and society. Strong pressure was put on research translating the social and political beliefs that knowledge transfer and research partnerships with the entrepreneurial world were crucial to enhance economic development and to face the worldwide competition in the globalisation arena' (Santiago et al., 2008, p. 495). In this context, the traditional protection of science from market and political pressures under the influence of the Mertonian social and epistemic system of beliefs, translated in the acronym CUDOS (Community, Universalism, Disinterestedness, Originality, Scepticism) (Merton, 1973; Hooker, 2003; Ziman, 2000; Sztompke, 2007), started to be replaced. New values based on the strategic, entrepreneurial or commercial research notions (Slaughter & Leslie, 1997), deriving from new forms of producing knowledge classified, following Ziman (1998, 2000), as 'post-academic/post-industrial science' or as Mode 2 knowledge production, according to Gibbons et al. (1994), started to be imposed. These new forms of knowledge production translate the new social and institutional conditions based on the acronym PLACE (Proprietary, Local, Authoritarian, Commissioned and Expert).

In this context, knowledge is not represented as being produced for its own sake but instead it is oriented to 'client satisfaction' strongly influenced by entrepreneurial values, with an important part of it being transformed into a private and commercial good. In this sense, knowledge is more influenced by policy and profit than by researchers personal interests leading to questions if and how the hoard of knowledge produced or preserved by universities is still available to society more broadly (Calhoun, 2006). The commercialization and privatization of knowledge question higher education's contributions to society as a whole, especially if one takes into consideration the way the accountability and market values have been translated in an increasing competitive and individualist culture in HEIs. Assessment mechanisms based on quantitative measures were defined for all academic roles. Institutions, research groups and academics are closely scrutinized by the university management concerning their productivity and research performance, mainly measured by the number of publications in international indexed journals. The access to this knowledge is, in this context, not accessible to those who are not able to speak English. Taking this into consideration, one can say that NPM and managerialism, in restricting the production and dissemination of knowledge, also promote societies to become more unequal not only because those who fund research benefit more from scientific knowledge but also because scientific knowledge in general is less accessible to the wider population.

These pressures are also applied to teaching, with utility and employability being elected as the main values concerning curriculum design (and even institutions evaluation) turning the economical dimension to become more relevant than any other teaching orientation (Amaral et al., 2003; Santiago & Carvalho, 2004). Critical perspectives on this have concerns that '(...) the current policy focus on labor market driven policies in higher education have led to an ever growing competition transforming this social institution to an ordinary market-place, where attainment and degrees are seen as a currency that can be converted to a labour market value. Education has become an instrument for economic progress moving away from its original role to provide context for human development' (Kromydas, 2017, p. 1).

The role of higher education is almost restricted to serve the interests of the economy relegating to a second, and almost inexistent place: its social role (Walker, 2009; McArthur, 2013). Following Jan McArthur's (2011) arguments, the employability perspective reveals a narrow and statistical vision of markets and economy. The emphasis in employability centres the learning process in a process of 'know who to' limiting the critical thought and transforming students not only into clients, instead of heirs of higher education (Cardoso et al., 2011), but also into a 'commodity with an exchange value' in the labour market (McArthur, 2011).

The consequences for social justice in higher education are probably more evidenced at the endogenous level. There is a relevant discussion in the literature about the possibility of NPM-inspired reforms promoting deprofessionalization (degradation of professional status and prestige due to loss of monopoly over knowledge and mistrust in professional ethics) and even proletarianization (degradation of labour relations) (Haug, 1972) in the academic profession. While there is a lack of consensus on the impact of NPM over academics professionalism, there are less doubts concerning the degradation of working conditions in academia. Stephen Ball (2003, 2008, 2016) argues that NPM leads academics to rely not on professional judgements but, instead, on decontextualized judgements and practices restricted to practices that can be measured and rewarded. However, based on empirical data, other studies conclude that academics are still framing their professional practices based on the traditional normative framework of the profession and even that they demonstrate antipathy to a market ethos and to the reduction of education to an economic function (Carvalho & Santiago, 2010; Carvalho, 2017; Winter & O'Donohue, 2012). Referring to the English context, Kolsaker (2008) argues that academics are being instrumental in supporting NPM ideas and practices assuming it as a facilitator of enhanced performance, professionalism and status.

Less controversial has been the analysis over the changes in academics' working conditions promoted by NPM-oriented reforms worldwide (Carvalho, 2017). There is a wide consensus about the degradation of working conditions, in terms of appointment and remuneration. The traditional full-time permanent or tenured position has been declining in academia in different contexts (Altbach, 2015; Liu & Mallon, 2004). In some countries, like in the UK, tenure ceased to exist by the end of the 1990s, with academics having the possibility to obtain a permanent position but not the tenured special protection (Karran, 2007). Even in countries with a tenured system, the non-tenured track appointments have been much more prevalently used (Liu & Mallon, 2004) with few professors being hired on the permanent and tenure track (Lassiter & De Gagne, 2010). In South Africa, for example, 65 per cent of academics are on short-term contracts. Although the conditions to obtain a tenured position vary widely between higher education systems and even between institutions, there is a consensus in the literature that research, publications and, more than ever, generation of external funding are crucial for obtaining promotion and tenure (Bhopal et al., 2016; Liu & Mallon, 2004; Carvalho et al., 2013; Wagner, 2006; Woods, 2006; Gentry & Stokes, 2015). This extensive focus on research also has implications for teaching and service and for the careers of junior faculty (Woods, 2006). In this context, it is undeniable that competition increased in the academic profession leading Kwiek (2012) to assert that in the European context, it is difficult to not only find high job security but also experience a relatively friendly, non-competitive workplace. These high levels of competition aligned with high levels of workload have a negative impact on academics', and even PhD students', mental health (Deem, forthcoming).

Non-tenured staff may have a multiplicity of contracts that include not only non-permanent positions but also part-time positions. This all adds to the exploitative nature of many non-tenured staffs' employment situation. This multiplicity is also evidence of an increasing division of academic work, with those working in a non-permanent position assuming more teaching duties, sometimes almost exclusively, with a heavy workload (Gale, 2011; Fogg, 2003; Gentry & Stokes, 2015). Along with this, new remuneration systems have been implemented based on merit pay systems, which in countries such as the United States, the United Kingdom and Australia (Gillespie et al., 2001) translated into academics' salaries falling in real terms. Given this, Musselin's (2006) argument that changes in academic working conditions transform academics into 'academic workers' similar to industry workers seems to be true. However, as Musselin recognizes, one cannot position academics as passive actors who have had changes imposed on them from the outside. On the contrary, some academics were actually active participants in higher education reforms. According to Musselin (2013) there is, in fact, a small group of academics who hold in their hands the professional self-regulation since decisions on hiring, promotion or assessment criteria depending on their decisions. This small elite group may actually have seen their power increase within HEIs since they seem to be aligned with the institutional power contributing to turn political will into institutional practices (Musselin, 2013).

Besides the position in the academic rank, two other variables have been identified as sustaining the segmentation and hierarchization of the higher education profession: age and gender. Concerning age, the empirical studies reveal that relevant generational differences in different national contexts. The new generations are better qualified, but they also experience more difficulties in entering and moving up in their career (Marquina & Jones, 2015; Höhle, 2015; Marquina et al., 2015), in having a permanent job (Höhle, 2015) and in participating in institutional decision-making (Santiago et al., 2015).

The first analysis on the impact of NPM and managerialism on gender composition of academic career suggested a very optimist perspective. The strong emphasis on efficiency and objective and quantified measures for academics performance was seen as a way to overcome the obstacles and bureaucratic structures imposed on women's progress, making their work more real and visible (Yeatman, 1995; Prichard, 1996). Nevertheless, the following analysis concluded that NPM has in fact reinforced gender inequalities. The increasing complexification of academic roles and the division of academic work have led to a tendency to delegate teaching duties, which are less valued in the new institutional culture, mainly to women (Angervall et al., 2015; Ryan, 2012; Acker & Dillabough, 2007; Davies & Thomas, 2002). This tendency led Angervall and Beach (2017) to conclude that 'women in teaching have been made into profitable workers for others to use'. Women are concentrated not only in teaching roles but also in non-secure positions, working on a part-time and temporary basis (El-Alayli et al., 2018; Fogg, 2003; Gentry & Stokes, 2015) and earning less than their male counterparts.

Adding to this, NPM imposes expectations of performativity that women can have more difficulties in satisfying, due to their traditional caring roles (Bailyn, 2003; Probert, 2005). Furthermore, some authors also emphasize how the culture of accountability and performance measure lead to an increase in administrative work that has been mainly conceded to women (Morley, 2005). The concentration in these roles ends up imposing more difficulties for women to progress to the top of the career since they are less concentrated in the roles more valued in the new context. In fact, although the proportion of women among all academics has increased in European countries, they are still less represented in senior categories (Goastellec & Pekari, 2013). According to Davies and Thomas (2002, p. 191), the new cultural environment of HEIs based on competition, individualism and accountability is also more aligned with a masculine culture, again imposing more obstacles for women.

The analysis of the literature on the impact of NPM over the academic profession reveals, in fact, an increasing segmentation and hierarchies within the profession. This segmentation is translated into the existence of a small group of elite academics with relevant working conditions coexisting with a significant 'reserve army' of young and less privileged academics who face precarious working conditions while competing for better positions.

In this context, the endogenous analysis also reveal that NPM and managerialism reforms are far from promoting social justice in higher education. But, it is relevant to highlight that endogenous and exogenous aspects of social justice in higher education are intertwined. Maria do Mar Pereira (2016) emphasizes precisely the way the demands for productivity and impact generate intense workloads that present increasing challenges to the balance between work and personal life and that prevent academics from being involved in other relevant activities such as social activism. This is especially true for women given that in most countries the traditional division of labour in the family context attributes more work to women. The way these changes have been framed as an individual problem also contributes to preventing academics from taking more collective action. Social justice is an essential concept to higher education; however, its implementation only seems possible if integrated in a counter-hegemonic reform of higher education.

Conclusion

NPM and managerialism have framed reforms worldwide in the last decades, influenced by a neoliberal political agenda. The reforms were designed in the name of the three E's: economy, efficiency and efficacy, emerging as part of a global trend in which market ideology and market, or quasi-market, modes of regulation are associated with a set of management policies and practices drawn from the corporate sector. In this context, an institutional culture that is market and economic oriented, and associated with increased productivity and accountability, has been imposed in HEIs.

The institutionalized social perceptions of higher education mission and goals have been questioned in this context, and the notion of social justice as one of higher education aims itself has also been questioned. Even if there are different conceptualizations of social justice, it is possible to summarize them in two main perspectives: one exogenous to higher education – considering that social justice translates higher education contribution to a better and equal society – and the endogenous one – assuring that HEIs promote equal access and equity in their staff. With the intrusion of NPM and managerialism, higher education became more socially unjust, taking both the endogenous and exogenous perspective. Actually, both are intertwined and cannot be separated. Changes in the way knowledge is produced and disseminated are an important source of inequality in higher education since the production of knowledge is increasingly oriented to those who can pay it. Simultaneously, knowledge dissemination is mainly based in international indexed journals, as well as registered patents, that restrict the access to scientific knowledge. This represents a major paradox within the so-called information and knowledge society. In an endogenous perspective, HEIs are also turning more unequal and unjust with an increasing internal segmentation, with women and young academics facing the worst working conditions. The culture of high workloads and control of academic work, based on accountability mechanisms, are in turn, maintaining academics' distance from non-work activities, including social activism.

References

Acker, S., & Dillabough, J. A. (2007). Women 'learning to labour' in the 'male emporium': Exploring gendered work in teacher education. *Gender and Education*, 19(3), 297–316.

Altbach, P. (2015). Knowledge and education as international commodities. *International Higher Education*, 28, 2–5.

Amaral, A., Meek, V. L., Larsen, I. M., & Lars, W. (Eds.). (2003). *The Higher Education Managerial Revolution?* (Vol. 3). Springer Science & Business Media.

Angervall, B., & Beach, D. (2017). Dividing academic work: Gender and academic career at Swedish universities. *Gender and Education*, 1–16.

Angervall, P., Beach, D., & Gustafsson, J. (2015). The unacknowledged value of female academic labour power for male research careers. *Higher Education Research & Development*, 34(5), 815–827.

Bailyn, L. (2003). Academic careers and gender equity: Lessons learned from MIT 1. *Gender, Work & Organization*, 10(2), 137–153.

Ball, S. (2003). The teacher's soul and the terrors of performativity. *Journal of Education Policy*, 18(2), 215–228.

Ball, S. (2008). New philanthropy, new networks and new governance in education. *Political Studies*, 56(4), 747–765.

Ball, S. (2016). Neoliberal education? Confronting the slouching beast. *Policy Futures in Education*, 14(8), 1046–1059.

Bhopal, K., Brown, H., & Jackson, J. (2016). BME academic flight from UK to overseas higher education: Aspects of marginalisation and exclusion. *British Educational Research Journal, 42*(2), 240–257.

Brennan, J., & Naidoo, R. (2008). Higher education and the achievement (and/or prevention) of equity and social justice. *Higher Education, 56*(3), 287–302.

Calhoun, C. (2006). The university and the public good. *Thesis Eleven, 84*(1), 7–43.

Cardoso, S., Carvalho, T., & Santiago, R. (2011). From students to consumers: Reflections on the marketisation of Portuguese higher education. *European Journal of Education, 46*(2), 271–284.

Carvalho, T., & Santiago, R. (2010). Still academics after all …. *Higher Education Policy, 23*(3): 397–411.

Davies, A., & Thomas, R. (2002). Gendering and gender in public service organizations: Changing professional identities under new public management. *Public Management Review, 4*(4), 461–484.

Deem, R. (In Press). Rethinking doctoral education: University purposes, academic cultures, mental health and the public good. In S. Cardoso, O. Tavares, C. Sin, & T. Carvalho (Eds.), *Structural and Institutional Transformations in Doctoral Education: (Mis)alignment with Doctoral Candidates' Career Expectations.* Palgrave Macmillan (In Press).

DoMar Pereira, M. (2016). Struggling within and beyond the Performative University: Articulating activism and work in an 'academia without walls'. In *Women's Studies International Forum.* Elsevier: Pergamon.

Dunn, W. N., & Miller, D. Y. (2007). A critique of the new public management and the neo-Weberian state: Advancing a critical theory of administrative reform. *Public Organization Review, 7*(4), 345–358.

El-Alayli, A., Hansen-Brown, A. A., & Ceynar, M. (2018). Dancing backwards in high heels: Female professors experience more work demands and special favor requests, particularly from academically entitled students. *Sex Roles, 79*(3–4), 136–150.

Fogg, P. (2003). So many committees, so little time. *Chronicle of Higher Education, 50*(17), A14.

Gale, H. (2011). The reluctant academic: Early-career academics in a teaching-orientated university. *International Journal for Academic Development, 16*(3), 215–227.

Gentry, R., & Stokes, D. (2015). Strategies for Professors Who Service the University to Earn Tenure and Promotion. *Research in Higher Education Journal, 29*, 1–13.

Gibbons, M. (Ed.). (1994). *The New Production of Knowledge: The Dynamics of Science and Research in Contemporary Societies.* Sage. London.

Gillespie, N. A., Walsh, M. H. W. A., Winefield, A. H., Dua, J., & Stough, C. (2001). Occupational stress in universities: Staff perceptions of the causes, consequences and moderators of stress. *Work & Stress, 15*(1), 53–72.

Goastellec, G., & Pekari, N. (2013). Gender differences and inequalities in academia: Findings in Europe. In U. Teichler & E. Ava Höhle (Eds.), *The Work Situation of the Academic Profession in Europe: Findings of a Survey in Twelve Countries*, 55–78. Dordrecht: Springer.

Gow, J. I., & Dufour, C. (2000). Is the new public management a paradigm? Does it matter? *International Review of Administrative Sciences*, 66(4), 573–597.

Habermas, J. (1975). *Legitimation Crisis* (Vol. 519). Beacon Press. Boston

Haug, M. R. (1972). Deprofessionalization: An alternate hypothesis for the future. *The Sociological Review*, 20(1_suppl), 195–211.

Höhle, E. (2015). From apprentice to agenda-setter: Comparative analysis of the influence of contract conditions on roles in the scientific community. *Studies in Higher Education*, 40(8), 1423–1437.

Hooker, C. (2003). Science: Legendary, academic – and post-academic? *Minerva*, 41(1), 71–81.

Hüther, O., & Krücken, G. (2018). *Higher Education in Germany: Recent Developments in an International Perspective* (Vol. 49). Berlin:Springer.

Karran, T. (2007). Academic freedom in Europe: A preliminary comparative analysis. *Higher Education Policy*, 20(3), 289–313.

Kolsaker, A. (2008). Academic professionalism in the managerialist era: A study of English universities. *Studies in Higher Education*, 33(5), 513–525.

Kromydas, T. (2017). Rethinking higher education and its relationship with social inequalities: past knowledge, present state and future potential. *Palgrave Communications*, 3(1), 1–12.

Kweik, M. (2012) *Knowledge Production in European Universities: States, Markets, and Academic Entrepreneurialism*. Frankfurt: Peter Lang.

Lassiter, E. B., & De Gagne, J. C. (2010). Academic Freedom and Tenure: Protective or Destructive to Academe. *Journal of Globalization and Higher Education*, 1(7), 1–7.

Liu, M., & Mallon, W. T. (2004). Tenure in transition: Trends in basic science faculty appointment policies at US medical schools. *Academic Medicine*, 79(3), 205–213.

Marquina, M., & Jones, G. A. (2015). Generational change and academic work: An introduction. *Studies in Higher Education*, 40(8), 1349–1353.

Marquina, M., Yuni, J., & Ferreiro, M. (2015). Generational change in the Argentine academic profession through the analysis of 'life courses'. *Studies in Higher Education*, 40(8), 1392–1405.

McArthur, J. (2011). Reconsidering the social and economic purposes of higher education. *Higher Education Research & Development*, 30(6), 737–749.

McArthur, J. (2013). *Rethinking Knowledge Within Higher Education: Adorno and Social Justice*. London: Bloomsbury.

Merton, R. K. (1973). *The Sociology of Science*. Chicago: University of Chicago Press.

Morley, L. (2005). Opportunity or exploitation? Women and quality assurance in higher education. *Gender and Education, 17*(4), 411–429.

Musselin, C. (2006). European academic labor markets in transition. *Higher Education 49*(1(2)): 135–154.

Musselin, C. (2013). Redefinition of the relationships between academics and their university. *Higher Education, 65*(1), 25–37.

Piketty, T., & Saez, E. (2014). Inequality in the long run. *Science, 344*(6186), 838–843.

Prichard, C. (1996). Managing universities: Is it men's work? In D. L. Collinson & J. Hearn (Eds.), *Men as Managers, Managers as Men: Critical Perspectives on Men, Masculinities and Managements*. London: Sage.

Probert, B. (2005). 'I just couldn't fit it in': Gender and unequal outcomes in academic careers. *Gender, Work and Organization, 12*(1): 50–72.

Ryan, S. (2012). Academic zombies: A failure of resistance or a means of survival? *Australian Universities Review, 54*(2), 3–11.

Santiago, R., Carvalho, T., & Relva, R. (2008). Research and the universities' image. *European Journal of Education, 43*(4), 495–512.

Santiago, R., Carvalho, T., & Ferreira, A. (2015). Changing Knowledge and academic profession in Portugal. *Higher Education Quarterly, 69*(1), 79–100.

Santiago, R. A., & Carvalho, T. (2004). Effects of managerialism on the perceptions of higher education in Portugal. *Higher Education Policy, 17*(4), 427–444.

Scott, P. (1995). *The Meaning of Mass Higher Education*. Buckingham: SRHE/Open University Press.

Scott, P. (2000). Globalisation and higher education: Challenges for the 21st century. *Journal of studies in International Education, 4*(1), 3–10.

Shepherd, S. (2018). Managerialism: An ideal type. *Studies in Higher Education, 43*(9), 1668–1678.

Slaughter, S., & Leslie, L. (1997). *Academic Capitalism: Politics, Policies and the Entrepreneurial University*. Baltimore: Johns Hopkins University Press.

Sztompke, P. (2007). Trust in science, Robert K. Merton's inspirations. *Journal of Classical Sociology, 7*, 211–220.

Wagner, N. R. (2006). *Getting Tenure at a University*. TX: San Antonio. http://cs. utsa. edu/~ wagner/creative_writing/tenure.

Walker, J. (2009). Time as the fourth dimension in the globalization of higher education. *The Journal of Higher Education, 80*(5), 483–509.

Winter, R. P., & O'Donohue, W. (2012). Academic identity tensions in the public university: which values really matter?. *Journal of Higher Education Policy and Management, 34*(6), 565–573.

Wong, C. A., Eccles, J. S., & Sameroff, A. (2003). The influence of ethnic discrimination and ethnic identification on African-American adolescents' school and socio-emotional adjustment. *Journal of Personality, 71*, 1197–1232.

Woods, D. R. (2006). A case for revisiting tenure requirements. *Thought & Action*, (Fall), 135–142.

Yeatman, A. (1995). The gendered management of equity-oriented change in higher education. In J. Smyth (Ed.), *Academic Work*, 194–205. Buckingham: Open University Press.

Zajda, J., Majhanovich, S., & Rust, V. (2006). Introduction: Education and social justice. *International Review of Education, 52*(1), 9–22.

Ziman, J. (1994). *Prometheus Bound: Science in a Dynamic Steady State*. Cambridge: Cambridge University Press.

Ziman, J. (1998). Essays on science and society: Why must scientists become more ethically sensitive than they used to do? *Science, 282*(5395), 1813–1814.

Ziman, J. (2000). *Real Science: What It Is, and What It Means*. Cambridge: Cambridge University Press.

3

Researching Social Justice in Higher Education from Both Insider and Outsider Perspectives

Vicki Trowler

Introduction

In her chapter, Jan McArthur foregrounds recognition as a mechanism of social in/justice: 'To deny or misrepresent recognition to another is to do injustice.' Fraser (2013, p. 176) distinguishes between 'injustices of distribution and injustices of recognition', stressing that while the latter are not reducible to the former, they are also not 'merely cultural' – a position attributed to her by critics including Butler (1997). In the context of higher education research, injustices of recognition can translate into injustices of distribution, should mis/recognition in re/presentation be translated uncritically into policy.

One can conduct research *into* social justice in higher education, and/or one can conduct research *for* social justice in higher education. Depending on one's orientation, one could argue that these ought – or ought not – to be the same. If one sets aside the myth of objectivity and steps outside of a positivist paradigm, one is further confronted with the question of whether research into social justice issues in higher education can – or ought to – be studied from outside, or from within.

Research – especially research into, or for, social justice issues in higher education – is often prompted by a recognition of injustice. As noted by Van Maanen (2010, p. 338),

> A grievance or sense of righteous indignation it seems can get one to the field and keep them there. … Without an affront, injustice, complaint, or beef to explore we might well become ciphers-qua-celebrants, happy agreeable sorts

who wallow in unmitigated delight … and, in the end, have little to say other than everything is hunky-dory.

I noted elsewhere (Trowler, 2014, p. 43) that 'it is a political choice to turn the spotlight onto the marginalised'; it is also important as an antidote to the partiality (in both senses) of accounts that consider only the experiences of the advantaged. Yet as bell hooks (1990) cautions, studying the experiences of others – especially where issues of social justice are concerned, and those under study may have relatively less power than the researchers – has moral implications:

> No need to hear your voice when I can talk about you better than you can speak about yourself. No need to hear your voice. Only tell me about your pain. I want to know your story. And then I will tell it back to you in a new way. Tell it back to you in such a way that it has become mine, my own. Re-writing you I write myself anew. I am still author, authority. I am still colonizer the speaking subject and you are now at the center of my talk.

This appropriation of the subaltern's experience by the researcher often results in injustices of recognition and, potentially, of distribution. Such injustices have led to researched populations including Inuit and First Nations in Canada, Australia and South Africa issuing codes of ethics with which any researchers are obliged to comply as a condition of access. Nordling (2017) quotes the head of the South African San Council in Upington, Leana Snyders, as saying thus:

> When a researcher comes they enrich themselves of our culture and our knowledge. But our communities remain in poverty; their daily life does not change. We want to change that.

The San Code of Research Ethics (South African San Institute, 2017) opens with the requirement for respect and recognition – of themselves and of their contribution to the research. 'Re-writing you' is a form of denying or misrepresenting recognition (Honneth, 1995, 2003, 2007). The term 'mis/recognition' is used to convey a process of not simply failing to recognize accurately but simultaneously delegitimizing. Fraser (1995, p. 280) describes mis/recognition as

> not simply to be thought ill of, looked down on, or devalued in others' conscious attitudes or mental beliefs. It is rather to be denied the status of full partner in social interaction and prevented from participating as a peer in social life – not as a consequence of a distributive inequality (such as failing to receive one's fair share of resources or 'primary goods') but rather as a consequence of institutionalised patterns of interpretation and evaluation that constitute one as comparatively unworthy of respect or esteem.

Issues of mis/recognition are thus pivotal in the re/presentation of marginalized, subaltern or less powerful subjects. One way to challenge that is through truly endogenous research – not just 'close up', but 'inside out'. This, however, presents its own challenges, since those subjects do not have access to the hegemonic discourse, as I noted (Trowler, 2014, p. 44) previously:

> Subalterns are rendered mute by the 'epistemic violence' of hegemonic discourse – in order to be heard, they must adopt the thought, reasoning and language of the dominant group, and can never express their own reasoning, forms of knowledge and logic.

Schultze (2000, p. 7) describes the 'constraints' under which a knowledge worker tries to convince others of the reliability and validity of their claims, in constructing new knowledge:

> constraints include the format that knowledge needs to take in order to be acceptable to others, the language or symbol system within which it must operate, and the evidence ... to support ... new knowledge claims.

For the subaltern researcher, then, the two identities are in opposition. As subaltern, one has 'insider' access to raw data – the lived experience of those being studied – but not to the discourse with which to make 'knowledge claims' that may be recognized as reliable or valid. As a researcher, one has access to the discourse with which to make, and defend, new knowledge claims, but not authentically to the lived experience of the subaltern. Schultze (2000, p. 8) captures it thus:

> Ethnographers ... are ... confronted with potentially conflicting demands. In their role as instrument they rely on their personal experience and subjective engagement with phenomena in the field to generate insights, whereas in their role as scientist they need to convince the scientific community of the trans-situational ... and reliable nature of these very phenomena.

This tension between researcher-as-instrument and researcher-as-scientist is particularly heightened when the researcher is conducting endogenous research.

Who Is an Insider?

Clegg and Stevenson (2013) argue that interviewing in higher education research is a form of ethnography, because as participants in the higher education system, we are 'insiders'. I have engaged more fully with this argument elsewhere

(Trowler, 2016), but it raises the question of exactly who can lay claim to 'insider' status. I propose that there are three dimensions to this:

- Location – how close the researcher is to the site of the study. Is it sufficient to be located in the same system, as Clegg and Stevenson propose, or does one need to be located in the institution, or even the department, that one is studying? Clearly the focus of the study matters here: if the focus is system wide, the researcher's own location matters less than it does if the focus is on a specific research centre situated in a different department to the researcher's home department, in a different institution to that which employs the researcher and with different disciplinary affiliations to those of the researcher.
- Time – in any direction. A researcher who is researching backward in time – for example, looking at the development of a policy, or researching a particular event – may share a systems/institutional/departmental or other specific location with that which they're researching, but may not have been present in that specific locus at the time of the policy development or event. Likewise, a researcher may return to a system or institutional (or departmental) context where they were once located, to conduct research in the present. They may extrapolate from their own experience backward or forward in time, but the magnitude of the changes prior to, or since, their being an insider may be sufficient to render them an 'outsider'.
- Subjectivities – especially relative to who holds power in that context. Researchers who are differently placed are likely to be granted different levels and kinds of access, leading to the 'Rashomon effect' (Heider, 1988) where different researchers produce different accounts of 'the same' event, process or situation. An example may be seen in considering two recent texts alongside each other: Council on Higher Education's (2016) 'Reflections of South African University Leaders' features a mix of self-penned reflective essays and interviews conducted by staff of the Council on Higher Education (CHE), while Jansen's (2017) 'As by Fire' draws on interviews the author – himself a vice chancellor (VC) at a South African university at the time – conducted with other VCs. While the former publication provides some interesting insights, these lack the intimate, immediate edge of the Jansen text, where one gets a real sense of the person rather than just the role.

While the above example illustrates nuances of gaining access 'upward', similar dynamics play out when conducting research among those who (perceive themselves to) have less power. Scott (1991) refers to 'hidden transcripts', the body of information and views shared by subalterns among themselves, which differs from the 'public transcripts' they share with others. These hidden transcripts are characterized by

- taking place offstage, away from public gaze, because of the risk to the subordinates;
- being accessible only to subalterns, and not shared with those who hold power and
- being rendered visible without decoding at the point of 'rupture' – certain events can force these hidden transcripts into view at moments of crisis and challenge.

As widening participation (or 'transformation') policies produce results, more researchers will emerge from historically underrepresented communities with assumed access to these 'hidden transcripts'. However, as I noted previously (Trowler, 2014, pp. 51–2), conducting research from within 'subaltern space' does not fully equate with acquisition of the 'hegemonic discourse'. Rather,

> analogous to Prensky's 'digital immigrants' who speak with an 'accent', it would appear that these subalterns master a dialect, or speak with a heavy accent, which continues to mark them out as different, and continues to exclude them [from the community of knowledge producers].

I will consider the issues of what constitutes 'insiderness' through reflecting on three studies, and my role and subjectivities vis-à-vis those who were being studied. A brief description of each of the studies will be followed by a fuller reflection, in the following section.

Study 1: A Study of 'Non-Traditional' Higher Education Students

This study (Trowler, 2016) set out to examine how students who define themselves as 'non-traditional' in their own study contexts perceive their institutions' attempts to engage them, and their own engagement practices, and how these affect their intentions to persist or withdraw from their studies. I interviewed twenty-three undergraduate students enrolled at Scottish universities three times each across a calendar year.

Was I an Insider?

What we shared:

- I was also a student registered at a Scottish university – but I was not an undergraduate student, nor was I enrolled at the same university as the overwhelming majority of my respondents, so the extent to which our 'being students at Scottish universities' qualified as shared experience is contestable.
- I shared some aspects of subjectivities with some of the students: I had been the first in my family to attend university; I had studied my undergraduate degree in a language not my first and attended a university whose culture was not my own; I had studied for two of my degrees part-time; I had worked while studying for two of my degrees; I had been a student-parent for some of my studies; I had been a mature student; I was an 'international' student, marked by accent; I had been a student of a 'race'/ethnicity that was a minority at a university at which I had studied.

What we did not share:

- I was not an undergraduate student at the same time as the students I interviewed.
- I had not been an undergraduate student in the same place as the students I interviewed.

Thus, while sharing elements of location, time and subjectivities, there was much (in terms of location, time and subjectivities) that I did not share. I could not legitimately lay claim to 'insider' status.

Reflections

With this study, the shared aspects of subjectivities helped to build rapport and to spark genuine interest in both directions. Providing points of connection for students who felt 'out of place' or 'marginal' in their study contexts seemed to help them to develop trust and open up. However, the very clear differences also aided, in reminding me of my role as researcher and thus allowing me to maintain a critical distance. The different contexts also foregrounded for me the necessity of checking assumptions: while shared subjectivities and experiences can lead to empathetic bonding, it can lead to projection if assumptions are not checked and details of experiences not elicited – and, in extreme cases, inadvertent misrecognition.

This study also caused me to reflect anew on the Clegg and Stevenson's (2013) argument of interviewing in higher education research having ethnographic overtones. My experience of being located 'in the system' did not locate me in the position, or the positionality, of my respondents. Sitting in a café in Glasgow interviewing a student did not magically transport me to the lived experience of entering a university from the college sector, which I had not personally experienced; spending time walking around a newer university with an informant who studied there observing the graffiti, the staffed access control and the deportment of many of the students, however, did give me at least some insight into the context behind his comments.

Wary of misrepresenting the students I interviewed, I made drafts of relevant sections (with explanatory notes) available to them for comment. Perhaps predictably, none of them offered any comment, and there was no discernible evidence that any of them had engaged with the drafts. While this allowed me to feel smugly compliant from an ethics perspective, it does surface concerns about how informed 'informed consent' actually is in practice. These were students literate and sophisticated – in comparison to some other researched populations. Their reluctance to engage with my drafts can be understood in many ways, but I suspect that for most of them it was yet another chore competing for their time, attention and intellectual effort, when they felt under siege by so much else, coupled with a naive faith in the academic system to which they had also committed themselves. (The 'sunk cost fallacy' argues that the more you invest in something, the harder it becomes to abandon it. These students had given generously of their time and engagement – disappointment in the results of their investment may have been a risk they were not willing to take.)

The San Code of Research Ethics (South African San Institute, 2017) requires high levels of transparency and informed consent, including the stipulation that complex issues be made accessible and communicated appropriately rather than assumptions being made about what the San can and cannot be expected to understand. While this seeks to avoid mis/representation and is clearly desirable, how is this translated into the context of social justice research in higher education in a way that is true to the spirit of the Code? Is it sufficient to make something available, knowing that in all likelihood it won't be read, or challenged? Or does the commitment not to mis/recognize and not to mispresent require a deeper, more informed form of informed consent?

Study 2: Comparative Study

The second study aimed to compare the engagement experiences of self-defined 'non-traditional' higher education students in Scotland (Study 1) with students who self-identified as 'non-traditional' in a different context (a university in South Africa). This was a collaboration with a former colleague, who was employed at the South African university at the time. A few hours after we'd met to discuss the project, student protests erupted and the study shifted its focus more explicitly to that, with data being generated primarily from social media posts.

Were We Insiders?

What we shared:

- We shared location, to an extent: we had both worked and studied at that university, and my former colleague was working there at the time.
- I was no longer at the university in any role, while my former colleague was; thus, our sharing of 'time' was mixed.
- With respect to subjectivities, we shared a political programme with the students, as it was recorded at the time. My former colleague was black, but not a student; I was a student, but not black.

What we did not share:

- Given the protest movement's foregrounding of intersectionality, we were very conscious of the extent to which we did not share subjectivities with many of the students, especially those aspects related to power and visibility. (Voices of LGBTQIA students, non-binary students and students with disabilities emerged strongly alongside discussions of race, class, gender and the urban/rural divide.) We became very conscious of relative privilege along many axes of difference.

While in many ways my former colleague had a greater claim to 'insider' status than I had at the time, neither of us could claim fully to be 'insiders'.

Reflections

With regard to the second study, the conflicts around 'insiderness' became more pronounced. As noted earlier, the original intention was to generate comparative data from a very different context, to compare experiences of students identifying as 'non-traditional' and to test out tentative theory emerging from the Scottish study (Study 1) in the very different context of a South African university.

With our decision to shift the focus to the protests, we were confronted by scope-creep and role-blurring. We had both been active in social justice structures and activities at the university and had a sustained history of activism on the issues that were the subject of the protests. We were thus drawn into providing support of various kinds to the protesting students – including providing advice and using our networks to secure legal, financial and other forms of assistance. This raised questions in our own minds about critical distance and 'objectivity', and where we located ourselves, in a climate where some university staff writing opinion pieces in the media were being accused of being 'mere apologists' for the protests movement and others of 'exploiting' the protest movement to boost their own profile. As McArthur notes in her chapter,

> There can be no greater injustice than to consider social justice as simply another topic of research: an interesting and perhaps vaguely honourable area of data to be mined and processed into academic papers and promotion applications.

This tension between our roles as social justice activists and as social justice researchers led us to stepping back once again to review our research purpose. We suspended data collection with a view to developing a larger research proposal and seeking funding, and continued in our roles as activists.

Study 3: Subordinate Estate of HEI

The third study (Trowler, 2014) focused on demographic shifts taking place within the 'non-academic' staff sector at a university in South Africa, where I was employed at the time on 'non-academic' conditions of employment.

Was I an Insider?

What we shared:

- We shared a location contemporaneously and shared aspects of subjectivities, especially our location in the subordinate estate in a highly hierarchical context.[1]

However:

- I occupied a privileged space relative to many of the colleagues among whom I was generating data. In part, this was due to my position in the staff union, which gave me access to social and cultural capitals (access to people in senior leadership roles, membership of committees and other governance structures). But it was also related to the study itself – as a postgraduate student (albeit at a different university) I was gaining access to the hegemonic discourse (though having spoken with an 'accent' – as noted earlier) that Spivak (1994) argues is denied to subalterns – who she claims are rendered mute by the 'epistemic violence' of the hegemonic discourse.

While I felt very much an insider, I occupied a privileged space within that role.

Reflections:

In reflecting on the third study, I am confronted to an even greater extent by issues of role-blurring and boundary confusion. I was very conscious throughout the study that my pre-existing relationships – as a colleague, as a line manager and as president of the staff union, for example – produced dynamics of power which shaped not only the extent to which I was granted or denied access but also the nature of the data which emerged. As I noted (Trowler, 2014, p. 50) elsewhere,

> While in theory I could step outside of one role and into another, in practice it was much more difficult, and I was aware that as I stepped into my 'researcher' role, I brought with me knowledge repositories and networks of access associated with the multiplicity of my other roles. My being an insider both allowed me access to, and contaminated, my data. I was acutely conscious of the idiosyncrasy of my data, and the questions of reliability and validity that this raised.

I was aware that I was utilizing knowledge, data, insights that I had gained in other roles, at other times, and for which I had never sought nor been granted access as a researcher. I needed to keep resurfacing those insights consciously, verbalizing them and asking permission to include them, knowing that I could not un-know them if permission was refused.

As an 'insider', unintended consequences (or 'observer effect') seemed far more acute. As I wrote up the study, I became aware that every African[2] respondent I was quoting had since left the university. I was crushingly familiar with the institutional climate that was perceived as hostile to black staff before undertaking the study, but reading the words of black staff who felt marginalized and alienated and noting that each of them had left since I'd captured those words, I could not help but wonder to what extent asking them to reflect on their situation had hastened their departure. While such consequences are not peculiar to insider research, endogenous researchers are more likely to be conscious of these, since they are closer to the lived realities of those they study. It is, moreover, possible that their closeness encourages more openness or reflectivity from their study participants and that this exacerbates these unintended consequences. This complicity will be considered further in the following discussion.

Discussion

As a disciplinary vagrant, I have passed through many paradigms, epistemologies and traditions along my meanderings, but I remember being taught that the central tenet of anthropology was 'to make the strange familiar, and the familiar strange'.[3] For the endogenous researcher, the 'culture', phenomenon or process under study is both familiar and strange: as an insider, it is familiar, but as a researcher, it is viewed as strange. The emic (endogenous) and etic (exogenous) perspectives are thus held in tension as one moves between one's positionalities as insider and researcher.

Reflexivity is important in any form of social research, but with endogenous research it becomes paramount. As Jones (2000, p. 159) notes,

> reflexive fieldwork strategies offer important opportunities to problematize knowledge production. They give us the chance – even force us – to re-think 'them/us'.

In my experience, gleaned from the three studies discussed earlier (and others), reflexivity is easier when there are at least some aspects of difference. No community or group is ever totally homogenous, and 'insiderness' is therefore always a question of degree rather than a binary yes/no. In my experience, however, the fewer the number of differences (or the less aware the researcher is of differences) between the endogenous researcher and the group under study, the easier it is to slip into assumptions without noticing, and the more tempting it is to project one's own understandings onto one's study participants. Markers of difference act as reminders to question assumptions, verify understandings and remain reflexive. They act not so much as a caution against 'going native', but against assuming that one already is.

Not being a complete insider also renders ethical considerations around access more straightforward. Because one is prompted by markers of difference into checking one's assumptions – or not making them in the first place – the researcher can feel more confident that the data or understandings have been generated overtly, as part of the research process, with the consent of the participants, rather than being imported from prior 'knowings', generated covertly without the conscious consent of participants. There is less role confusion, for both researcher and informants.

Maruyama (1981) argues for a 'polyocular' anthropology, which combines endogenous and exogenous epistemologies. (Binocular anthropology would combine a single endogenous viewpoint with a single exogenous one; truly polyocular anthropology would require a team of researchers representing several 'subcultures', within the group being studied, and several exogenous cultures.) As a first step towards this, he argues for endogenous research, since it combines conceptualization, design and execution from within the epistemology and structure of relevance of the culture under study. Beyond epistemological considerations, he claims endogenous researchers bring heightened awareness of other critical aspects that might otherwise distort the research.

The first of these concerns the philosophy regarding communication. Without fully understanding the role of communication in the group under study, an exogenous researcher may deploy research methods that trigger resistance or produce inauthentic responses. This has resonance with Scott's (1991) description of the 'public transcripts', which are offered to researchers or outsiders, unlike the 'hidden transcripts', which are shared 'offstage' among the group themselves. An example from Study 2 was the use of Twitter as a 'public transcript' and WhatsApp groups (of known, trusted insiders) as a 'hidden transcript'. Relying only on Twitter, as several studies have done, thus skews the data towards only the 'outward facing'.

However, as Scott also notes, 'hidden transcripts' can become public at the point of rupture, and Study 3 included an example of that with the use of the (public) listserv to voice frustrations in the wake of a faculty meeting held to discuss the depressing findings of the organizational climate survey, which indicated severe unhappiness among 'non-academic' staff in the faculty. The presence of both academic and 'non-academic' staff at the meeting, the venue of the meeting, and the tone set by the first speaker (an academic Head of Department) acted to silence the 'non-academic' staff, who then found other media to air their views (notably the listserv and an anonymous webform). This example illustrates Maruyama's point: the organizer of the meeting (the dean, an academic with little insight into the concerns of 'non-academic' staff) had – and shared with many of the academic staff – a different philosophy of communication, which involved debate, assertion and refutation. For the majority of the 'non-academic' staff, such combative discussion was read as conflict and not a 'safe space' in which to discuss their concerns around the discrimination, harassment and bullying they had reported in the survey.

The second aspect raised by Maruyama concerns relevance dissonance. By this, he means the understanding of the purpose of collecting data as understood by the group being studied. Maruyama (1981, p. 231) gives the example of white middle-class people having faith that data being collected will further their well-being, while Native Americans have the opposite expectation – that the data will benefit the researchers, but not themselves. He argues that endogenous researchers are more likely to share research goals with the group they are researching, and are thus less likely to receive inauthentic responses.

An example from Study 1: during my first interviews with the students, there was little alignment to our goals. I was seen to be 'collecting' data towards a PhD; the students had volunteered to be interviewed mostly because of wanting to be visible. As a result, some of the responses were probably closer to what they thought they ought to say than what they may really have wanted to say. As rapport developed over the years, a greater awareness of a shared goal emerged – to convey authentically the experiences of those students who considered themselves to be 'non-traditional' in their study contexts. Thus, with subsequent interviews, responses developed in nuance and shifted to include more 'oppositional' forms of engagement rather than recounting their behavioural compliance.

Criticality dissonance is the third aspect listed by Maruyama. This concerns exogenous researchers being unaware of the dangers posed by the generation of the research data because of their lack of familiarity with the context. As an example, Study 3 might have involved direct risk to participants. Detailed data I generated could have been used to negative effect – with regard to job grading, performance assessment or disciplinary action, for example – in the wrong hands, despite my best efforts to pseudonymize data. An example from Study 2 relates to the identity and roles of the protest 'leadership' – because of the threat of physical, economic and academic harm to some of the more visible protesters, some data was extremely sensitive. Arrests, suspension from studies, protracted legal and disciplinary (within the university) proceedings compromised the data that could safely be generated for use in the study.

This returns the focus to those occasions where, as a social justice researcher, one finds one's role as a researcher in tension with one's commitment to social justice. There are times when one's most useful contribution to social justice would be the generation and dissemination of data. There are other times when that feels like self-enrichment at the expense of those one is studying, when the need for more 'hands on' activism surpasses the need for data – at least in one's own mind. Like the photographer torn between recording the atrocity to make the world aware and stepping in to stop it, the tension between the roles of activist and researcher can sometimes surface into open conflict, obliging one to step back from at least one of the roles to reflect.

This is further complicated by issues of complicity, as intimated earlier in the reflections on Study 3. As an 'insider', you are implicated in that which you are studying – which may at times seem damning to those concerned with social justice. Foucault's (1980) construct of the 'specific intellectual' may be usefully deployed here. In contrast to the notion of the 'universal intellectual', who is concerned with the 'just-and-true-for-all', the specific intellectual works 'within specific sectors, at the precise point where their own conditions of life and work situate them' (Foucault, 1980, p. 126). Rather than trying to uncover what might be inside someone's head, the specific intellectual's project is to uncover 'the political, economic institutional regime of the production of truth' since 'truth is linked in circular relations with system of power which produce and sustain it, and to effects of power which it induces and which extend it' (Foucault, 1980, p. 133). The work of the specific intellectual is not invalidated ethically or politically by their complicity, but politically important because of it, since specific intellectuals have both complicity and agency. As Jones (2000, p. 168) notes, the 'specific intellectual is someone positioned in a specific power/knowledge nexus, and therefore uniquely qualified and empowered to reflexively critique the nexus itself'. As insiders, our complicity empowers us uniquely to pull back the covers and expose the truth regime which governs the space, time and subjectivities where we are situated.

Conclusion

'Close-up' research can be conducted exogenously – by 'outsiders' – or endogenously – by 'insiders'. Maruyama (1981) argues for an ideal of 'polyocular' research, combining multiple exogenous and endogenous perspectives, towards which endogenous research is an important first step. Reflecting on three research projects in which I held different degrees of 'insiderness' – based upon the varying extents to which I shared location, time and subjectivities with those being studied – I would suggest that it is not just possible, but important, to hold both emic and etic perspectives in tension. Researching reflexively requires critical awareness of one's own positionality in relation to those one is studying – especially when concerned with issues of social justice.

I have argued that rather than clinging to a binary of 'insider' versus 'outsider', recognizing that groups and communities are not homogenous but riven with multiple power differentials compels one to recognize that 'insiderness' is not absolute but a matter of degree. Such dichotomies are unhelpful, as McArthur stresses in her chapter, when pursuing social justice research. Utilizing reflexive strategies to problematize 'us/them', as Jones (2000, p. 159) suggests, can help in this regard. Being attuned to points of connection can enhance empathy and help to sensitize researchers to relevance dissonance and criticality dissonance, while remaining cognizant of markers of difference can prevent projection of assumptions and alert researchers to epistemological differences and different philosophies of communication. This 'situated sensitivity' requires honesty about one's own positionality as a researcher, even where one might consider oneself a 'true' insider. Recognizing our complicity in situations where we are conducting 'inside out' research brings with it a recognition of our being uniquely 'qualified and empowered' to deploy our insights – as 'insiders' and as researchers – in the pursuit of social justice.

Notes

1 At the time of the study, there were marked differences in conditions of employment between academic and 'non-academic' staff. The former qualified for sabbatical leave and ad hominem promotion, could compete for research-related funding and retired at the age of sixty-five, while the latter retired at the age of sixty and were subject to micromanagement.
2 As they were categorized for the purposes of monitoring employment equity. These were black African South African citizens, a category that – together with other black ('Indian', or 'coloured') people, people with disabilities and women – qualified for restorative measures in appointment and promotion.
3 Quote originally attributed to eighteenth-century German poet Novalis.

References

Butler, J. (1997). Merely cultural. *Social Text, 52*(53), 265–277.

Clegg, S., & Stevenson, J. (2013). The interview reconsidered: Context, genre, reflexivity and interpretation in sociological approaches to interviews in Higher Education Research. *Higher Education Research & Development, 32*(1), 5–16.

Council on Higher Education (2016). *Reflections of South African University Leaders, 1981 to 2014*. Cape Town: African Minds and Council on Higher Education.

Foucault, M. (1980). Truth and power. In C. Gordon (Ed.), *Power/Knowledge: Selected Interviews and Other Writings 1972 – 1977* (pp. 109–133). New York: Pantheon.

Fraser, N. (1995). From redistribution to recognition? Dilemmas of justice in a 'Post-Socialist' age. New Left Review, *212*, 68–94.

Fraser, N. (2013). *Fortunes of Feminism: From State-Managed Capitalism to Neo-Liberal Crisis*. London: Verso.

Heider, K. G. (1988). The Rashomon effect: When ethnographers disagree. *American Anthropologist, 90*(1), 73–81.

Honneth, A. (1995). *The Fragmented World of the Social*. Albany, NY: State University of New York Press.

Honneth, A. (2003). Redistribution as Recognition: A Response to Nancy Fraser. In *Redistribution or Recognition? A Political-Philosophical Exchange*, 110–197. London: Verso.

Honneth, A. (2007). *Disrespect: The Normative Foundations of Critical Theory*. Cambridge: Polity Press.

Hooks, B. (1990). Marginality as a Site of Resistance. In R. Ferguson (Eds.), *Out There: Marginalization and Contemporary Cultures*, 341–343. Cambridge, MA: MIT.

Jansen, J. (2017). *As by Fire: The End of the South African University*. Cape Town: Tafelberg.

Jones, D. (2000). Knowledge Workers 'R' Us: Academics, Practitioners and 'Specific Intellectuals'. In C. Pritchard (Eds.), *Managing Knowledge: Critical Investigations of Work and Learning*, 158–175. Houndmills: Macmillan Business.

Maruyama, M. (1981). Endogenous Research: Rationale. In P. Reason & J. Rowan (Eds.), *Human Inquiry*, 227–238. Chichester: John Wiley & Sons.

Nordling, L. (2017). San People of Africa draft code of ethics for researchers. *Science*, 17 March 2017. doi: 10.1126/science.aal0933.

Schultze, U. (2000). A confessional account of an ethnography about knowledge work. *MIS Quarterly, 24*(1), 3–41. doi: 10.2307/3250978.

Scott, J. C. (1991). *Domination and the Arts of Resistance: Hidden Transcripts*. New Haven: Yale University Press.

South African San Institute (2017). *San Code of Research Ethics*. Kimberley: South African San Institute. Retrieved from http://trust-project.eu/wp-content/uploads/2017/03/San-Code-of-RESEARCH-Ethics-Booklet-final.pdf.

Spivak, Gayatri C. 1994. Can the Subaltern Speak? In P. Williams & L. Chrisman (Eds.), *Colonial Discourse and Post-Colonial Theory: A Reader*, 66–111. New York: Columbia University Press.

Trowler, V. (2014). May the subaltern speak? Researching the invisible 'other' in Higher Education. *European Journal of Higher Education*, *4*(1), 42–54, doi: 10.1080/21568235.2013.851614.

Trowler, V. (2016). *Nomads in Contested Landscapes: Reframing student Engagement and Non-Traditionality in Higher Education*. University of Edinburgh: Unpublished PhD thesis.

Van Maanen, J. (2010). You gotta have a grievance: Locating heartbreak in ethnography. *Journal of Management Inquiry*, *19*(4), 338–341. doi: 10.1177/1056492610370284.

4

Understanding Social Justice through the Lens of Research Impact across the Academy

Sharon McCulloch and Karin Tusting

Introduction

One popular stereotype of the academic is that of the wild-haired genius in the metaphorical ivory tower, pursuing arcane knowledge for its own sake with little regard for the 'real world'. For example, in 2016, a British MP tweeted that he did not view academics as 'experts' since they have no experience of 'the real world' (Sheppard, 2016). A contrasting view is that of the academic as a passionate, left-wing intellectual, committed to changing the world (c.f. Carl, 2018; Solon, 2015). The reality is that academics' perspectives on the idea of social justice are likely to be characterized by difference, with understandings of what social justice means and its relevance to their work varying more widely than stereotypes might suggest. A recent change in the way academic research is evaluated in the UK might influence this, since it encourages academics to demonstrate the impact of their scholarly work beyond academia, and it is this notion of impact and how it relates to academics' understandings of social justice that this chapter focuses on.

The chapter reports on an ESRC-funded research project entitled 'The Dynamics of Knowledge Creation: Academics' writing practices in the contemporary university workplace',[1] based at Lancaster University from 2015 to 2017. Through detailed investigation of the writing practices of academics in three different disciplines and institutions in England, the project aimed to explore how knowledge is produced and distributed through academics' writing practices and how these are shaped by the contemporary context of higher education, including managerial practices and evaluation frameworks.

One important aspect of the UK's REF is the notion of impact. Impact, as defined in the REF, means 'an effect, change or benefit beyond academia, in areas such as the economy, environment, policy, culture, health, or society at large' (HEFCE, 2016). Unlike the 'impact factor' of a journal, which measures the impact of research on other researchers through citation counts, this concept represents one of the ways in which academia can make itself accountable, reach out to more diverse communities and potentially ensure that research makes a positive impact on society.

In this chapter, we consider how academics across different disciplines and institutions interpret policies requiring them to demonstrate economic and social impact and how this interacts with their views on the wider role of academic work in society. We begin by outlining some of the changes that have taken place in higher education in England, where this study was situated, over the past few years, and discuss how these have shaped the role of academics and their writing practices. We then briefly discuss the UK's REF, the notion of impact embedded within this and how these interact with the idea of social justice. Next, we describe the context for and design of our study, before discussing the findings. Specifically, we report on interviews conducted with academics in which they share their perspectives on impact and how this relates to the notion of social justice. We discuss whether some disciplines lend themselves to social justice more readily than others and the extent to which social justice is understood to be a collective or individual responsibility for academics. Finally, we explore the interaction between national and institutional policies on research quality, on the one hand, and academics' ability and willingness to pursue social justice goals on the other.

Background

A Marketized Perspective on Higher Education

Higher education in England has undergone many of the changes that took place in other European countries over the past few decades associated with a process of marketization, whereby universities are run along increasingly commercial lines (Deem, Hillyard & Reed, 2007). These changes influence the perspectives both students and staff are encouraged to take regarding the purpose of universities in society and their own role within them.

Higher education is treated as a kind of global marketplace, where universities compete with each other for students, who, in turn, are positioned as consumers who can use information such as university rankings and student satisfaction survey scores to make informed choices about where to spend their money. Such a perspective means that students are positioned as customers (Bunce, Baird & Jones, 2017; Ingleby, 2015) and knowledge is viewed as a commodity that can be quantified via rankings and 'bought' via tuition fees. In this conceptualization, the purpose of higher education is primarily seen in terms of instrumental and economic goals, while other purposes, such as self-fulfilment or contributing to a more just society, are downplayed (Naidoo & Williams, 2015). This position thus also involves a number of dichotomies similar to those outlined by McArthur in Chapter 1; most notably that between service provider (university) and consumer (student).

Of course, universities do make an important economic contribution to society, and getting a better job is one reason for getting a degree, but these utilitarian aspects of higher education are not the only, nor arguably the most, important functions of universities. We must look beyond the binary distinctions or dichotomies. Universities also have a social, moral and cultural role to play. Higher education creates graduates such as lawyers, doctors, teachers and artists who can contribute to society as a whole in the fields of justice, health, education and culture. Universities should foster values such as tolerance and freedom of speech, which are essential to any just society. Higher education may also promote social mobility, which benefits society by enabling people to live more fulfilled lives.

Amartya Sen links the purpose of education to the notion of 'human flourishing', understood as people's freedoms and opportunities to live a life that is of value to them (Sen, 2009). Many scholars (c.f. Molesworth et al., 2011; Naidoo & Williams, 2015) have argued that an increasingly marketized view of higher education contributes to a weakened commitment to the transformative or emancipatory aspects of higher education (Beetham, 2016).

How Marketization Affects Academics

Much of the research on education and social justice has focused on students' experience through issues such as access to and participation in higher education (Furlong & Cartmel, 2009) and on the role of assessment in facilitating social justice (McArthur, 2016). However, an emphasis on instrumental goals and the economic value of higher education also affects university staff in a wide range of ways.

As higher education has become more commercialized, academics as well as students have found many aspects of their role changing. In this chapter, we argue that the research academics do, and the scholarly writing associated with it, are coming under similar pressures to those experienced by higher education as a whole (Deem, Hillyard & Reed, 2007) and that understandings of social justice are influenced by the competing and sometimes contradictory pressures academics experience with regard to their writing.

The changes in higher education outlined earlier influence the ways in which academics' scholarly writing is produced and published and the ways in which findings are disseminated and promoted. Competition for research funding has become more intense since universities in England now receive less funding from direct government grants, and the results of national research evaluation exercises are used to assess research quality and allocate funds accordingly. It would be fruitful to undertake further work on the extent to which similar pressures and influences are found in other higher education systems.

England's national research evaluation scheme, the REF, is conducted every five to six years. Star ratings are awarded to each piece of published research, and funding is allocated to departments in accordance with their aggregated ratings along with assessments of the research environment and of impact (see below). Most universities therefore encourage or require their academics to submit work to the REF, often incentivizing the production of publications in high-ranking journals by linking this to probation and promotion criteria. The Stern report criticized the 'tying of research quality too closely with individual performance' (Stern, 2016, p. 15) for having adverse effects on academics' career choices.

While one could argue that rewarding 'good' publications is perfectly reasonable, the REF and universities' responses to it risk overemphasizing quantitative aspects of scholarship in the form of measurable outputs at the expense of more diverse forms of scholarship that reach wider audiences (McCulloch, 2017). The way the REF is configured tends to reward academics for their individual measurable 'outputs' rather than, for example, pushing the boundaries of the discipline or doing innovative forms of research. The close linking of the REF to academics' career advancement also encourages an orientation towards entrepreneurialism and individual career success rather than commitment to the more difficult-to-measure goals of social justice (Taylor, 2016; Tourish & Willmott, 2015), which remains one of the aims of higher education. Thus, for academics, there is a potential tension between the drive to perform well in terms of the REF and any desire to contribute more broadly to 'civic virtues' such as advancing democracy and social justice.

The Relationship between 'Impact' and Social Justice

One change brought about as part of the 2014 REF was that university departments in England were, for the first time, expected to demonstrate that their research had economic or social impact beyond academia (HEFCE, 2016). This encourages academics to disseminate findings to non-academic audiences, which entails engaging in forms of writing that differ markedly from the traditional monograph or academic journal paper written by and for expert audiences. Genres of writing for this purpose could include policy statements, reports for business or government bodies, websites, blogs, documents or other artefacts to be used by practitioners or the general public. Many academics also use social media as a means of reaching wider audiences. These forms of writing are not usually peer-reviewed nor would they typically generate many academic citations.

This 'impact agenda' is one of the ways in which scholarly research may engage with the notion of social justice, and it may counteract some of the disincentives to civic values created by the REF by enabling academics to reach wider and more diverse communities. However, some have argued that impact is more complex and cumulative in nature than is accounted for in research assessment exercises like the REF (Ashwin, 2016), which tend to focus on direct, relatively short-term and measurable effects which can be clearly linked to specific publications. As well as being difficult to measure in the short term, impact may also be interpreted in different ways across different disciplines (Cruickshank, 2015), with some lending themselves to social justice more readily than others. It is therefore important to investigate the role that social justice plays in academics' research writing, how they understand social justice and how it interacts with factors such as disciplinary tradition and research evaluation policies.

The Study

The study we report on here takes a broadly social practice approach to literacy, in which reading and writing are seen as practices developed and maintained within their social contexts and shaped by aspects of people's purposes, histories and institutional positionings (Barton & Hamilton, 2000; Barton, 2007). In this sense, the research considers the interaction between policy frameworks and the values and practices of the academics who work within them.

The data reported in this chapter comes from interviews conducted with seventy academics working at three different universities in England. Participants were recruited from three disciplinary areas at each of these institutions. The disciplines chosen were mathematics, to represent the STEM disciplines, history as a humanities discipline and marketing as an example of a professional/applied discipline. We also conducted preliminary interviews in our own disciplines in the social sciences, some of which are included in the data reported in this chapter. All participants held research-active posts, in roles from lecturer to professor,[2] thirty-two of whom were women, while thirty-eight were men.

The participants were interviewed about their writing practices within the context of the university as a workplace, in order to understand how their writing practices were changing in light of some of the broader changes in higher education outlined above, as well as the impact of digital communications technologies. We asked academics about their pedagogical, administrative and scholarly writing, and it is the latter that we focus on in this chapter, particularly where it relates to the notion of 'impact' as defined in the REF.

The interviews were recorded, transcribed and anonymized, then analysed using ATLAS.ti qualitative data analysis software. Coding of the data focused on content. The initial coding framework developed aspects of the research questions, with subsequent codes and sub-codes being added as they emerged through our engagement with the data. We did not set out to investigate academics' attitudes to social justice specifically, but we were interested in the factors that influenced their decisions about what to write and where to publish their work, and this led to discussions about the purpose and audiences for their research and how these interacted with notions of impact and social justice. The findings reveal a range of different perspectives on social justice and how it might be achieved, reinforcing the point made in the introductory chapter of this volume that we need to be open to different interpretations and experiences of social justice.

Results and Discussion

Academics' Understandings of 'Impact'

Understandings of what 'impact' meant varied widely among the participants of the current study. When asked about impact-related writing, some talked about blogs and social media, while some described 'trade books' aimed at outsiders such as professionals or young people. Some participants included consultancy work and commissioned research within their definition of impact. Those working in applied or professional disciplines tended to talk about enabling outsider agencies to understand complex issues or make direct changes as a result of research:

> But often trying to write for people like the Environment Agency, who haven't really got a statistical background, who still very much care about the type of things I do, but it needs to be presented to make it accessible to as many of the people there as possible. (Gareth, mathematics)

> Writing reports for the consultancies I do ... can have very direct impact. Those reports can sometimes make ... the organisations that they review [their products] completely, ... they've changed them on the basis of my findings or recommendations. (Juliette, social science)

Like Juliette, many academics talked about making a difference in utilitarian terms in that they wanted their research to be useful or actionable, but the perceived beneficiaries of changes resulting from research included not only students or groups usually thought of as disadvantaged but also commercial companies and government agencies.

In a 2017 study conducted in the UK and Australia, Chubb and Reed interviewed academics about their views on the impact agenda. They found that most of their participants saw the sharing of knowledge and findings beyond the academy as a duty or moral responsibility. This perspective shares some commonalities with the current study. In our study, several participants mentioned the notion of responsibility, but this was not always framed in terms of social justice as understood by Sen (2009). Some interpreted impact in terms of financial transparency, seeing this as a form of social justice towards taxpayers:

> It's an accountability thing. If you're paid through public money then I think part of the duty is then to try to engage with the public about what the money is used for. (Robert, mathematics)

As well as the diversity of understandings of impact and its relationship with social justice, three other main themes emerged from the interview data as influencing academics' perspectives on social justice, namely the role of discipline in shaping perspectives on social justice, the extent to which individual academics were seen to be responsible for social justice and the effects of national and institutional policies on academics' engagement with social justice. These themes are discussed in turn below, with reference to further data from interviews with academics.

How Discipline Interacts with Perspectives on Social Justice

Most of the academics interviewed for this study agreed with the notion that research should be made accessible to wider audiences. They valued the notion of 'making an impact' or 'making a difference' in principle, but the extent to which this was a driver for their research and the extent to which this was framed in terms of social justice varied. One of the factors that influenced academics' perspectives on social justice was their discipline.

One professor of marketing referred to her research as 'engaged' and spoke of making a difference to the lives of those who use her research.

> A lot of my work is engaged research, so I think I do make a difference to managers' lives, helping everything think through, helping them work out what they want to do. I don't have any of the answers, but actually the symbiotic relationship I find quite rewarding and exciting. (Diane, marketing)

Although Diane's work is aimed at managers, who might not be seen as the prototypical targets of a social justice agenda, her description of her work as enabling others to think through ideas and 'work out what they want to do' is in keeping with Sen's (2009) notion of people being enabled to live lives *they* regard as good. A marketing lecturer in a different university made a similar comment about making a difference, albeit to businesses:

> I try and make sure that my research is actually actionable, and makes a difference to some business somewhere. (Emma, marketing)

Emma's comment appears to reflect an understanding of a fairly direct relationship between research and impact. Her perspective differs from Diane's, however, in that she frames the difference being made by her work in terms of action rather than influencing thinking or raising awareness.

The relevance of their research to professionals outside of academia may be particularly important to academics working in applied disciplines such as marketing. However, not all marketing academics saw impact or social justice as important drivers of their research work. James, for example, who was a lecturer in marketing, but whose PhD was in history, explained:

> I don't start off a research project with the thought of, 'How is it going to affect people today?' Part of that is because I was trained as a historian. Historians don't set out to change people's lives in the same way that a social worker might, even here in the school a marketing person might do. (James, marketing)

James's view may reflect not a complete disregard for the notion of social justice, but a different perspective on the value of knowledge informed by his background in a humanities discipline, where the impact of research might be seen as more indirect than is typical for disciplines with close links to the professions. Chubb and Reed (2017) also found disciplinary variation in the perspectives of academics on impact. Specifically, those working in arts and humanities disciplines were more likely to see the value of knowledge as aligned with Sen's (2009) understanding of social justice. As one participant put it, 'it [humanities] gives one the wherewithal to live a certain kind of life' (Chubb & Reed, 2017, p. 2). Such a perspective contrasts with the more direct and instrumental understanding of how disciplinary knowledge might make a difference expressed by Emma and reflects a view of impact as something more diffuse and gradual, to do with changing mindsets rather than generating specific actions.

The ways in which social justice informs academics' thinking were not, therefore, always straightforwardly linked to the department in which they were currently located, but were also shaped by their background and disciplinary training.

The disciplinary tradition in which academics worked also exerted influence on both the extent to which they saw social justice as relevant to their work and the extent to which impact was seen as achievable. For example, Ian, a lecturer in pure mathematics, explained that he did not use social media to disseminate his findings or communicate about this research to the wider public because of the complexity of his subject area:

> I mean, for mathematicians, hardly anybody can understand what our research is about. (Ian, mathematics)

This is similar to a comment by one of Chubb and Reed's participants (2017, p. 3), who also worked in pure mathematics and expressed some concern about trying to communicate this to the general public, saying that impact was important only 'as far as it is helpful'. The view that engagement with wider audiences was not important to mathematics academics was by no means universal. Some of our participants who worked at the more applied end of the discipline, in the realm of statistics, for example, saw public engagement as a major part of their social responsibility. For example, Robert, a professor in applied mathematics, saw promoting mathematical knowledge in society in general as an important part of his role. For him, this involved both policy-level decision-making and writing maths books aimed at non-experts:

> I've been vice president of Institute X and so there's a policy side of what I do as well. I also do popular maths things. I see that all as part of the same job. (Robert, mathematics)

The finding that one's position on the applied-pure continuum is a factor influencing the way academics interpret and take on board the drive to engage with wider audiences finds support in Oancea's (2013) study into disciplinary differences in academics' framings of impact, which also found that the applied or non-applied nature of research influenced academics' understandings particularly in physical sciences and engineering.

Likewise, in a study based in South Africa, Walker and McLean (2015) interviewed university students and staff in a range of professional fields such as law, social work and engineering and found that they conceptualized social justice differently, emphasizing different qualities as important in graduates from their fields and seeing their contribution to the public good, as being more or less direct. The current study suggests that even though disciplinary differences were a factor in shaping understandings of social justice, difference and diversity persisted. Thus, even within disciplines, difference is found in how academics conceptualize and attempt to implement social justice.

Impact as Collective or Individual Responsibility

The second issue to emerge from this study relates to who was seen as being responsible for social justice, particularly how this was seen: whether as an individual or a collective responsibility. Certainly, it can be argued that impact builds over time in complex ways and that this is not generally taken into account in the way the national research assessment exercise aims to measure it (Ashwin, 2016). The REF focuses on direct, relatively short-term and measurable effects that can be clearly linked to specific academic publications, but impact, particularly in the complex arena of social justice, may be indirect, multifaceted and difficult to measure. By its very nature, academic research entails building on or refuting the work of others; thus, it could be argued that impact is a collective endeavour. Oancea (2013, p. 246) has argued that the contribution of social sciences in particular to social and intellectual life is collective in nature, occurring through public debate and the diffusion of ideas. Similarly, Chubb and Reed (2017) found that some academics saw impact as a community responsibility, and not necessarily the responsibility of each individual. In the current study, Robert, for example, takes a collective perspective on this issue, seeing the responsibility as lying with 'the university' as a collective body:

> Until 10 or 15 years ago, it was seen as wasting your time doing something like that. I think more and more the university has become aware that they have

a responsibility beyond academia and to communicate and so on. (Robert, mathematics)

He goes on to note that engaging with the wider public was not something that every academic could or should do and that age and career stage had a bearing on the extent to which any individual might do less prestigious work such as writing popular books:

> Once you've reached a certain age, it's not a bad thing to be thinking about explaining maths. Also trying to get the next generation of mathematicians engaged and interested. (Robert, mathematician)

Despite the above claim that historians do not set out to change the world, they nevertheless may find themselves writing about aspects of history that are relevant to global issues today. One of our participants, a professor of history, found himself being approached by the media to write on current events relating to social justice because these intersected with his own historical specialism. He describes the responsibility towards social justice as a pledge that 'the university' rather than himself as an individual has made, although he does go along with it:

> The university is committed to something called social responsibility. Well, I am very happy to sign up to that ... I think we are citizens. If we have something worthwhile that we think we can contribute, then I think we should do that. (Colin, history)

When asked what counted as success for his department, Matt, who was the head of the department, talked about impact beyond academia, but framed this in terms of its contribution to the success of the university as a whole:

> In terms of research it's around a combination of volume and academic impact ... increasingly non-academic impact as well ... that's sometimes a case of success is more a measure of how you're supporting the broader university activity rather than how it contributes to yourself or individual student success. (Matt, mathematics)

How National and Institutional Priorities Shape Perspectives on Social Justice

The third factor that mediated the extent to which the academics in this study engaged with social justice was the effect of the REF as a system of research evaluation in universities in England. The demands that the REF placed on academics to produce specific types of research output, evaluation of which still formed the majority proportion of the REF evaluation in 2014, meant that writing directed at contributing to social justice by reaching wider audiences or achieving societal impact sometimes took second place.

As noted in the previous section, historian Colin was keen to get involved in writing for the media and talked about the contribution this might make to the wider public debate given the reach such journalistic writing would have. However, he also expressed concern that it conflicted with other demands on his time, adding:

> It's just that it [writing about social justice issues for the media] is extra and it's quite demanding, and I wouldn't like it to take over my writing life. (Colin, history)

Colin's conceptualization of social justice is framed more in terms of morality than in terms of instrumentality, perhaps in recognition that the contribution of his discipline to society is likely to be indirect or to accumulate over longer periods, as discussed earlier (Oancea, 2013). Colin values social responsibility, but he sees the forms of writing it entails as an additional burden on top of the work already prioritized by his institution. Social responsibility is thus seen as secondary to his existing work, which included, in his view, a duty to his students and colleagues. Colin's perspective on social justice was to see it as a symbolic goal, and as supplementary to, rather than embedded within, his writing work. Colin's comment reveals something of the pressures that academic writing is under in the era of research evaluation. He is already busy and his 'writing life' primarily involves producing scholarly, peer-reviewed work and marking student work (in our data, journal articles and feedback on student work were by far the most commonly mentioned genres of writing). Students' work has to be marked in increasing numbers, and scholarly writing aimed at other researchers is the form of writing that contributes most to the REF and therefore to universities' ranking and incomes. Publications in high-ranking journals were also the form of writing that most of our participants described as being assessed on when it came to probation or promotion. Thus, this is the form of knowledge creation that is prioritized by universities. The tension between what is valued by institutions in terms of allocation of time and resources and what is valued mainly in symbolic terms is highlighted by David:

> I'm doing a lot of work now on people trafficking and sexual exploitation. A lot of the work is grey literature where people have written blog pieces. [...] I think that's opened my eyes to what's possible in that area but yes, if there's time – I think it's always a question of time. Again, that work is not valued by the

university as far as I can see but it is important in terms of generating impact. (David, mathematics)

David clearly considers blog posts as making an important contribution to an area of social justice, but they do not count as scholarly publications for the purposes of the REF and do not carry much kudos in the university's perspective. David's frustration echoes that of one of the participants in Teelken's (2011) study into academics' responses to managerialism in universities in three European countries, including the UK. Teelken's participants lamented that the emphasis on producing measurable research outputs of a certain type narrows the range of audiences one can reach through one's writing (2011, p. 280).

The tension between career progress and social justice orientations is also evident from the perspective of an academic in the middle of his career in the following comment:

> My humble little collection of work, such as it is, the only life I really expect it to affect or alter is mine in a professional sense. You've written enough articles, at some point maybe get promoted or do this or do that or you'll be REF-able, or you won't be REF-able, this kind of thing. (James, marketing)

These comments illustrate the influence of what Wilsdon (2016) calls 'cultures of counting' on what is valued by institutions and, in turn, prioritized by academics. In other words, because academics must produce a certain number of publications of a certain calibre in order to keep their job or obtain promotion, they feel compelled to focus on these individual career goals, which may come at the expense of goals directed at their desire to make a difference to society.

In addition to the REF, institutional priorities and the availability of funding opportunities also influence academics' understandings of which communities can be served by the social justice agenda. For example, Mark was interested in doing research into improving teaching and learning for Chinese students, but said,

> Because they [his institution] were working to their targets ... my topic area had very little interest. So if it was looking at underachieving white males from lower social areas in Area X in England, they would have jumped on that, because there was some funding relating to that. (Mark, marketing)

Mark's research interests appear to be informed by his own experience and expertise, while he characterizes those of his institution as driven by the availability of funding. Where social justice comes into these decisions is clearly constrained by whose understandings of social justice take precedence. These academics' comments demonstrate that the factors driving the ways in which social justice is understood and the research agenda directed at addressing it go beyond both the intellectual interests of individual academics and their particular disciplinary traditions and also encompass institutional strategies in response to policy.

Conclusion

Overall, the findings from the current study indicate that the forms of knowledge creation valued in the working lives of our participants are complex and contested. No unified notion of social justice across the disciplines emerged, nor did any single understanding of how this might be achieved. Instead, perspectives on impact and social justice were characterized by difference. The ways in which social justice is conceptualized by the participants in our study and the extent to which serving society is a driver for the choices they make interact with a number of factors, and several contrasting perspectives on these issues emerged from the data. Specifically, participants varied in terms of whether they took an instrumental or a less direct perspective towards how impact could be achieved in their disciplines. Impact was seen as both more relevant and easier to achieve in some disciplines than others.

Another difference related to the language used to talk about impact, as well as the nature of the perceived beneficiaries. Some academics described the impact of their research in the kind of language adopted by university management, highlighting financial accountability as a responsibility, while others focused more on the ways in which they could influence the terms of a wider debate. Similarly, the participants also varied in the extent to which they took an individual or collective perspective towards impact and social justice, with some claiming that they had individually made an identifiable difference to society, while others aligned themselves with a set of values they ascribed to 'the university' as a whole.

Finally, academics' willingness and ability to do writing related to social justice goals interacted to some extent with their own professional goals and career stage and were constrained by the policies and targets of their institutions. There was, at times, a perceived tension between the forms of knowledge creation and research agendas that were prioritized by institutions and those that enabled academics to pursue their preferred goals with regard to social justice. Many academics were under pressure to produce a certain quantity and quality of outputs and focused their efforts on this, seeing social justice as secondary to their main priorities, despite the fact that they subscribed to a social justice agenda in principle.

Perspectives on social justice were influenced by academics' disciplinary traditions, their career trajectories, their personal priorities and aspirations, as well as how they interpret policy on impact. The extent to which the work of academics advances the cause of social justice is not fully determined by them as individuals despite their purported autonomy in setting their own research agenda, but is shaped in part by wider forces including pressures regarding workloads and priorities, and dominant discourses around what counts as success for individual academics. These factors ultimately influence the choices academics make in their writing practices.

Notes

1 See http://wp.lancs.ac.uk/acadswriting/about for more information.
2 The names of universities and individuals have been anonymized, and some identifying details have been changed.

References

Ashwin, P. (2016). From a teaching perspective, 'impact' looks very different. *Times Higher Education*, 21 March. Retrieved from https://www.timeshighereducation.com/blog/teaching-perspective-impact-looks-very-different.

Barton, D. (2007). *Literacy: An Introduction to the Ecology of Written Language*. Oxford: Wiley-Blackwell.

Barton, D., & Hamilton, M. (2000). Literacy practices. In D. Barton, M. Hamilton, & R. Ivanič (Eds.), *Situated Literacies*, 7–15. London and New York: Routledge.

Beetham, H. (2016). Employability and the digital future of work. In S. Cranmer, N. B. Dohn, M. de Laat, T. Ryberg, & J. A. Sime (Eds.), *Proceedings of the 10th International Conference on Networked Learning 2016*, 47–55.

Bunce, L., Baird, A., & Jones, S. E. (2017). The student-as-consumer approach in higher education and its effects on academic performance. *Studies in Higher Education*, 42(11), 1958–1978. doi: 10.1080/03075079.2015.1127908.

Carl, N. (2018). The political attitudes of British academics. *Open Quantitative Sociology & Political Science*. doi: 10.26775/OQSPS.2018.01.16.

Chubb, J., & Reed, M. (2017). Epistemic responsibility as an edifying force in academic research: investigating the moral challenges and opportunities of an impact agenda in the UK and Australia. *Palgrave Communications*, 3(20). doi: 10.1057/s41599-017-0023-2.

Cruickshank, J. (2015). Neoliberalism, the 'scientific enterprise' and the 'business of people': Comments on the sociology and politics of knowledge production. *Social Epistemology Review and Reply Collective*, 4(8), 53–65.

Deem, R., Hillyard, S., & Reed, M. (2007). *Knowledge, Higher Education, and the New Managerialism: The Changing Management of UK Universities*. Oxford: Oxford University Press.

Furlong, A., & Cartmel, F. (2009). *Higher Education and Social Justice*. Maidenhead: Open University Press and McGraw-Hill Education.

HEFCE (19 February 2016). *REF Impact*. Retrieved from http://www.hefce.ac.uk/rsrch/REFimpact/.

Ingleby, E. (2015). The house that Jack built: Neoliberalism, teaching in higher education and the moral objections. *Teaching in Higher Education*, 20(5), 518–529. doi: 10.1080/13562517.2015.1036729.

McArthur, J. (2016). Assessment for Social Justice: The role of assessment in achieving social justice. *Assessment and Evaluation in Higher Education*, 41(7), 967–981.

McCulloch, S. (2017). Hobson's choice: The effects of research evaluation on academics' writing practices in England. *Aslib Journal of Information Management*, 69(5), 503–515.

Molesworth, M., Scullion, R., & Nixon, E. (2011). *The Marketisation of Higher Education and the Student as Consumer*. Abingdon, OX: Routledge.

Naidoo, R., & Williams, J. (2015). The neoliberal regime in English higher education: Charters, consumers and the erosion of the public good. *Critical Studies in Education*, 56(2), 208–223. doi: 10.1080/17508487.2014.939098.

Oancea, A. (2013). Interpretations of research impact in seven disciplines. *European Educational Research Journal*, 12(2), 242–250.

Sen, A. (2009). *The Idea of Justice*. Cambridge, MA: Harvard University Press.

Sheppard, E. (2016). Real world academics: A response to Glyn Davies MP. *Times Higher Education*, October 31. Retrieved from https://www.timeshighereducation.com/author/emma-sheppard.

Solon, I. (2015). Scholarly elites orient left, irrespective of academic affiliation. *Intelligence*, 51, 119–130.

Stern, N. (2016). *Building on Success and Learning from Experience. An Independent Review of the Research Excellence Framework*. Ref: IND/16/9. Department for Business, Energy & Industrial Strategy. Retrieved from https://www.gov.uk/government/uploads/system/uploads/attachment_data/file/541338/ind-16-9-ref-stern-review.pdf.

Taylor, Y. (6 May 2016). Occupying academia: Stretching the meaning of 'career'. *Social Theory Applied*. Retrieved from http://socialtheoryapplied.com/2016/05/06/occupying-academia-stretching-meaning-career/?utm_campaign=shareaholic&utm_medium=facebook&utm_source=socialnetwork.

Teelken, C. (2011). Compliance or pragmatism: How do academics deal with managerialism in higher education? A comparative study in three countries. *Studies in Higher Education, 37*(3), 271–290.

Tourish, D., & Willmott, H. (2015). In defiance of folly: Journal rankings, mindless measures and the ABS guide. *Critical Perspectives on Accounting, 26,* 37–46.

Walker, Melanie and McLean, Monica (2015). *Professional Education, Capabilities and the Public Good.* Abingdon: Routledge.

Wilsdon, J. (2016). *Cultures of Counting: Metrics through a Critical Lens.* Paper presented at the Designing the Academic Self seminar series at Lancaster University. 24 May 2016.

Part Two

Locating Social Justice in Higher Education Pedagogies

5

Higher Education Research to Investigate Epistemic In/Justice

Monica McLean

Introduction

It can be useful to think of the injustices of higher education as occurring in three phases: coming into higher education (access), being at university (participation) and going out of university into the rest of life (outcomes). I bracket for now all the systemic inequalities of access, that is, the barriers to entering higher education connected to poverty and deprivation; social class, age and ethnic background; type of school; and geographical location. Bracketed, too, are the systemic inequities when students leave universities to go into employment, whereby, on the one hand, the graduate premium appears to be lessening for poorer students and, on the other, students from high-status universities monopolize high-status, well-paid jobs in the global labour market (Brown & Lauder, 2017). From this view, a higher education qualification has become a positional good of diminishing value to historically excluded groups.

This chapter focuses on what happens when students participate in a university education and on the outcomes of that education other than employment. It is social fact that globally students from poorer backgrounds who, against the odds, get into university are more likely than wealthier students to attend considerably less well-resourced universities, which also appear lower in league tables than in rich universities (e.g. Boliver, 2011). In these circumstances, it is pertinent to investigate what relatively disadvantaged students take from their university courses that they value, in addition to employment possibilities. The key question for the chapter is whether the academic (rather than social) 'goods' that can accrue from a university education are equally distributed. So I will discuss the evidence that students' educational experiences and outcomes *are* unfairly differentiated and stratified along hierarchical lines in terms of 'epistemic justice' taken from the work of the philosopher Miranda Fricker (2007, 2015). Epistemic injustice thus stands as a particular way of understanding social justice.

First I propose that whether students experience injustice or justice at a university can be illuminated by the concept of epistemic injustice as advanced by Fricker. I argue that epistemic justice at university is served by students gaining 'epistemological access' to the disciplines, interdisciplines and fields that they study. From there, I discuss how 'close-up' research allows explorations of whether or to what extent epistemic justice is being satisfied. Throughout the chapter, I hope to convey that researching epistemic justice at university is an important element of researching social justice.

Defining of Epistemic In/Justice

Fricker's interest lies in the relations between rationality and power. Her starting point is that the power of reason is a natural, complex human phenomenon, but that the interpretative or reasoning practices of the powerful are privileged unfairly structuring our understandings of the social world. In other words, the epistemic perspectives of some groups eclipse those of others. Fricker introduced the idea of 'epistemic injustice' in a seminal book called *Epistemic Injustice: Power and the Ethics of Knowing* (2007). She has developed her ideas since then by proposing that being able to make an epistemic contribution in society is a basic human 'capability' to which all humans have a right (see Martha Nussbaum, 2000 and 2013 for discussions of human capabilities). The capability for epistemic contribution means having opportunity and means to contribute on an equal basis to the stock of concepts and meanings in society (whether at work or in other sociopolitical activity).

In Fricker's view, people-as-knowers can be epistemically wronged in two ways. The first way that a person-as-knower can be wrong is by way of 'testimonial injustice'. Put simply, testimonial injustice means that the person is wronged by not being listened to because of who they are (that is a person is not seen as a source of knowledge because of social class, gender, ethnicity, etc.). In other words, when someone is telling something, or making a suggestion or an argument, airing an idea, putting forward a hypothesis or trying to persuade, they are not seen as credible by the hearer who is prejudiced. Fricker's example is from *To Kill a Mocking Bird* in which Tom Robinson is not believed in the courtroom because he is black; she also uses the example of the Stephen Lawrence murder when the testimony of his black friends was not taken seriously by the police.[1]

There is a salient example of testimonial injustice operating when students leave different universities and seek employment. Testimonial justice demands that we ask whether 'identity prejudices' (Fricker, 2007, p. 4) or stereotyping are operating when employers select from graduates from different universities. Given that Oxbridge graduates and those from a few of the higher ranking universities pull away from other universities in the labour market (Brown & Lauder, 2017; Hussain, McNally & Telhaj, 2009; Tholen et al., 2013), it is plausible to suggest that they enjoy a 'credibility excess' (Fricker, 2007, p. 21). We can speculate that when students from lower ranking universities write CVs or go to job interviews, they are systematically less epistemically credible or trusted than students from higher ranking universities.

The second way a person-as-knower can be wrong is by way of 'hermeneutic injustice' which is done when someone is prevented from accessing the pool of available concepts and meanings in a society that allows that person to be a trustworthy knower. With hermeneutical injustice, a speaker's lack of knowledge blocks their capacity to reason and to interpret and therefore to claim a hearing for her or his own experiences. One of Fricker's examples is when someone experiences domestic abuse without being able to know or name it. While the opportunity and means to know and reason are not developed in formal education systems only, and although Fricker herself does not dwell much on education, it must play a large role. The example of hermeneutic injustice I will develop in this chapter is when students are not offered curriculum and pedagogy which give them access to the specialized ways of thinking and reasoning in (inter)disciplines and professional fields.

It is worth noting that 'hermeneutic justice' cannot be absolute; that is, the extent to which people have equal access to the means and opportunities to contribute to the stock of concepts and meanings in society is an empirical question. University education should have something to do with the means and opportunities to becoming a credible knower, but there is considerable doubt about whether they are equally distributed in the system. It needs investigation. The types of research questions which arise from the perspective of hermeneutical justice are thus: Do graduates who have studied the same disciplines in different universities acquire comparable knowledge-derived confidence to speak and expect to be heard in the public sphere? Are students who attend lower ranking universities having their academic, personal or professional aspirations curtailed by acquiring less credible knowledge? Are working-class students systematically epistemically wronged when they attend higher-status universities? If we find the answers to these questions as 'yes', as might be suggested by league tables and some studies, then the system is perpetuating hermeneutical injustice by putting one group at a disadvantage to another.

Epistemological Access at University

My proposal is that in formal education, including universities, hermeneutical justice is served by 'epistemological access': a term introduced by the South African philosopher of education Wally Morrow (2009) in the early 1990s and taken up by researchers in higher education since then. Before I define 'epistemological access', my justification for using the term as well as 'epistemic access' is to indicate that what students need access to is more than propositional knowledge, which I think is suggested by 'epistemic' – the use of 'epistemological' is intended to denote not only what is learned but also *how* to learn or practise it.

The starting point for defining epistemological access is the work of the sociologist of education Basil Bernstein (2000) which shows how knowledge in society is unequally distributed according to social hierarchies by way of education. Below, I reproduce a small experiment that colleagues conducted with schoolchildren during the 1970s which vividly illustrates how certain types of knowledge bestows power:[2]

> 7 year-old school children were divided into two equal groups of 30 working-class and 30 middle-class children and given 24 cards with food on them: potatoes, ice cream, fish fingers, milk eggs and so on. They were asked to put the foods together which they thought went together-using all or only some of the cards (that is they could choose to put the cards together in any way they wanted for any reason they wanted). When the children had made their groups, Bernstein and his researchers asked them why they'd grouped them as they had. There were two types of reasons: the first had something to do with the child's life, for example, 'I eat these for breakfast'; 'I like these'. 'My Mum cooks these for tea'; the second type of reason referred to a more abstract commonality, for example, 'These are vegetables'; 'These come from the sea'. (adapted from Bernstein, 2000, p. 19)

In Bernstein's sociological terms, the first set of reasons has a direct relation to a specific material base – it is embedded in the child's local experience – and the second set has an indirect relation to a specific material base (so the two sets of reasons have different relations to a material base). At this stage of the experiment, the working-class children were 'much more likely' (Bernstein, 2000, p. 19) to offer reasons that had a direct relationship to their lives and the middle-class children to offer reasons with an indirect relation. The researchers then asked the children to put the cards together in a different way. This time, many of the middle-class children changed their reason to refer to a local experience, while the working-class children continued to give local reasons. The conclusion was that the middle-class children possessed two principles of classification of reasons which stood in hierarchical relation to each other – so the reasons that had an indirect relation to the material base were privileged and offered first. While the working-class children recognized the instruction as referring to a non-specialized domestic context, the middle-class children *initially* recognized the instructions as specialized because they were in school. Bernstein's view was that the middle-class children recognized a strong boundary between home and school, which the working-class children didn't. In technical terms, this means recognizing the dominance of 'official pedagogic meanings' over 'local meanings'. It is this dominance which bestows a position of relative power and privilege to the middle-class child.

So following this kind of analysis, knowledge that is powerful for the knower tends to be equated with knowing that (propositional knowledge). As in Michael Young's *Bringing Knowledge Back In* (2008), powerful knowledge is characterized as providing reliable explanations; the basis for suggesting realistic alternatives; enabling acquirers to see beyond their everyday experience; conceptual as well as based on evidence and experience; open to challenge; acquired in specialist educational institutions, staffed by specialists; and, organized into domains with non-arbitrary boundaries and specialist communities. The preoccupation for those who describe themselves as social realists using Bernstein to gain insights (as I do) has been to look for the balance between conceptual knowledge (known as specialized/vertical/sacred discourse) and contextual knowledge (known as everyday/horizontal/mundane discourse) to see whether the knowledge allows students to transcend the local (e.g. Muller, 2014; Wheelahan, 2010).

However, findings from the 'Quality and Inequality in First Degrees' project (RES-062-23-1438), comparing the quality of sociology-based degrees in four different status universities, complicate this formulation (McLean, Abbas & Ashwin, 2017). We found that students engage with and understand the discipline when the curriculum is structured so that knowing that (propositional knowledge) and knowing how (procedural knowledge) are developed progressively. In curriculum, what propositional knowledge is taught is a matter of what Bernstein calls 'recontextualization' which involves taking the disciplinary knowledge produced by researchers or scholars or scientists and making decisions about selecting, sequencing and pacing this knowledge for the purpose of teaching and learning. Procedural knowledge involves the same kind of recontextualizing and refers to knowledge about how specialized knowledges are produced: for example, learning how to argue in the discipline, or evaluate claims, or carry out research. Another element to epistemological access was identified by Bernstein as the 'regulative or moral discourse' of the discipline, whereby it is conveyed to students what kind of values they should aspire to (e.g. working hard, thinking for themselves, grasping the importance of theory).

Added to this, in the research about sociology, students appeared to grasp the power of concepts, theories and methodologies in what Bernstein called the 'discursive gap' between the abstraction of discipline knowledge and knowledge of everyday issues and experiences (McLean, Abbas & Ashwin, 2017). Finally, there appeared to be more success in engaging students in disciplinary knowledge when teachers were reflective and possessed principled ways of 'framing' pedagogical experiences so that students could 'recognize' (in Bernstein's terms) what was expected and so were able to develop the necessary 'conceptual pile' of propositional and procedural knowledge (Muller, 2014, p. 7).

In sum 'epistemological access' is both epistemic (i.e. about knowing that, knowing how and a set of values in relation to specialized disciplinary or interdisciplinary fields) and pedagogical (i.e. about *how* the knowledge and students can meet so that their capability to make epistemic contributions is enhanced). The pedagogical endeavour is to bring knowledge, knowers and knowing need together.

Researching Epistemic Justice

This chapter explores why 'close-up' research might shed light on whether in any university course hermeneutical justice is being done. In this section, I first look briefly at some of the existing higher education research that focuses on 'epistemological access' that can be employed and built on. I've chosen two sets: work framed by Pierre Bourdieu's concepts of habitus, cultural capital and field and that framed by Basil Bernstein theories about knowledge distribution and social hierarchy.

Bourdieu himself has shown how in France social classifications are turned into academic ones and then treated as if they are natural. Educationalists

Stephen Ball (2003), Ann-Marie Bathmaker (2016), Gill Crozier and Diane Reay (2008, 2011), Miriam David (2014), Caroline Hart (2012) and David James (2015) have employed Bourdieu's concepts to analyse empirical data to show how working-class students' experience of higher education is different and more difficult than that of middle-class students. This body of work reveals that before arriving at university, working-class students' pathways into higher education are often characterized by ambivalence, shame and doubt, involving self-exclusion or finding out where they couldn't go and then looking at what was left. When at university, these students find that universities comprise a 'field' of discursive practices which mesh with the 'habitus' of middle-class students and exclude working-class and ethnic-minority students from mainstream university experience. Working-class students face a middle-class world without the right kind of cultural and social capital and so (like Bernstein's working-class seven-year-olds) find it harder than their middle-class peers to engage in the wider university, to fit in and to develop strong, confident learner identities. Moreover, different inequities operate at universities of different status: in higher-status universities, working-class students are less likely to feel part of the university than those in lower-status universities (where they regard other students as 'like us'). But students at lower-status universities (at least in those discussed in these studies) are not encouraged to work as hard as students at higher-status universities and are anxious not to be thought of as 'nerdy'. Sometimes this Bourdieuian-informed research portrays working-class students as agents responding in multiple ways to their university education and shows them successfully dealing with challenges (mainly in the higher-status universities). But overall, the findings are pessimistic, indicating unequal access to academic goods and therefore to hermeneutic justice.

David James (2015) has drawn attention to one aspect of a Bourdieu-framed study he was involved in, which I think has relevance. The study is not of higher education but of middle-class parents who chose local failing schools 'against the grain'. This is what James quotes from the original study:

> The interviews with parents contained many mentions of 'bright' and 'brightness' [in reference to their child], plus [...] close synonyms including having something 'extra' or being 'special'. [...] Middle-class 'brightness' was the main way in which middle-class distinction was characterised and expressed: Across 251 interview transcripts there were a staggering 256 references to brightness [...] without prompting by the interviewers. [...] Such discourses position middle-class brightness as both normative and a justification for middle-class privilege, [and] are one of the main means through which the middle classes defensively use

their own investments in class hierarchies to distinguish themselves as superior to others. [...] Brightness then becomes a rationalisation for holding on to more: educationally, socially and economically. (James, 2015, p. 105)

For James, this is an example of what Bourdieu calls 'misrecognition' and it also illustrates how testimonial injustice is already at play in school, with some children unjustly designated as less effective knowers than others.

So studies by framed Bourdieu can unpick what Fricker calls 'dysfunctional' (Dieleman, 2012, p. 256) practices. But his concepts are not designed to explore the mechanisms by which curriculum and pedagogy interact with and produce habitus. For this, we need work framed by Basil Bernstein's theories.

Bernstein revealed how messages about power and control are sent as knowledge is transmitted in formal educational settings, which reproduces social hierarchies. In South Africa there is a solid scholarship of curriculum in higher education (motivated by the transformation agenda of 1994 and following a series of seminars by Bernstein the same year). In higher education,[3] Jenni Case (2011, 2013), Kathy Luckett (2009, 2012), Shalem and Slonimsky (2010) and Suellen Shay (2011, 2013, 2015), among others, have investigated curriculum in different disciplines. Using Bernstein and Karl Maton's (2014) Legitimation Code Theory, which builds on Bernstein, these studies shed valuable light on how knowledge is recontextualized in curriculum and how curriculum and pedagogy project specific learner identities. The context in South Africa is one in which schooling is rated as very poor, so the many students who historically were unable to go to university are ill-prepared. These scholars rightly point out that discussions about what higher education teaching and learning would support these students largely neglect questions of curriculum and knowledge. This lacuna results in those students who are identified as 'less prepared' being taught too little specialized knowledge, which curtails the possibilities for what they can do or be in the future. So within this body of work, the extent to which epistemic justice is being done tends to be the extent to which students are being presented with coherent bodies of disciplinary knowledge.

Both sets of work discussed above reveal epistemic injustice. Bourdieu and Bernstein were not determinists, but decidedly pessimistic, with reason- the domination of some groups over others prevails and both authors have it that education is one of the fundamental agencies of the maintenance of the prevailing social order.

Yet, while we certainly need to know when and understand how injustice is occurring, we also need to know when arrangements are just and what they look like. Is what happens in universities' teaching spaces *always* complicit in reproducing social inequality? I think the answer surely must be 'no'. Universities, like schools, reflect what Habermas (1984) called the 'dual potential' of modernity: they are ambiguous sites – places where it is possible to prise open spaces for hope. At this point, I want to be clear that I take Amartya Sen's (2009) position that justice need not be perfect – injustice tends to gain ascendancy and the effort is to put a brake on it. So, as educators, rather than focusing on what would count as completely overcoming inequalities in the system, our interest can be in understanding what constitutes epistemic injustice and what might challenge and reduce it.

To illustrate this point, I'll return now to the 'Quality and Inequality in First Degrees' project. It was framed by Bernstein's concepts and used a wide range of methods to explore how sociology-related knowledge was distributed in four universities of different status. The big picture was that the pedagogic quality of the degrees was not distributed unequally according to status and that in all universities very similar kinds of identities and capabilities were formed as a result of academic learning. A more nuanced reading of the data showed a complex, subtle patterning of epistemic justice and injustice across the universities, but still no clear relationship between the students' social grouping, status of university, acquisition of knowledge and the types of capabilities being (imperfectly) formed.

To illustrate how epistemic justice was being done in one lower-status university, I will focus on the curriculum and pedagogy of the university we called Diversity, which was an inner-city, teaching-led, recruiting, ex-polytechnic, with a large proportion of black and minority ethnic and working-class students, and it ranked low in league tables. However, in our research, Diversity confounded league tables: for example, in our survey of over 700 students in all four universities, Diversity ranked second on the scale 'A change in personal identity and an intention to change society for the better', second on the 'Engagement with academic knowledge' scale and first on the 'Good teaching' scale and 'Enhanced employability skills' scales.

In the following passage, I quote from an account by Celia Jenkins and Caroline Barnes who were, at the time of our research, two of the lecturers of the sociology degree at Diversity. What makes it a valuable account is that following their involvement in the research as co-researchers, they have used the language of Bernstein to explain how they attempted to open up epistemological access to their students.

> We wanted to engage students through their lifeworlds but also to achieve an academic orientation and personal transformation. Emphasis was thus placed upon academic rigour to assist in bringing about the reconceptualization

of experience. [...] [W]e were trying to merge the horizontal and vertical discourses, so that students treat their lifeworlds as potential objects of analysis and critique, thereby centralising the transformative impact of thinking sociologically about society and their place within it. [...] We required students to do academic research from the outset, the pinnacle of which is their final year dissertations, which we fought hard to keep against pressure from other subject areas to drop it because it was deemed too challenging for the sort of students we recruit. After all, students like ours, with relatively low entry requirements are assumed not to 'read' a degree but need it to be simplified and taught to them. [...] From the beginning of their degree students analyse their everyday lives and denaturalize the taken-for-grantedness of their experience. [...] For us, research methods best encapsulate our approach to both curriculum and pedagogy. We had consistently and painfully failed to engage students' interest through the whistle-stop lecture tour of different methods and related seminar exercises, however interactive we made the experience. [...] So, across the academic year, we give the students two research tasks only. [...] Through establishing the practice of doing research in the first year, we constantly attend to the processes of abstraction, conceptualisation and theorisation associated with vertical discourse. (Jenkins et al., 2017, pp. 52–3)

Bernstein (1999) regretted the use of horizontal/mundane/everyday discourse in school classrooms in the 1970s to engage the 'less able' students because it denies them access to the type of knowledge which lifts their minds from their local contexts. Nevertheless, he did concede the possibility of creating a 'discursive gap' between horizontal and vertical discourse where new, original, transforming knowledge can emerge (Bernstein, 1996, 2000). This is the achievement Jenkins and Barnes describe. They show how opening this gap depends on making explicit or 'visible' to students what is expected of them. For Bernstein (1975) 'invisible pedagogies' which leave much implicit, benefit middle-class learners who have been better enculturated into what is expected in formal educational settings. Arguably, when students have little knowledge of higher education, this observation holds in universities where the degree of control and guidance is considerably less than that in school. So for Jenkins and Barnes, the means of epistemological access was the recontextualization of sociological knowledge in curriculum and pedagogy that foregrounded a principled juxtaposition of vertical and horizontal discourses and made explicit to students the kinds of efforts necessary to develop a powerful sociological identity. Jenkins and Barnes call what they do 'clevering up' (2017, p. 53) to set it against the accusation of 'dumbing down' that can sometimes be heard in relation to universities like theirs.

In Muller's (2014) view, 'it remains tragic how little is known about how [epistemological access] works, circulates and becomes productive' (p. 10). So what can be said about what kind of research would continue to build knowledge about epistemological access? It is not straightforward to understand the complex patterning of the exclusions and inclusions which result in forming or not forming the capability of social epistemic contribution. This indeterminate nature arises from both the (inter)disciplinary specificity and the subtle and intangible processes of transmission and acquisition of knowledge which shape students' consciousness. It seems to me that if research is to teach us about how epistemological access works, circulates and becomes productive, these are the main characteristics:

- First, it needs to be close-up. That is, it should be near the curricular and pedagogical action and fine-grained. We need more studies of epistemological access which are specific to subjects or disciplines. Such studies need to generate multiple data sets (talking to the actors, observing, analysing documents and texts, including student work) and to combine them for analytical purposes.
- Secondly, despite the difficulties of funding, we need more longitudinal studies which track students from specific courses for a few years after leaving university.
- Thirdly, research needs to be more cumulative than it now appears. That is, how do we build knowledge from different close-up studies of curriculum and pedagogy and their effects on students. This will help us think about what we can learn from variations.
- Finally, the accounts need to be theorized to be open to discussion and have wider application. And this points to something of a difficulty in higher education research: researchers or research teams need a deep understanding of both the discipline or field being studied *and* what might be called the 'sociological imagination' because even though epistemic injustices are experienced and performed individually, they emanate from and refer back to social fabric.

Conclusion

To conclude the chapter, I return to Fricker who reminds us that power creates and preserves social hierarchies, enabling some groups to speak and silencing others. So some groups enjoyed 'a credibility excess' (like David James's middle-class 'bright' students) and others 'a credibility deficit' (like students from lower-status universities), thereby enhancing or restricting social epistemic capability.

What I have proposed in this chapter is that close-up higher education research focuses on what Fricker calls 'tracker prejudices' (2007, p. 27) which systematically track a person of a social type or kind across an entire lifetime of being and doing. So, some children arrive at school less attuned than others to what is expected and are therefore seen as 'less bright'. These children then aspire to university, realizing that some are barred to them because they are 'less bright'. At university, they will be anxious about debt and their chances in the labour market, and they might or might not feel they fit in. In and out of university, they are then treated as less credible knowers than those who go to different, higher-status universities. Yet, despite all this, they might, as Muller puts it, be learning 'to do things with knowledge' (2014, p. 10) which they think is valuable (e.g. form an identity, have confidence in power to think, talk to others in the same field, instruct people outside the field or discipline).

Universities undoubtedly maintain differentiation by exclusion and ranking, contributing to enduring inequalities, but they also disrupt inequalities by offering life-changing opportunities. Some students from 'less prepared' backgrounds are being given the opportunities and means to develop the capability of social epistemic contribution. *Not* recognizing and acknowledging when epistemological access is opened is committing a form of misrecognition whereby specific groups are denigrated; that is, students and teachers in lower-status universities are unjustly not taken as seriously as knowers in comparison to those students and teachers in higher-status universities. This is testimonial injustice and causes harm to these people.

To sum up, in our world it might seem small fry to worry about the inequities between university students, but the problem has global reach and influences the moral tenor of societies. Higher education is highly and increasingly sought after for its potential for social mobility because it can disrupt the connections between origins and destinies. And it can do more. It can address an overemphasis on economic wealth and individual prosperity by producing graduates who also value personal transformation and being democratic citizens. It can produce graduates interested in solving the complex and serious problems of the contemporary world: poverty, threats to the environment, war and conflict. Close-up research can play a part in understanding how universities might more frequently and sustainably achieve such goals.

At least one powerful means to bring this vision about is trying to understand and pursue epistemic justice in all its forms.

Notes

1 Stephen Lawrence was an eighteen-year-old black boy who was murdered by strangers in 1993. His parents' persistent campaign led to a public inquiry which in 1999 revealed that the police investigation into Stephen's death was incompetent and characterized by institutional racism.
2 Similar experiments were carried out by Hoadley (2005) and Holland (1981) with the same results.
3 There is substantial research emanating from South Africa which uses Bernstein to research schooling.

References

Ball, S. J. (2003). *Class Strategies and the Education Market*. London: Routledge.
Bathmaker, A. M., Ingram, N., Abrahams, J., Hoare, A., Waller, R., & Bradley, H. (2016). *Higher Education, Social Class and Social Mobility*. London: Palgrave MacMillan.
Bernstein, B. (1975). *Class, Codes and Control Vol. III: Towards a Theory of Educational Transmission*. London: Routledge.
Bernstein, B. (1996). *Pedagogy, Symbolic Control and Identity: Theory Research Ad Critique*. London: Taylor and Francis.
Bernstein, B. (1999). Vertical and horizontal discourse: An essay. *British Journal of Sociology of Education*, 20(2), 157–173.
Bernstein, B. (2000). *Pedagogy, Symbolic control and Identity: Theory, Research and Critique*. Revised ed. Oxford: Rowman and Littlefield.
Boliver, V. (2011). Expansion, differentiation, and the persistence of social class inequalities in British higher education. *Higher Education*, 61(3), 229–242.
Brown, P., & Lauder, H. (2017). Higher education, knowledge capitalism and the global auction for jobs. In P. Scott, J. Gallacher & G. Parry (Eds.), *New Landscapes and Languages of Higher Education*, 240–255, Oxford: Oxford University Press.
Case, J. (2011). Knowledge matters: Interrogating the curriculum debate using the sociology of knowledge. *Journal of Education*, 51, 1–20.
Case, J. (2013). *Researching Student Learning in Higher Education: A Social-Realist Approach*. London: Routledge.
Crozier, G., & Reay, D. (2008). *The socio-cultural and learning experiences of working class Students in HE*. Full Research Report, ESRC End of Award Report, RES-139-25-0208, June. Swindon: ESRC.

Crozier, G., & Reay, D. (2011). Capital accumulation: Working-class students learning how to learn in higher education. *Teaching in Higher Education, 16*(2), 145–155.

David, M. E. (2014). *Feminism, Gender and Universities: Politics, Passion and Pedagogies.* Farnham: Ashgate.

Dieleman, S. (2012). An interview with Miranda Fricker. *Social Epistemology, 26*(2), 253–261.

Fricker, M. (2007). *Epistemic Injustice: Power and the Ethics of Knowing.* Oxford: Oxford University Press.

Fricker, M. (2015). Epistemic contribution as a central human capability. In George Hull (Ed.), *The Equal Society,* 73–90. Lanham: Lexington Book.

Habermas, J. (1984). *Theory of Communicative Action Volume 1: Reason and the Rationalisation of Society,* trans. T. McCarthy, Boston: Beacon Press.

Hart, C. S. (2012). *Aspirations, Education and Social Justice: Applying Sen and Bourdieu.* London: Bloomsbury.

Hoadley, U. K. (2005). *Social Class, Pedagogy and the Specialization of Voice in Four South African Primary Schools,* unpublished PhD thesis, Cape Town, University of Cape Town.

Holland, J. (1981). Social class and changes in orientations to meaning. *Sociology, 15,* 1–18.

Hussain, I., McNally, S., & Telhaj, S. (2009). *University Quality and Graduate Wages in the UK.* IZA Discussion Paper No. 4043.

James, D. (2015). How Bourdieu bites back: Recognising misrecognition in education and educational research. *Cambridge Journal of Education, 45*(1), 97–112.

Jenkins, C., Barnes, C., McLean, M., Abbas, A., & Ashwin, P. (2017). Sociological knowledge and transformation at 'Diversity University', UK. In M. Strydom Wilson & M. Walker (Eds.), *Socially Just Pedagogies, Capabilities and Quality in Higher Education,* Studies in Global Cultures, Education and Democracy series, 45–68, London: Palgrave MacMillan.

Luckett, K. (2009). The relationship between knowledge structure and curriculum: A case study in sociology. *Studies in Higher Education, 34*(4), 441–453.

Luckett, K. (2012). Disciplinarity in question: Comparing knowledge and knower codes in sociology. *Research Papers in Education, 27*(1), 19–14.

Maton, K. (2014). *Knowledge and Knowers: Towards a Realist Sociology of Education.* London: Routledge.

McLean, M., Abbas, A., & Ashwin, P. (2013). The use and value of Bernstein's work in studying (in)equalities in undergraduate social science education. *British Journal of Sociology of Education, 34*(2), 262–280.

McLean, M., Abbas, A., & Ashwin, P. (2015). 'Not everybody walks around and thinks "That's an example of othering or stigmatisation"': Identity, pedagogic rights and the acquisition of undergraduate sociology-based social science knowledge. *Theory and Research in Education, 13*(2), 180–197.

McLean, M., Abbas, A., & Ashwin, P. (2017). *Quality in Undergraduate Education: How Powerful Knowledge Disrupts Inequality*. London: Bloomsbury.

Morrow, W. (2009). *The Bounds of Democracy: Epistemological Access in Higher Education*. South Africa: HSRC Press.

Muller, J. (2014). Every picture tells a story: Epistemological access and knowledge. *Education as Change*, 18(2), 255–269.

Nussbaum, M. (2000). *Women and Human Development: The Capabilities Approach*. Cambridge University Press.

Nussbaum, M. (2013). *Creating Capabilities: The Human Development Approach*. Harvard: Harvard University Press.

Sen, A. (2009). *The Idea of Justice*. London: Allen Lane.

Shalem, Y., & Slonimsky, L. (2010). Seeing epistemic order: Construction and transmission of evaluative criteria. *British Journal of Sociology of Education*, 31(6), 755–778.

Shay, S. (2011). Curriculum formation: A case study from history. *Studies in Higher Education*, 36(3), 315–329.

Shay, S. (2013). Conceptualizing curriculum differentiation in higher education: A sociology of knowledge point of view. *British Journal of Sociology of Education*, 34(4), 563–582.

Shay, S. (2015). Curriculum reform in higher education: A contested space. *Teaching in Higher Education*, 20(4), 431–441.

Tholen, G., Brown, P., Power, S., & Allouch, A. (2013). The role of networks and connections in educational elites? Labour market entrance. *Research in Social Stratification and Mobility*, 34, 142–154.

Wheelahan, L. (2010). *Why Knowledge Matters in Curriculum*. London: Routledge.

Young, M. F. D. (2008). *Bringing Knowledge Back In: From Social Constructivism to Social Realism in the Sociology of Education*. London: Routledge.

6

The Promise of Community-Based Research for Greater Social Justice through Higher Education

Carolin Kreber

Introduction

What does it mean to do social justice research in higher education? Who is involved in research that addresses social justice issues? Where does the expertise reside in social justice research in higher education?

Typically, social justice research in higher education, here on referred to as SJRHE, has centred on the issue of access and has linked improved access with greater chances of social mobility. This research seeks to reveal and better understand the relationships between socio-economic status, type of institution and programme entered, and success in gaining access to certain occupations (e.g. Croxford & Raffe, 2012; The Sutton Trust, 2012; UK Government, 2014). Many higher education researchers have focused attention on the institutional policies and support processes necessary to achieve greater equity in the opportunities underrepresented groups are afforded once they have been admitted into HEIs. Cautioning not to 'confuse wider access with social justice' (Furlong & Cartmel, 2009, p. 103), these researchers argue that it is often through the implementation of appropriate equity, diversity and inclusion policies that full participation in higher education becomes possible, which then enhances the chances of student success (e.g. Richardson, 2010; Riddell et al., 2004; Tackey, Barnes & Khambhaita, 2011). Research aimed at better understanding and enhancing access and participation in higher education, underpinned by the goal of greater equity, inclusion and social mobility, is of fundamental importance in a society that values social justice. It is for this reason that higher education researchers who are committed to these questions may indeed be conceived of as agents of social justice. Notwithstanding the social significance of this work, I propose in this chapter that the meaning of SJRHE can be interpreted also from a different angle.

At the centre of the perspective I will be discussing are two questions: first, where does the expertise reside in SJRHE and second, how do we prepare higher education students for their participation in a complex society characterized by a myriad of conflicting perspectives, uncertainties and drastic social inequalities? Concretely, I suggest that another way of understanding SJRHE is to focus attention on how we prepare students to participate, take action and make a positive contribution to the world we live in, and on the role of research in such preparation. This is a perspective where higher education pedagogy and social justice research become fully integrated (Strand et al., 2003), and where the student is afforded opportunity to learn how to engage in participatory research (Chevalier & Buckles, 2013; Reason & Bradbury, 2008) with communities to support communities in addressing the concerns they identified.

While this integration of pedagogy and research has been noted to be relevant with respect to all students studying in higher education (e.g. Strand et al., 2003), I propose that it takes on special significance with students studying on programmes preparing for a 'profession'. Acknowledging that 'professions' do not represent equal homogenous entities (Saks, 2014), the term 'profession' is used here to refer to an (ever changing) set of occupations that are distinguished by a knowledge base of abstract theories and complex skills acquired through study in HEIs, relative self-regulation supported by professional bodies and associations, the need to exercise personal judgement and, importantly, a commitment to public service (Freidson, 2001). Professional programmes here refer to university degree programmes that prepare students for the profession of public health specialist, nurse, lawyer, teacher, accountant, engineer, social worker, architect, journalist, doctor, dentist and so forth.

The argument and proposal I put forward in this chapter are overtly ideological and presupposes that those responsible for professional programmes in universities not only routinely ask 'What is the professional ideal we hope our students will form identities around?' but, in addition, have reached three concrete conclusions: (1) our professional ideal involves a commitment to public service by supporting the well-being of individuals and communities; (2) supporting well-being involves assisting individuals and communities in having fundamental choices or freedoms over how to live and act; and (3) professionals have a moral responsibility to work towards this ideal.

In this chapter, then, I take the position, as have Walker and McLean (2013) previously, that helping build capabilities in society (Nussbaum & Sen, 1993; Nussbaum, 2011) is a professional responsibility (Kreber, 2016, 2017) and closely attuned to greater social justice. Helping expand capabilities in society means to contribute to interventions that provide more people with real chances and substantial freedoms to pursue a good life; or, to use Nussbaum and Sen's language, to afford people the freedom to be or *do* what they have reason to value (e.g. Nussbaum & Sen, 1993). Drawing in part on Aristotle, Nussbaum contends that capabilities need to be informed 'by an intuitive idea of a life that is worthy of the dignity of the human being' (Nussbaum, 2000, p. 5). Her list of ten central capabilities, which, as she explains, is 'the result of years of cross-cultural discussions' (Nussbaum, 2011, p. 76), incorporates the following (each further specified in her books (Nussbaum, 2000, 2011)): (1) life; (2) bodily health; (3) bodily integrity; (4) senses, imagination and thought; (5) emotions; (6) practical reason; (7) affiliation (being able to live with as well as towards others and being treated with respect); (8) other species; (9) play; (10) control over one's political and material environment (pp. 78–80). Each of these capabilities, sometimes referred to as comprehensive capabilities, represents a sphere of life over which individuals must have real choices. Only if persons have real freedom to choose their functioning in *each* of these spheres, Nussbaum (2015) suggests, can we speak of a life that people have reason to value. Nussbaum claims that her list has applicability across different cultures and traditions as it is both thin and narrow in its claims: it is *thin* as it does not prescribe how a person must live but emphasizes real choices; and it is *narrow* as the list of ten capabilities leaves many matters of life unaddressed, thus respecting individuals' own conceptions of the good life. Nussbaum's claim to universality has been contested (e.g. Jaggar, 2006; Robeyns, 2011), but this chapter is not the place to enter into this debate. I do, however, need to defend the decision I take in this chapter to single out four of the ten capabilities on Nussbaum's list, for she argues that all ten, together, are needed to afford a life of human dignity.

My choice to concentrate on the four capabilities of (1) senses, imagination, and thought, (2) practical reasoning, (3) affiliation and (4) having control over one's political (and material) environment is driven by the focus of this chapter. These four capabilities are essential for individuals to participate in decision-making or public deliberation on issues affecting their lives and, I shall argue, are furthered through involvement in community-based research (Strand et al., 2003). According to Strand et al. (2003) community-based research 'is a partnership of students, faculty and community members who collaboratively engage in research with the purpose of solving pressing community problems or effecting social change' (p.3). It is research *with* and for community and is grounded in an explicit social justice agenda. Importantly, community members, students and teachers are all participants and learners in this research. To be clear though, the argument here is not that professionals should contribute only to interventions that support these four capabilities. I also do not mean to suggest that these four capabilities are more important than any others. Moreover, capability expansion expects more of professionals (and 'professionals-in-the-making' (i.e. students)) than just involvement in community-based research. However, I do contend that when teachers and students are involved in community-based research, this is one form of SJRHE with strong potential to support in our communities the four capabilities of (1) senses, imagination and thought, (2) practical reasoning, (3) affiliation and (4) having control over one's political (and material) environment.

I will make two further theoretical connections in this chapter. I will propose that the notions of task sharing (Dzur, 2008) and *action* (Arendt, 1958) can enlighten us as we contemplate how these four capabilities can be enabled through involvement of students ('professionals-in-the-making') in community-based research. The students, and their teachers, involved in community-based research, may then be conceived of as democratic professionals (Dzur, 2008) who enable democracy through task sharing and sharing of expertise. They also may be conceived of as individuals who, together with others, are involved in public deliberation and *action* where they recognize the perspectives of others, engage in representational thinking and thus enable freedom to appear.

Each of the concepts referred to in this introduction will now be elaborated in the following sections. The chapter is organized into four short sections entitled 'Capability expansion as a professional ideal', 'Enabling democracy and freedom through community-based research', 'Community-based research as pedagogy' and 'SJRHE reconsidered'.

Capability Expansion as a Professional Ideal

A decent society, Nussbaum (2013, 2015) argues, is one that upholds the premise of equal respect for persons and diversity grounded in Rawls's (1986) concept of political liberalism; it also allows each person a certain threshold of capabilities that enables a good life. Importantly, as we saw earlier, a society which fosters basic human capabilities does not prescribe functionings but enables people's fundamental choices about how to live. If professionals, as one subsection of society, also were to uphold the premise of equal respect for persons and diversity and were committed to supporting individual and community well-being on these grounds, then two conclusions would follow.

First, in exchange of the privileges they enjoy, think of status, wealth, prestige, professions would be committed to employing their knowledge (and other forms of social capital) to advance the life circumstances of others, including the least advantaged. In drawing this conclusion, I am inspired by a frequently cited section from A Theory of Justice:

> All social goods – liberty and opportunity, income and wealth, and the (social) basis of self-respect – are to be distributed equally *unless an unequal distribution of any or all of these primary goods is to the advantage of the least favoured.* (Rawls, 1971, p. 303, emphasis added)

As we have seen in the introduction to this chapter, access to higher education, and by extension to the professions, is a primary social good, which continues to be distributed unequally in society. The privileges associated with being part of a professional group, therefore, lie in the hands of a select few. This unequal distribution of professional privilege, we might say, should be tolerated only if ultimately it were to result in the least advantaged of society being better off than would be the case if these privileges were not extended to a select few. Hence, professionals who believe in equal respect for persons and diversity would seek to employ their accumulated knowledge, networks and skills to the advantage of those with fewer privileges, including the least favoured.

Second, professions would not prescribe courses of action but provide the enabling conditions for people to practise their agency in the key areas of life that Nussbaum (2000, 2011) identifies in her list of ten comprehensive capabilities. In other words, professionals would recognize their purpose as helping to build capabilities, or freedoms to choose certain ways of functioning (e.g. voting, playing, eating, being healthy, becoming educated and participating in political life), in society. This is a radical departure from the paternalistic attitude of the professions where clients are looked after by (sometimes) well-meaning authorities which make decision for them in terms of certain functionings rather than letting them take responsibility for their own lives. To be clear then, capabilities are not just personal innate characteristics; rather, the conditions of the environment in which one is placed play a crucial role in terms of whether a person is afforded certain capabilities. For example, a person may have no difficulty understanding and identifying the key flaws in the health care system but may live in a community that does not afford access to resources that would offer the opportunity to challenge existing policies. In this example, the capability of control over one's political environment is not given. Alternatively, having the capability of challenging authority does not prescribe that I must do so; the capabilities approach does not prescribe functionings but emphasizes real choices.

Extrapolating from Nussbaum's (2013) idea of a decent society, I proposed the idea of a 'decent profession' as one that is committed to the ideal of contributing to capability expansion (Kreber, 2017). By extension, and building on the pioneering work of Walker and McLean (2013), I view the purpose of professional education as socializing students into capability expanding practices that professionals ought to engage in. One of these, I suggest here, is involvement in community-based research.

Enabling Democracy and Freedom through Community-Based Research

In community-based research, the issues to be addressed are determined by the community, and every further step of the research is negotiated with the community including how and with whom the work is shared. Strand et al. (2003) point out that community-based research

> challenges the exclusive authority of the trained researcher and argues for the value of nonspecialist participation in decisions relating to research processes and practices ... CBR also challenges conventional assumptions about knowledge itself: what constitutes valid knowledge, how it is best produced and acquired, and who gets to control it. (p.13)

The assumptions and principles guiding community-based research parallel those which inform the practice of democratic professionalism. Dzur (2004, 2008) introduced his notion of democratic professionalism as an alternative to both the social trustee model of professionalism that had developed by the 1950s (e.g. Goode, 1957; Marshall, 1963; Parsons, 1954) and its radical critique of the 1970s (e.g. Larson, 1977). Social trustee professionalism is based on the principle of trust. As Dzur notes,

> The public places trust in the professional to self-regulate and determine standards of practice, while the professional earns that trust by performing competently and adhering to the socially responsible normative orientation. (Dzur, 2008, p. 98)

While the social trustee model is socially responsible in its intention, Dzur cautions that it fails to recognize how essential it is to include members of the public, who are directly affected by professional action, in the process of defining what their social interests are. He observes that the radical critics of social trustee professionalism, writing in the 1970s, already had realized the dangers of professional task monopoly. Ivan Illich (1977) and his colleagues exposed the disabling function of the professional elite as they take away from ordinary citizens the opportunity to decide for themselves on significant matters concerning their lives.

While critical of both social trustee professionalism and the radical critique, Dzur (2008) sees some value in each of these two perspectives. Concurring partially with the social trustee model, he recognizes the enduring social and political significance of the professions; and concurring partially with the radical critique he argues that the paternalistic attitude of the professions needs to be challenged, especially in light of media-reported abuses of power in some professions. However, the shortcomings he sees in each of these models leads him to propose an alternative which assigns to professions a distinctive function. Specifically, he argues that the professionals' most fundamental function in society should be to empower lay citizens to become participants in the process of making decisions on issues associated with vital social interests – decisions typically made only by professionals. Citizens then are not just customers but real participants in the practice and the democratic process. Dzur's democratic professionals focus their work on helping citizens to organize themselves. They enable task sharing and citizen participation in decision-making. While the professionals' professional expertise still counts, they appreciate that important expertise lies with the public itself and see the mobilizing and furthering of this public expertise as an important task. Democratic professionalism acts in the interests of society but emphasizes that these interests, and appropriate responses, must be negotiated with the public.

Teachers and students on professional programmes who collaborate together with community members in community-based research (Strand et al., 2003) learn about the practice of democratic professionalism. Saltmarsh and Hartley (2012) commenting on the role of higher education in promoting a more engaged citizenry likewise argue that such community partnerships seek 'the public good *with* the public, and not merely *for* the public, and as a means of facilitating a more active and engaged democracy' (Saltmarsh and Hartley, 2012, p. 20, emphasis in original). These ideas in turn have strong resonance with Hannah Arendt's notion of *action*, which refers to a particular form of human togetherness that can be observed when and wherever people participate in public deliberation. Public deliberation is a condition of freedom, which disappears if there is no space or opportunity for action. When Arendt argues that action leads to individuals being free, the freedom she has in mind is not individual sovereignty or autonomy where one person can rule over others but collective freedom (Biesta, 2012). One might say that the bureaucracy associated with how policy decisions are made in the fields of public health and education, for example, poses a threat to people's freedom – a threat which can be reduced by involving community members in public deliberation on these issues.

Arendtian action is made possible by two conditions: natality and plurality. When individuals participate in *action*, new opportunities are generated for renewal and change, akin to a new beginning inherent in birth. While natality emphasizes each person's uniqueness and thus the possibility for change that comes with each person who makes an appearance in the world through action, plurality recognizes that we share the common world as equals which involves respecting and engaging the multiple perspectives and values of others. Arendt also argued that action relies on a particular form of reasoning, noting that in representative thinking we 'think with an enlarged mentality' and train our 'imagination to go visiting' (Arendt, 1982, p. 43). Democratic professionals who 'listen carefully to those outside their walls ... encourage co-ownership of problems previously seen as beyond the laypeople's ability or realm of responsibility' (Dzur, 2013, electronic source) seek to know how issues appear and are processed from the public's perspective; as such, they too are engaged in representative thinking. They make efforts to imagine what a given situation looks like from the point of view of others with whom they share a common world. In this way, they enable public deliberation, and thus *action*.

Arendt's work is not routinely evoked in discussions on professional learning and professional practice although exceptions exist (e.g. Kreber, 2016), but its significance has been recognized for higher education pedagogies (e.g. Nixon, 2012; Walker, 2004). My purpose of bringing Arendt's work into this discussion is not to claim any new contribution to our understanding of higher education pedagogies but rather to point to the linkages between community-based research, democratic professionalism and action – all three aimed at creating a public space through which freedom can occur.

Community-Based Research as Pedagogy

Community-based research functions as a powerful pedagogy, and it does so on two levels. On the first level, employed as a university pedagogy, students learn a great deal about relevant research skills (Strand, 2000) and they learn to work collaboratively with communities on issues these communities have identified as a need. Rather than learning in university courses to see ordinary community members as 'needy, victimized, and requiring rescue by educated elites' (Boyte, 2004, p. 113), which presents a serious challenge to democratic professionalism, training in and exposure to community-based research will help shape professional identities and practices to make them more public. On a second level, I suggest, community-based research also functions as a *public* pedagogy (Biesta, 2012) that can help strengthen the public sphere and ultimately democracy. It is community-based research as a pedagogy on this second level that I shall say more about now.

Biesta (2012) distinguished three types of 'public pedagogy': a pedagogy *for* the public, a pedagogy *of* the public and a pedagogy that generates space 'through which freedom can appear' (p. 683). A pedagogy *for* the public is a kind of community education that is informed by a motivation to do things *for* others – a service ethic characterizing social trustee professionalism. A pedagogy *of* the public is a form of community education where the public organizes itself. Professionals involved in this second type of public pedagogy will share their expertise, but at the same time recognize the expertise of citizens and be careful not to deny community members the opportunity to act as civic agents. In articulating the third type of public pedagogy, one that generates space 'through which freedom can appear' (p. 683), Biesta (2012) is inspired by Arendt's theory of action. When people come together, there is an opportunity of deliberation and through this the potential for something new to begin arises. Although there are clear similarities between Biesta's type 2 and type 3 pedagogy, his argument for keeping them separate is that the third type of public pedagogy cannot be planned in the same way that the other two might be planned in advance. The key issue here is that action, for Arendt, is spontaneous. It is up to the actors or citizens themselves, given the opportunity, to seize the moment and do something. Thus, when the community organizes itself (type 2) for a particular purpose, for example to tackle the inadequate health care provision in their local community, this can be considered as being conceptually different from the community gathering to deliberate or debate particular issues which are of importance to them (type 3). In type 2, the activity is planned; in type 3, *action* may or may not occur. This distinction is significant in conceptual terms, but in practice I would argue it fades. Let's look at an example.

When teachers and students on professional programmes, or professionals in their own practice, provide opportunity for collaborative community-based research, there is space provided for deliberation and action can arise spontaneously. The community may or may not decide to engage in the partnership when approached by the university (or professionals themselves). Yet, at a formal town hall meeting or an informal community BBQ members might have deliberated on the health issues affecting their communities and might have decided to seek a partnership with the local university (or professionals from the local health authority). In this case, it is *action* that leads to the partnership. Yet once a partnership is formed in the form of a community-based research initiative, in accordance with the arguments presented earlier in this chapter, then this partnership would be characterized by continued deliberation and strengthening of the public's agency (Boyte & Fretz, 2012). This, in turn, involves both offering ongoing support for the public to organize itself (Dzur, 2008) and the space for further 'action'.

SJ*RHE* Reconsidered

This book is about social justice research in higher education. I suggested that SJ*RHE* has a strong tradition of being focused on greater access and participation in higher education, and on the processes and policies necessary to achieve a better experience, better outcomes and better employment opportunities for equity-seeking groups. Notwithstanding the importance of such continuing work, I proposed that SJ*RHE* can be conceptualized differently, turning the gaze on the question of who is involved in the research and whose expertise counts. I argued that community-based research, especially as conceptualized by Strand et al. (2003), is both a powerful pedagogy and professional practice that is grounded in the spirit of equal respect for persons and diversity. Community-based research involves community members, students and higher education teachers/researchers as equal partners and is focused on issues that matter to the community. As such, it has an explicit social justice agenda. Since this chapter is about researching social justice in higher education, I focused on students and their teachers. However, occasionally I made reference to practising professionals, referring to community-based research as a professional practice. To be clear, my suggestion to introduce students to community-based research in the first place is grounded in the idea that it would prepare them for a later professional life that would integrate community-based research.

I made a case in this chapter that community-based research (Strand et al., 2003) resonates strongly with Dzur's (2008) model of democratic professionalism.

As students on professional programmes engage in community-based research, they learn that a key contribution their profession can make to society is not just to provide efficient and useful services but to facilitate public understanding and practical abilities by stimulating open debate around decisions important to communities. Rather than learning that professions simply do things *for* the public, students learn that society may be served better if professionals do things *with* the public. Ideally, the knowledge, experience and skills students gain through this process they would then take with them into their future life as professionals and citizens.

I also suggested that community-based research was one way by which teachers and students on professional programmes, and of course graduates (practising professionals) themselves, could contribute to capability expansion (Nusbaum & Sen, 1993; Nussbaum, 2000, 2011). Arguably, as students and later graduates collaborate with community members within a community-based research framework, they are involved in interventions that afford participants at least four of the capabilities that Nussbaum considered as essential for a decent life: imagination, senses and thought are typically afforded through education and community-based research is one form of community education; the capability of practical reasoning refers to the freedom to form a conception of the good life which in community-based research is enabled through the validation of and respect for different forms of knowledge, and task sharing; affiliation is enabled by having the opportunity to collaborate with others to address common concerns; and, finally, control over one's political and material environment is afforded through direct participation in all steps of the community-based research projects, enabling community members to have a say in the decisions affecting their lives.

Although community-based research is practised on several campuses, such initiatives are not the norm (Strand et al., 2003). Community-based research can be observed, for example, in work in the field of Indigenous health and well-being in Canada (e.g. Etowa et al., 2011; Ford et al., 2016). In the model I'm proposing, community-based research becomes incorporated into professional programmes as a pedagogy so that students learn the skills of negotiating with the public and the public is afforded certain freedoms. Of course, and as has been outlined by several authors, involving undergraduate students in community-based research has its challenges (e.g. Kravetz, 2004). Undergraduate students may not have the skills that are required to successfully address the issues identified by the community, and it will not always be possible for students to complete these projects within the parameters of a course or programme. Moreover, academics employing community-based research together with students may feel discouraged by the criteria against which their research is assessed within the academy. Woodrow Presley (2012) argued that the culture of the academy 'Will not notice or value community-based research until and unless it is published in a first-tier, peer reviewed journal' (p.133). Nonetheless, witnessing capability-building community-based research modelled by their teachers and having some engagement with such work during their years at university is valuable preparation for students' later professional practice.

Those responsible for professional programmes in universities, therefore, may need to ask themselves whether they incorporate into their programme any opportunities for students to become involved as facilitators of shared decision-making, allowing clients or citizens to make their views on issues heard. Do they attempt to prepare students for a professional practice that seeks to break down traditional barriers between citizens and professionals? Is it their sense that they are preparing students as enablers of democracy, and facilitators of Arendtian action? And more fundamentally, do they believe that higher education programmes, in particular professional programmes, should equip students with the knowledge, skills and values that would enable them to work towards capability expansion? Four of the ten capabilities Nussbaum (2000, 2011) identified, namely (1) senses, imagination and thought, (2) practical reasoning, (3) affiliation and (d) control over one's environment, I argued, can be supported through the processes that characterize community-based research; other capabilities may be supported as well depending on the focus of a particular community-based research project.

References

Arendt, H. (1958). *The Human Condition*. Chicago, IL: University of Chicago Press.
Arendt, H. (1982) [1970]. *Lectures on Kant's Political Philosophy*, ed. R. Beiner. Sussex: The Harvester Press Limited.
Biesta, G. J. (2012). Becoming public: Public pedagogy, citizenship and the public sphere. *Social and Cultural Geography*, *13*(7), 683–697.
Boyte, H. (2004). *Everyday Politics: Reconnecting Citizens and Public Life*. Philadelphia, PS: Pennsylvania University Press.
Boyte, H. C., & Fretz, E. (2012). Civic professionalism. In J. Saltmarsh and M. Hartley (Eds.), *To Serve a Larger Purpose. Engagement for Democracy and the Transformation of Higher Education*, 82–101. Philadelphia, PS: Temple University Press.

Chevalier, J. M., & Buckles, D. (2013). *Participatory Action Research: Theory and Methods for engaged Inquiry*. Abingdon-on-Thames: Routledge.

Croxford, L., & Raffe, D. (2012). Social class, ethnicity and access to higher education in the four countries of the UK: 1996–2010. *International Journal of Lifelong Education, 33*(1), 77–95 (CES Ref 1222).

Dzur, A. (2004). Democratic professionalism: Sharing authority in civic life. *The Good Society, 13*(1), 6–14. Retrieved from http://www.jstor.org/stable/20711151

Dzur, A. (2008). *Democratic Professionalism: Citizen Participation and the Reconstruction of Professional Ethics, Identity, and Practice*. Pennstate: Pennstate University Press.

Dzur, A. (2013). Trench Democracy: Participatory innovation in unlikely places. *Boston Review*. http://www.bostonreview.net/blog/dzur-trench-democracy-1

Etowa, J., Matthews, V., Vukic, A., & Jesty, C. (2011). Uncovering aboriginal nursing knowledge through community based participatory research. *Indigenous Policy Journal, XXII*(1), Retrieved from http://indigenouspolicy.org/index.php/ipj/article/viewFile/3/82. Accessed 23 March 2019.

Ford, J. D. et al. (2016). Community-based adaptation research in the Canadian Arctic. *WIREs Climate Change, 7*, 175–191. doi: 10.1002/wcc.37.

Freidson, E. (2001). *Professionalism: The Third Logic*. Chicago: The University of Chicago Press.

Furlong, A., & Cartmel, F. (2009). *Higher Education and Social Justice*. Maidenhead: Society for Research into Higher Education and Open University Press.

Goode, W. J. (1957). Community within a community: The professions. *American Sociological Review, 22*, 194–200.

Illich, I. (1977). Disabling professions. In I. Illich, I. Zola, J. McKnight, J. Caplan and H. Sharken (Eds.), *Disabling Professions*. London, UK: Marion Boyars.

Jaggar, A. (2006). Reasoning about well-being: Nussbaum's methods of justifying the capabilities. The Journal of Political Philosophy, *14*(3), 301–322.

Kravetz, K. (2004). *Undergraduates and Community-Based Research: Benefits, Challenges and Opportunities*. COMM-ORG Papers. Retrieved from https://comm-org.wisc.edu/papers2004/kravetz.htm#elements. Accessed 23 March 2019.

Kreber, C. (2016). *Educating for Civic-Mindedness: Nurturing Authentic Professional Identities through Transformative Higher Education*. London and New York: Routledge.

Kreber, C. (2017). The idea of a decent profession: Implications for professional education. *Studies in Higher Education*. doi: 10.1080/03075079.2017.1395405.

Larson, M. S. (1977). *The Rise of Professionalism: A Sociological Analysis*. Berkeley, CA: University of California Press.

Marshall, T. H. (1963). The recent history of professionalism in relation to social structure and social policy (first published in 1939), reprinted in *Sociology at the Crossroads*. London, UK: Heinemann.

Nixon, J. (2012). *Interpretive Pedagogies for Higher Education*: Arendt, Berger, *Said, Nussbaum and their Legacies*. London, UK: Continuum International Publishing Group.
Nussbaum, M. (2000). *Women and Human Development. The Capabilities Approach*. Cambridge, NY: The Cambridge University Press.
Nussbaum, M. (2011). *Developing Capabilities*. Cambridge: The Cambridge University Press.
Nussbaum, M. (2013). *Political Emotions: Why Love Matters for Justice*. Cambridge, MA: Harvard University Press.
Nussbaum, M. (2015). Political liberalism and global justice. *Journal of Global Ethics*, *11*(1), 68–79.
Nussbaum, Martha, & Sen, Amartya (Eds.) (1993). *The Quality of Life*. Oxford: Clarendon Press.
Parsons, T. (1954). Professions and social structure. In *Essays in Sociological Theory*. Glencoe, IL: The Free Press.
Rawls, J. (1971/1999). *A Theory of Justice*. Cambridge, MA: Harvard University Press.
Rawls, J. (1986). *Political Liberalism*. New York, NY: Columbia University Pres.
Reason, P., & Bradbury, H. (Eds.) (2008) *The Sage Handbook of Action Research: Participative Inquiry and Practice*. Sage, CA. ISBN 978-1412920292.
Richardson, J. T. E. (2010). Widening participation without widening attainment: The case of ethnic minority students. *Psychology Teaching Review*, *16*(1), 37–45.
Riddell, S., Tinklin, T., & Wilson, A. (2004). Disabled Students in Higher Education: A reflection on research strategies and findings. In C. Barnes & G. Mercer (Eds.), *Disability Policy and Practice: Applying the Social Model*, pp. 81–98. Leeds: The Disability Press.
Robeyns, Ingrid. (2011). *Comment for Author Meets Critic. Martha Nussbaum's Creating Capabilities. 2011 Eastern APA Authors Meets Critics Session: Martha Nussbaum, Creating Capabilities: The Human Development Approach*. The Belknap Press of Harvard University Press, 1 December 2011. Retrieved from https://www.academia.edu/1145709/Comment_for_author_meets_critics_Martha_Nussbaums_Creating_Capabilities_session_at_the_2011_Eastern_APA_meeting. Accessed 10 March 2019.
Saks, M. (2014). Professions, marginality and inequalities. *Sociopedia.isa*. doi: 10.1177/205684601411. Retrieved from http://www.sagepub.net/isa/resources/pdf/ProfessionsMarginality.pdf. Accessed 10 March 2019.
Saltmarsh, J., & Hartley, M. (2012). Democratic engagement. In J. Saltmarsh & M. Hartley (Eds.), *To Serve a Larger Purpose. Engagement for Democracy and the Transformation of Higher Education*, 14–26. Philadelphia, PS: Temple University Press.
Strand, K. (2000). Community-based research as pedagogy. *Michigan Journal of Community Service Learning*, *7*, 85–96.
Strand, K., Marullo, S., Cutforth, N., Stoeckel, R., & Donohue, P. (2003). *Community-Based Research and Higher Education: Principles and Practices*. San Francisco: Jossey-Bass.

Tackey, N. D., Barnes, H., & Khambhaita, P. (2011). *Poverty, Ethnicity and Education. Institute for Employment Studies.* York, UK: Joseph Rowntree Foundation. Retrieved from www.jrf.org.uk/publications/. Accessed 10 March 2019.

The Sutton Trust (2012). *Social Mobility and Education Gaps in the Four Major Anglophone Countries. Social Mobility Summit.* London, UK.

UK Government. (2014). *Elitist Britain.* London, UK: Child Poverty and Social Mobility Commission. Retrieved from https://www.gov.uk/government/news/elitist-britain-report-published. Accessed 10 March 2019.

Walker, M. (2004). Pedagogies of beginning. In M. Walker and J. Nixon (Eds.), *Reclaiming Universities from a Runaway World*, 131–146. Maidenhead, Berkshire: The Society for Research into Higher Education and Open University Press.

Walker, M., & McLean, M. (2013). *Professional Education, Capabilities and Contributions to the Public Good. The Role of Universities in Promoting Human Development.* London, UK: Routledge.

Woodrow Presley, J. (2012). Chief academic officers and community-engaged faculty work. In J. Saltmarsh & M. Hartley (Eds.), *To Serve a Larger Purpose. Engagement for Democracy and the Transformation of Higher Education*, 130–154. Philadelphia, PS: Temple University Press.

Twitter and Social Media as Critical Media Pedagogy 'Tools' in Higher Education

Natasa Lackovic

Introduction

Information that students read on social media globally comes from a fantastic range of resources and platforms (Burnett & Merchant, 2011). Students use social media significantly in relation to discussing and finding information related to academic or any personal matter (Junco, 2014). As such, these media, albeit all media are social, have become a fundamental part of students' experience – a part of *being a student at university*. 'Being at university' (participation) is what McLean, in Chapter 5, sees as one phase where social injustice of higher education occurs. She identifies two further phases: students' access to university and moving to post-university life. With regard to 'being at university', such being does not happen only via curricular academic engagement and a student's physical presence but also, virtually, via students' online presence and engagement that connects to their real-life experiences. I propose that the injustice the students might experience concerning their social media presence is linked to their lack of *access* to critical media pedagogy and literacy practice. Regardless of the subject, this would enhance students' understanding of social media's varied nature, roles and functions. I also argue that this type of pedagogy, practice and training is necessary for any subject, discipline and programme, and goes beyond *transactional* media literacy role of acquiring some literacy 'skills' (Mihailidis, 2018). Rather, it should also support higher education's civic role in building more socially just societies (McArthur, 2010). This view aligns with 'civic media literacy' to 'produce and reproduce the sense of being in the world with others towards common good' (Mihailidis,

2018, p. 1). I develop the rationale for the aforementioned arguments in the remainder of this chapter, mainly building on the work in critical social media by Christian Fuchs (2017), related perspectives by Paul Mihailidis (2018) and Jan McArthur (2010). The overall approach adopted is one of a critical theory of social media.

In terms of a particular social media platform focus, the chapter refers to all social media, but foregrounds Twitter as the social media in the chapter's background study. The definition of Twitter is adopted from Murthy (2013, p. 10) who posits that this microblogging platform operates via public profiles by users who send short messages (of up to 140 characters up to 2017 – the year when it changed to 280 characters), which become publicly aggregated across users who are able to decide whose messages they receive/view, but not necessarily who receives and/or use their messages. The content of the messages have evolved over time: from instant news update of any kind to advertising, personal endorsement and social activism.

I first present the rationale for the argument opened at the beginning of the chapter about why critical pedagogy with social media is needed via the discussion about the link between social media and social injustice, and then expand this discussion in relation to higher education. This is followed by sketching the background study for these considerations. The study explored students' contribution to a Twitter-based learning activity and students' perceptions of Twitter (and social media in general) in relation to learning (Lackovic et al., 2017). What is unpacked in this chapter is the absence of any social justice or 'for-critical-reflection' roles of social media that are spontaneously reported by students, that is, when they are not prompted to think about it. I conceptualize this absence as a sign, and as an impetus, to think more deeply about social media and social justice relationships in higher education teaching-learning. I comment on the implications and tensions surrounding these issues.

I neither perceive students' lack of engagement with Twitter as something negative nor do I propose that students should or have to be active participants of social media. Rather, I am building an argument for critical dialogic teaching-learning/pedagogy with social media in higher education. This is the first step. Other steps in developing this pedagogy involve students as contributors to the development of related pedagogical activities, as well as university management support.

Why Criticality with Social Media? The Link Between Media and Social (In)Justice

Non-Neutrality and Othering in Social Media: Discourse, Affordances and Use

Social media can act as 'tools' or artefacts that can help make *a contribution* to social justice since they allow publication of user-generated content and thus provide outlets for public opinion on any social issue, supporting multiple voices and activist community building (Fuchs, 2017, 2014). On the other hand, social media, including Twitter, are also considered as 'cyber utopia' tools of oppression with regard to data storing, surveillance, coercion, control and prosecution threats (Fuchs, 2017). A salient reason as to why social media need to be critically examined is that digital technologies and the virtual world contribute to social injustice by being hegemonic and 'non-neutral' in terms of discourse, access, economies, affordances and use (Fuchs, 2017). Mihailidis (2018) adds to these concerns by emphasizing that social media require a theoretical framework not only towards critique but also towards socially just action. In relation to social justice pedagogy, McArthur (2010) similarly suggests that critical pedagogues need to find avenues to move closer from the culture of critique to the culture of action for change. As such, these approaches (Mihailidis, 2018; McArthur, 2010) suggest that critically deconstructing social media's 'non-neutrality' needs to be expanded with a holistic approach to critical student and pedagogue's engagement with social media, since both media and education are messy and complex.

How are social media 'non-neutral'? Fuchs (2017, p. 10) argues that, although many people benefit from using communication and transport technologies, 'the history of these technologies is deeply embedded into the history of capitalism, colonialism, warfare, exploitation and inequality'. He observes that 'corporate, military, or state interests often stand above the interest of humans' (Fuchs, 2017, p. 10). Furthermore, in his book *Social Media: A Critical Introduction*, he weaves together a strong argument that social media connectedness to social inequalities is orchestrated by neoliberal and hyper-neoliberal streams, which reproduce inequalities via the class-based system, racism and hijacking any 'social' purpose (of social media) for economic capital accumulation (Fuchs, 2017). It is not that accumulating wealth is a bad thing per se. Rather, the mechanisms surrounding it should be subject to scrutiny, so that everyone has better possibilities of earning more, and more equally and equitably. In terms of change, this means to think about action needed for more positive futures (McArthur, 2010).

The 'non-neutrality' of social media is embedded in discourses that are created on social media, regardless of their subject/profession/discipline background, and are not politically or ideologically neutral (Gajjala, 2012). They may be disguised in rationalist, business, scientific, professional, entertainment or other nice 'clothing' (e.g. attractive design or imagery may serve to draw attention away from an exclusive discourse). These discourses commonly operate with the concept of 'othering' and 'otherness' – the differentiation (commonly of some group of people) according to a dominant standard (commonly as defined by some dominant group of people) (Roberts & Schiavenato, 2017). To illustrate this point of 'non-neutral' and 'othering', Zhang, Gajjala and Watkins (2012, p. 4) refer to Hobson's (2008) concept of 'digital whiteness'. The concept reproduces 'whiteness' as an ideal state of being from 'real life' and 'gains power not only through access but, more importantly, through the "cultural scripts" that associate "whiteness with 'progress', 'technology', and 'civilization', while situating blackness [and other marginalized identities] within a discourse of 'nature', 'primitivism', and pre-modernity"' (p. 114). Such discourse propagated in media and social media further branches into many dichotomies under singular labels: one should consider that 'whiteness' is also not the same depending on a region/country of birth.

For example, Neumman (1999) provides an historical account of 'othering' looking at identity relationships in European history and nations, the East as juxtaposed with the West. At a more micro level, 'Balkanist' discourses and presentation across media, including microblogging, can turn the entire region of the Balkans and the people of the Balkans into something of a negative connotation (Kolstø, 2016; Čolović, 2013; Velickovic, 2010; Grubačić, 2012). This is first of all evident in an English verb 'to balkanise', the meaning provided in Oxford online dictionary being 'to divide (a region or body) into smaller mutually hostile states or groups'. The definition implies a distinct 'othering' of one group of people positioned together under the adjective 'hostile' and the premise of 'mutually hostile states or groups'. As Kolstø (2016, p. 1245) notes, 'The word "Balkans" often functions as a stigma.' All these issues are social justice issues when 'othering' is reinforced via identity politics and the politics of difference. A struggle for power and dominance is often behind such politics. This politics of difference is not a one-way street happening and is promoted just in the West, far from it – the politics of difference has been a crucial weapon of division and destruction in all contexts (e.g. the Balkans, South East or Central Europe, Middle East, Far East) in relation to some 'other'. However, if one considers the power as generated from accumulated economic wealth, this means that Western global influences are still most powerful and dominant (albeit China and India are on the rise); hence, (social) media discourses and possibly other types of influences and interventions would be expected to be orchestrated from the Western context, at a global level (Fuchs, 2017). If we consider social media headquarters, all major social media headquarters – Facebook, Twitter, YouTube, Airbnb and more – are located in the United States, currently the world's leading economic and media power.

Of course, digital technologies and social media can offer a space for emancipatory information and grouping that challenge societal status quo, and offer opportunities for educators' grassroots action (McArthur, 2010), just as it promotes problematic discourses and images (Fuchs, 2017). I do not wish to align myself with any dualistic positioning, technological pessimism or optimism, dystopia or utopia, the so-called 'vanilla' or 'radical' critical pedagogy. I also do not argue in favour of Twitter or student social media participation per se. Rather, my arguments are in favour of an informed and critical engagement with social media and Twitter, as mediators of social support and connectedness, togetherness towards change, preservation and highlighting of shared (rather than dividing) values, as well as civic media literacies. I acknowledge that some might see this as utopian, but I do not.

Unless the above-mentioned issues of contemporary society are discussed with students, valuable opportunities for discussion and also practicing critical social media pedagogy and challenging social injustice are simply lost. This does not mean to inoculate students in 'personal ideologies' though, as some might fear, since a critical pedagogue needs to be open to students about their position, as much as general education is not. Put it simply, all education is ideological. In addition, the proposed views on critical pedagogy in some higher education contexts and under particular state policies might have limited scopes to be practiced, let alone thrive. All the reasons mentioned in this section make a potent case to practice critical social media pedagogy.

Critical Pedagogy with Social Media in Higher Education

In the opening of this chapter, I argue in favour of critical social media information pedagogy or training as necessary for any subject, discipline and programme, to support a higher education civic role and duty in building more socially just societies. However, there is a tension in academic understanding of what this 'training' and critical engagement entails. This tension is with regard to approaches to media format, characteristics, analysis procedures and aims, as well as theoretical and conceptual lenses (Pangrazio, 2016). Therefore, different terminologies are used to connote the need for critical engagement with media, foregrounding new notions of 'literacy'. Some of the terms include critical media literacy (Kellner & Share, 2007), critical digital literacy (Pangrazio, 2016), critical information literacy (Elmborhg, 2006), critical media pedagogy (Morell & Duncan-Andrade, 2006). Shared messages of all these approaches could be summarized and presented to various extents for each approach such as the following:

1) Media and social media messages are not neutral, but deeply entwined with sociocultural histories, systems and ideologies; hence, they need to be questioned and examined critically.
2) Media and social media critical examination require training and active practice.

In addition to these approaches, 'civic media literacies' foregrounds the role of critical pedagogy and theory (such as that of Freire and bell hooks), in students' social media literacies (Mihailidis, 2018). This aligns with the observations by Giroux (1988) who questions an education that promotes the language of critique (critical thinking) only, and not the language of possibility that could lead to action and change (critical pedagogy); basically, a possibility of/for action in real life. Aligned with this proposition, Burbules and Berk (1999) suggest that there is a difference between critical thinking and critical pedagogy. The former, they argue, is more rooted in the tradition of scientific reasoning and search for factual evidence, and the latter is focused more on social justice and emancipation (Burbules & Berk, 1999). The former can also be observed in light of neoliberal obsession with performance and skills, such as 'employability skills' or 'literacy skills' or any other skills. Mihailidis (2018) criticizes media literacies skill building as a transactional approach, claiming that this approach, although very useful, needs definitional and practical expansion ('practical' meaning pedagogy, action and change). McArthur (2010) similarly identifies the need for and challenges in moving from critique to desired change. However, McArthur (2010) also rightly *emphasizes the importance of coming together* as both critical thinkers and pedagogues, whether this is radical pedagogues or not. Only such a union and the formation of critical mass could bring about some change, rather than pockets of thinkers and approaches that do not talk to and criticize each other, although they subscribe to the same broader strivings (McArthur, 2010).

In terms of defining critical social media pedagogy, I am cautious about its discourse of 'empowerment' and 'student voice' if it fails to acknowledge the inherent power in relationships between tutors and students. Other issues include the impossibility of having complete knowledge of some oppressions unless having lived them, and the failure to acknowledge the complexity of individual identities as well as personal privileged positions (Ellsworth, 1989). There will always be some social injustice that is not clearly under one's radar. Even if an educator is an ardent proponent of social justice and critical pedagogy, this educator will never be aware of all injustices and marginalization because the experience of each person is limited, and mostly linked to what they have encountered in their life, whether directly or via others they have encountered.

I define critical pedagogy with social media adapting Ellsworth's (1989, p. 324) definition as follows:

> Critical pedagogy with social media entails tutor and student dialogue and actions in relation to social media discourse and its effect in the society that support an understanding that students' or pedagogues' knowledge of anyone, the world and 'the Right thing to do' will always be partial, interested, and potentially oppressive to others. Such pedagogy is directed towards shaping and reshaping circumstances in which all students and ultimately people of difference can thrive.

This critical inquiry with social media resembles the idea of 'technoliteracy from below', that is, pedagogical initiative to look out for and legitimize 'counter-hegemonic needs, values and understanding (…) as opposed to the largely functional, economistic, and technocratic technoliteracy "from above" that is favoured by many industries and states' (Suoranta & Vadén, 2007, p. 159, quoting Kellner & Kahn (2006)). Mihailidis's (2018) views on civic media literacies further expand the stated definition. Civic media literacies 'support students' sense of care for and engagement with the society, their persistence in action and emancipation'. As Mihailids (2018, p. 11) explains the concept,

> Media literacies that are designed with civic intentionality challenge existing systems and structures that restrict or constrain individuals and communities in their pursuit of bringing people together in pursuit of a common good.

Mihailidis (2018) further comments that 'these approaches do not start with media texts, platforms, or modalities. Instead, they ask how media can support civic outcomes that bring people together in support of a common good'. This is similar to McArthur's (2010) calls for united and unifying critical pedagogy for change. However, few studies have looked at critical pedagogy or critical media literacy and thinking in higher education in relation to particular social media. An exception is, for example, Suoranta and Vadén's (2007) study in relation to

Wikis. Most Twitter studies in higher education are concerned with the role of Twitter for learning. Lackovic et al. (2017) conceptualized students' absence and lack of contribution to a Twitter learning initiative due to student–teacher power relationships and students' subsequent feelings of incompetence and subordination, as well as particular students' perceptions of Twitter, such as entertainment and career enhancement purposes (all of these perceived roles also noted by Fuchs, 2017). This Twitter study is the background for this chapter.

Background Study Context of the Chapter: The Missing 'Function' of Twitter

The mentioned empirical study (Lackovic et al., 2017) involved an entire cohort of students – forty-three Year 1 Physiotherapy students – at a UK university who were encouraged by researchers (the project leader and I, then in the role of researcher assistant) to contribute to Twitter with critical commentary and examination of module-related information. A Physiotherapy-specific hashtag, titled as a specific module's abbreviation, was created by one of the module tutors (who was also one of the project researchers) in addition to the regular lectures and seminars. It was stressed that lack of engagement would bear no consequences on assessment. Individual support was offered and detailed instruction on how to use Twitter was provided, including how to create Twitter profiles if students did not have any, but the majority of them did. One of the tutors on the hashtag module, the project leader, mentioned to students after each lecture that he would tweet a question for them and pose a challenge for their answers to be within the limit of 140 characters. Upon the end of the Twitter hashtag life planned for this project – eight weeks – it was clear that students showed little interest in the hashtag and there was no participation (other than one tweet). The hashtag developed a life of its own, and many professionals and a few students from other universities were tweeting, possibly due to the tutor's rather large Twitter network. The content of tweets contained a high number of critical questions and commentaries related to the subject of the hashtag.

We organized two focus groups with twelve student-volunteers (six male, six female) within the target physiotherapy students. These were to explore students' opinions and reactions to the hashtag, in order to answer how students perceive social media and Twitter, their engagement with the created Twitter hashtag and Twitter in general, and what factors discouraged and would encourage students to use Twitter for learning. A structured focus group schedule was followed, with questions such as these: Can you tell us a bit about Twitter? What is Twitter for? What is social media for? What about the Twitter hashtag for your course? Have you viewed it? Why? Why not? Do students tweet? Do they tweet in relation to their study? Why not? What would inspire you to engage with Twitter? We audio recorded the conversations, addressing students with pseudonyms (each was given a pseudonym name tag to protect their identity). The audio recordings were transcribed verbatim. The study was done in accordance with strict ethical research requirements, approved by the host university's ethics committee.

Although the research team's initial rationale was to support critical and participatory thinking under a module hashtag as a form of a Twitter 'community', my personal interest developed further here is contemplating the absence of students' perception of social media and Twitter in relation to critical social media pedagogy or critical analysis in any way. I do not claim that students were not aware of any social justice or 'for-critical-reflection' role of social media, or that they had not known about it or engaged with it prior to the focus group. Rather, their *choice of foregrounding* other uses of Twitter – for entertainment and business (Lackovic et al., 2017) – and not mentioning anything else, signals the marginal role of critical and social justice considerations of Twitter (and social media in general), and also for learning. I proceed with a focused discussion of the 'entertainment' positioning of social media and Twitter by students, followed by the consideration of the challenge of standardized practice in higher education that can stifle critical pedagogy with social media.

Twitter and Social Media as Spectacle Entertainment and Conduit for 'Othering'

Students' view of Twitter as primarily an entertainment tool aligns with how Twitter is still dominantly perceived by the general population, at least in the United States (Fuchs, 2017). It resembles the conceptualization of Twitter as a *spectacle* platform, a spectacle to watch (Mihailidis, 2018) and a spectacle to cheer to (likes) and regurgitate (retweet without looking into the URL that is shared on Twitter, for example). Both Mihailidis (2018) and Fuchs (2017) have commented on the spectacle character of social media and the spectatorship attitude in terms of how it fosters social passivity, as opposed to social action and civic engagement. It also fosters a consumerist culture as opposed to creative culture, where information is quickly consumed and promoted, without much time to reflect on it or create something of a substance. Since information and services are increasingly automated, this automation of life leads to an automation of response, the creation of a consumption habit and passive spectatorship, in contrast to real-life grouping and organized action (Fuchs, 2017; Mihailidis, 2018).

This passivity is apparent in social media acting as silos for critical commentary rather than action, occupying insulated networked communities. Such communities are not only common to student grouping but generally consist of like-minded people discussing in online 'echo chambers' without any challenging points of view to 'disturb' these insular online groups' entrenched views and comfort zone (Mihailidis, 2018; McArthur, 2010). Another form of passivity is stated by Mihailidis (2018) who claims that the rise of distrust and scepticism in social media is influencing students to distance themselves from social media, especially in terms of any social media civic engagement in practice. Such scepticism is one of the markers of the so-called 'post-truth' era we are currently living in (Peters, 2018). These are all the reasons why the 'entertainment' spectacle role of social media needs to be explored.

Furthermore, a spectacle can be not only pleasant but also gruesome – the high number of views of violent videos on YouTube, for example, confirm this unsettling appetite for shocking gory spectacles and spectatorship practice. When violence happens in societies, social media can feed this disheartening appetite, and it can be also 'blamed' for supporting it, by applying 'surveillance, law and order' discourse, much present in neoliberal politics. To illustrate the latter, in the case of looting during London and UK riots of 2011, the rioters were labelled in the news (by many news media in the UK) as 'Twitter mobs'. This is because they, among other things, used Twitter to provide information on available spots for looting. Of course, looting is not a desirable social behaviour; however, this labelling does not solve social discontent, inequalities and crisis, which are the root cause of any unrest.[1] Rather, it highlights and identifies 'the other' who has to be blamed by the public and other social media users; the common destructive culprit that effectively distracts public attention away from the sociocultural issues and problems that are at the core of socially organized violence and unrest. This further promotes passive spectatorship and the culture of 'blaming and shaming', and these issues are a part of social justice issues that can trigger discussion with students. Another issue with social media and internet *spectatorship* (White, 2006) is that it might serve corporate profit and wealth accumulation much more than common social communication and good (Fuchs, 2017). It isn't that we (people, society) should not engage in watching informative and entertaining media content or earn from it, far from it. I am not proposing some perpetual and grim state of critical inquiry to dampen and destroy the pleasures and joys of media entertainment, and the laughs at social media videos of cute cats doing silly things (no reason why this should stop). Nonetheless, I am proposing civic media literacies for critical engagement with social media, and relevant action: this is needed as much as savouring entertaining content.

Civic Media Literacy Challenge: Action, Standardized Practice and Knowledge Power

Stressing the importance of action in critical media literacy, Mihailidis (2018, p. 8) argues that

> if media systems and structures must be reformed, people cannot simply understand how they work but must translate their capacity to understand media with taking deliberate civic actions to improve, reform, or re-imagine media's role in our civic systems.

I would like to add to this that what is of paramount importance is to practice an *informed* action. Otherwise, an action can endanger someone's or group's earning status and even safety; hence, an important part of action is discussing what this entails and what implication and consequences it might bring to the acting person or a group, and how to mitigate those. When it comes to higher education pedagogy, civic media literacy cannot be achieved if there is no alignment between civic efforts and the ways universities operate. To reform and challenge power structures in higher education and especially the meaning of empowering knowledge, which was one of the issues identified in the Twitter background study, educators could also rethink and re-imagine academic definitions that identify such knowledge.

Academic knowledge–power relations are embedded in what Bernstein calls horizontal–vertical discourses (McLean, Chapter 5). Vertical discourse is official (schooled) knowledge, a highly conceptual academic discourse, whereas horizontal is the everyday, 'mundane', popular discourse and knowledge. Social media is some sort of such 'horizontal' discourse. In Chapter 5 McLean links horizontal discourses to less powerful knowledge. She refers to 'lower' social class students' disadvantage since they might have developed weaker vertical discourses, having had limited access to them from their families. This indeed happens in higher education, and it is problematic. However, the 'higher' level discourse can be considered as the one that does not only empower students but also exhort power structures, pedagogical traditionalism, standardized and authoritative knowledge (that has been created 'to empower' by some people who were at some time recognized to be leading academic minds, mainly Western, male and white). There is of course value in standardized knowledge and practice, but also much contestation surrounding the nuances of knowledge provenance, legitimization and the *separation* of those discourses in higher education, without more meaningful attempts to create links between them. This is yet another area for critical social media pedagogy. Social media are not recognized as an avenue for higher (vertical) academic knowledge, and hence practices with social media as related to knowledge creation are marginal pedagogic practices. Since social media have become such a powerful force that influences lives in the era of digital reason (Peters and Jandric, 2015) and even dictate what the 'truth' is (Peters, 2018), is the civic duty of higher education then to include them as legitimate and integral knowledge content, and consider these media critically with students?

Standardized practices can often stifle the spreading of critical media literacies simply because this is not endorsed by all practitioners, and standards apply to all. Higher education staff are already burdened with all sorts of higher education market place obligations and targets. Universities operate via many rules of a standardized practice. In the case of the background study's Twitter hashtag creation and student engagement, this had to be a strictly optional activity, and also not embedded in the classroom, so as not to impinge on university's and programme's standardized pedagogic practice. As much as this makes sense, such situation can create 'desired activity-prescribed outcomes' tensions and reproduce the same 'traditional' structural, curricular and pedagogical hierarchies and linearity (Ross, 2011) of digital environments, just as it existed in traditional educational formats. Furthermore, there may be a form of contrived and polished reflection enforced in group-shared social media commentary due to its visibility and asynchronous linearity, acting as a type of surveillance mechanism (Ross, 2011). Perhaps that is why it was not attractive to students to contribute on Twitter, and rightly so. Critical consideration of social media can shed light on all those issues; hence, it can bring empowering and informative experiences for both teachers and students. A change via an organized, management-supported joint action for critical social media civic literacy in higher education is needed.

Implications: Social Media and Critical Pedagogy

Social media are 'media', and they do not do any action in real life; action requires humans. People take action themselves that is increasingly mediated by machines and social media. Social media *mediates* information dissemination and exchange; therefore, it is a mediating artefact. However, social change can only happen via social action, which the information exchange can support. Such is the case of the commonly called 'Arab spring' – it is not the media that caused it, but the humans who organized it in real life that used social media to act, get organized and mobilized. Yet, in this very case, it has acted in dual way. This duality is evident in the testimony from one of the participators that social media both invigorated and destroyed civic action (Mihailidis, 2018). Indeed, social media are perceived as supporting both liberating social change (techno optimism) and social control and oppression (techno pessimism).

If its negative role is considered, social media can easily support moral panic, othering and divisions in the society. To counteract these forces, critical pedagogy with social media should do more to encourage positive 'uses' of social media and ways to develop alternative engagements towards informed student action. This is an action that challenges social injustice and encourages grassroots participation, towards intended change (McArthur, 2010). Similarly, Fuchs (2017) suggests that another way forward is to consider social media in alternative ways, as created, moderated and managed by groups who are oriented towards the betterment of diverse communities and alternative economics. Along these lines, students can participate in training that empowers them to create alternative social media platforms, or at least curate them.

Yet, critical pedagogy with social media is not at all straightforward. For example, critical pedagogy and its calls for emancipatory use of social media can also be seen as 'cyber-utopian' (Schneider & Goto-Jones, 2014). The 'ruling powers' have developed ways to 'manage political discontent' via social media (Schneider & Goto-Jones, 2014, p. 5), creating a culture of surveillance and fear, especially in some national contexts. The boundaries between students' emancipatory social media (Twitter) participation and the one that leads to social and personal vulnerability, stigmatisation and threat (of coercion) are indeed fragile and shaky (Schneider & Goto-Jones, 2014). Furthermore, it might be that some groups of extreme ideologies paradoxically see themselves as 'supporting civic outcomes that bring people together in support of a common good' (Mihailidis, 2018), but this is the good of their exclusive group or nation, which they see and defend as the common good. It is a rather hard task for educators on where to draw the line, and both invigorate students to *act* for social justice relating to social media towards change (McArthur, 2010), yet protect them from any threats and indoctrinations, even their own, and the ones that present themselves as 'socially just' and empowering. In terms of pedagogic practice, it is desirable and needed to develop and research possible pedagogic methods and approaches, although this is not possible here as the scope of the chapter is limited. For example, teachers could apply media artefacts inquiry methods building on critical media literacy (Tisdell, 2008), multi-modal critical discourse analysis (Ledin & Machin, 2017) and visual semiotics (Lackovic, 2018; Hallewell & Lackovic, 2017; Lackovic, 2010).

I am aware that I have spent much space on critique, but I am a firm proponent of thinking about what good one group can *do to support social connectivity and change via social media, rather than just criticize.* McArthur (2010) rightly suggests that more attention and energy should be spent on analysing and understanding how socially just change *actually* occurs. Twitter as a social media platform can bring many social benefits, such as virtual connectedness and encounters that lead to real-life social connectedness. These can be encounters that are empowering, fruitful and a catalyst for collaborations and positive change. Social media can also play a positive role in alleviating loneliness, a grave problem of a modern human, by providing platforms where people can connect and then meet in real life. Twitter can contribute to the creation of socially and mutually supportive networks, including the ones advocating social justice. This is indeed the role and use that needs to be foregrounded, understood and practiced more by educational staff and students in higher education.

All in all, education with or on Twitter, just like in general education practice, is a field of struggle for legitimacy and status, as the students' perceptions of Twitter reflected (Lackovic et al., 2017). The current climate of global university competition, prestige, publication and the research funding rat race are all markers of power games that all HEIs and their staff are invited to play. To acknowledge these is also a part of socially just discussions with students and colleagues.

Conclusion

I have argued in this chapter for the need to develop critical social media pedagogy/literacies in global higher education. I have strongly built on the work of Mihailidis (2018), Fuchs (2017) and McArthur (2010), coming from the contexts of Western and European academic institutions. However, I have included some critical voices from different global contexts and experiences. The arguments were triggered by an empirical study about student Twitter disengagement, and the absence of any critical and for-social justice role of social media reported by the students (Lackovic et al., 2017). Navigating media literacy and critical media literacy, pedagogy, and civic media literacies is not an easy task for educators. It involves a level of risk taken from both the educators' and students' side, and a sound decision in terms of what it entails, when and how to do so, especially in terms of implications and consequences. I have not tackled here the when and how of doing this practice, but this is desirable. Critical social media pedagogy-in-action is not that widely spread since it includes many possibilities of coercion. Critical pedagogues might be in a constant state of (existential) dilemma. Their struggle is further amplified by accusations (e.g. by neo conservatives in the United States) that higher education students are being indoctrinated into left-wing ideology, stifling intellectual diversity (Applebaum, 2009).

Importantly, as McArthur (2010, p. 501) argues, 'Critical pedagogy needs to develop a critical mass if it is to achieve real emancipatory change.' Above all, students must make their decisions of action or inaction, contribution or not, without any pressure. It is also fair to say that at the moment, most educators (including myself) in higher education are contributing to some extent to social injustice and its perpetuation by exercising criticism and no action, daily consumerist activities, academic elitist discourses and strivings, and/or tensions between espoused and enacted believes in social justice. To acknowledge these, and that we have all taken actions that might have had a negative impact on others, is the first step towards a more harmonious and socially just society. This step needs to be cultivated by higher education and via exploration of ways in which social media can support human togetherness and social justice. A risky business it is, but one that can build momentum and become a larger educational and social movement that is supported by social media, towards a more equal world of fulfilled communities and diverse individuals and groups within them. Even if some would see these strivings as romantic utopianism, I think that they are worth striving for, and my hope is that I have provided, to both national and international readers, enough rationale for it in this chapter.

Note

1 For related C. Fuchs's comment and accompanying discussion in the commentary section, please see Fuchs's blog post (August 2011): http://fuchs.uti.at/667/

References

Applebaum, B. (2009). Is teaching for social justice a 'liberal bias'. *Teachers College Record*, *111*(2), 376–408.

Burbules, N. C., & Berk, R. (1999). Critical thinking and critical pedagogy: Relations, differences, and limits. In Thomas Popkewitz & Lynn Fendler (Eds.), *Critical Theories in Education: Changing Terrains of Knowledge and Politics*, 45–65. New York: Routledge.

Burnett, C., & Merchant, G. (2011). Is there a space for critical literacy in the context of social media? *English Teaching*, 10(1), 41.

Čolović, I. (2013). Balkanist discourse and its critics. *Hungarian Review*, 2, 70–79.

Ellsworth, E. (1989). Why doesn't this feel empowering? Working through the repressive myths of critical pedagogy. *Harvard Educational Review*, 59(3), 297–325.

Elmborg, J. (2006). Critical information literacy: Implications for instructional practice. *The Journal of Academic Librarianship*, 32, 192–199.

Fuchs, C. (2014). *OccupyMedia!: The Occupy Movement and Social Media in Crisis Capitalism*. John Hunt Publishing.

Fuchs, C. (2017). *Social Media: A Critical Introduction*. Sage.

Gajjala, R. (Ed.). (2012). *Cyberculture and the Subaltern: Weavings of the Virtual and Real*. Rowman & Littlefield.

Giroux, H. A. (1988). *Teachers as Intellectuals: Toward a Critical Pedagogy of Learning*. Greenwood Publishing Group.

Grubačić, A. (2012). Balkanization of politics, politics of Balkanization. *Globalizations*, 9(3), 439–449.

Hallewell, M. J., & Lackovic, N. (2017). Do pictures 'tell' a thousand words in lectures? How lecturers vocalise photographs in their presentations. *Higher Education Research & Development*, 36(6), 1166–1180.

Hobson, J. (2008). Digital Whiteness, primitive Blackness: Racializing the 'digital divide' in film and new media. *Feminist Media Studies*, 8(2), 111–126.

Junco, R. (2014). *Engaging Students through Social Media: Evidence-Based Practices for Use in Student Affairs*. John Wiley & Sons.

Kellner, D., & Share, J. (2007). Critical media literacy: Crucial policy choices for a twenty-first-century democracy. *Policy Futures in Education*, 5(1), 59–69.

Kolstø, P. (2016). 'Western Balkans' as the new Balkans: Regional names as tools for stigmatisation and exclusion. *Europe-Asia Studies*, 68(7), 1245–1263.

Lackovic, N. (November 2010). Creating and reading images: towards a communication framework for Higher Education learning. *Seminar. net* 6(1), 121–135.

Lackovic, N. (2018). Analysing videos in educational research: an 'Inquiry Graphics' approach for multimodal, Peircean semiotic coding of video data. *Video Journal of Education and Pedagogy*, 3(1), 6.

Lackovic, N., Kerry, R., Lowe, R., & Lowe, T. (2017). Being knowledge, power and profession subordinates: Students' perceptions of Twitter for learning. *The Internet and Higher Education*, 33, 41–48.

Ledin, P., & Machin, D. (2017). Multi-modal critical discourse analysis. In John Flowerdon and John E. Richardson (Eds.), *The Routledge Handbook of Critical Discourse Studies*, 60–76. Abingdon and New York: Routledge.

McArthur, J. (2010). Achieving social justice within and through higher education: The challenge for critical pedagogy. *Teaching in Higher Education, 15*(5), 493–504.

Mihailidis, P. (2018). Civic media literacies: Re-Imagining engagement for civic intentionality. *Learning, Media and Technology, 43*(2) 152–164.

Morrell, E., & Duncan-Andrade, J. (2006). Popular culture and critical media pedagogy in secondary literacy classrooms. *International Journal of Learning, 12*(9), 273–280.

Murthy, D. (2013). *Twitter: Social Communication in the Twitter Age*. John Wiley & Sons.

Neumann, I. B. (1999). *Uses of the Other: 'the East' in European identity Formation* (Vol. 9). University of Minnesota Press.

Pangrazio, L. (2016). Reconceptualising critical digital literacy. *Discourse: Studies in the Cultural Politics of Education, 37*(2), 163–174.

Peters, M. A. (2018). The history and practice of lying in public life. In *Post-Truth, Fake News*, 77–88. Singapore: Springer.

Peters, M. A., & Jandric, P. (2015). Philosophy of education in the age of digital reason. *Review of Contemporary Philosophy, 14*, 162–181.

Roberts, Mary Lee A. and Schiavenato, M. (2017). Othering in the nursing context: A conceptual analysis. *Nursing Open, 4*(3), 174–181.

Ross, J. (2011). Traces of self: Online reflective practices and performances in higher education. *Teaching in Higher Education, 16*(1), 113–126.

Schneider, F., & Goto-Jones, C. (2014). Revisiting the emancipatory potential of digital media in Asia–Introduction to the inaugural issue of Asiascape: Digital Asia. *Asiascape: Digital Asia, 1*(1–2), 3–13.

Suoranta, J., & Vadén, T. (2007). CHAPTER 7: From social to socialist media: The critical potential of the Wikiworld. *Counterpoints, 299*, 143–162.

Tisdell, E. J. (2008). Critical media literacy and transformative learning: Drawing on pop culture and entertainment media in teaching for diversity in adult higher education. *Journal of Transformative Education, 6*(1), 48–67.

Velickovic, V. (2010). Against Balkanism: Women's academic life-writing and personal and collective history in Vesna Goldsworthy's Chernobyl Strawberries. *Woman: A Cultural Review, 21*(2), 172–188.

White, M. (2006). *The Body and the Screen: Theories of Internet Spectatorship*. MIT Press.

Zhang, Y., Gajjala, R., & Watkins, S. (2012). Home of hope: Voicings, whiteness, and the technological gaze. *Journal of Communication Inquiry, 36*(3), 202–221.

Part Three

Locating Social Justice in the Preparation of Graduates to Contribute to Societies

8

Engaging the Normative with the Analytical in Higher Education Research

Jennifer M. Case

The notion of 'social justice' considers the distribution of wealth (and related aspects of well-being) in society as a matter of justice. In contexts like the United States and the United Kingdom, social justice tends to stand in for a broad critique of the neoliberal political project that has been associated with an erosion of public institutions and an increase in income inequality – a rolling back of the post-war commitments of the social welfare state. In these contexts of relatively high participation in higher education, questions around how class continues to impact on educational experiences and life opportunities have not been resolved, with elite institutions continuing to draw largely from middle and upper classes (Reay et al., 2001) and questions raised around commitments to the discourse of 'widening participation'. A social justice stance on higher education also provides the starting point for a necessary pushback to a related set of justifications for higher education that sees these predominantly in instrumental and economic terms, focusing attention on issues of efficiency with educational outcomes characterized in 'evidence-based' terms.

In post-apartheid South Africa, it is relatively recent that 'social justice' has entered the lexicon of higher education scholarship (see Hlalele & Alexander, 2012; Leibowitz & Bozalek, 2015; Wilson-Strydom, 2011) – these issues used to be more signalled with the term 'transformation' in the context of transforming a system from the legacy of apartheid. The emerging use of social justice can be associated with a sharply growing sense that the democratic government has not been able to address the inherited inequities from colonial and apartheid times – both access to and success in higher education remain skewed by race (Cooper & Subotzky, 2001).

Scholars such as Melanie Walker and Elaine Unterhalter (2007) have found value in engaging with Amartya Sen's (2011) critique of the concept of social justice as brought into contemporary times by John Rawls (1971). In short, Sen finds Rawls's abstract ideal notion of limited utility when faced with real-world contexts, where ideals are seldom attained but the necessity for moral judgements is important. Sen has offered what can be considered a more 'close-up' notion of social justice, grounded in his conceptualization of human flourishing – the possibility for humans to accomplish things that they value doing in life. There is an immediate appeal to this argument in that human flourishing feels so close to an intrinsic understanding of the purposes of education.

In this chapter, I want to consider what are the implications and potential pitfalls especially for scholars taking a social justice stance on higher education. My thinking is particularly influenced by current developments in the South African context, where extreme social inequity sharpens the debate. I am also concerned that taking the lead from deliberations in contexts such as the United Kingdom and the United States, with very different contemporary social arrangements, might lead to some blind spots in our thinking. It seems that in order to find a useful position around higher education and social justice, we need to go back to some foundational issues.

Just over twenty years after the democratic dispensation, the South African social landscape continues to be structured by its legacy of colonialism and apartheid. These were systems that regulated life opportunities for South Africans in distinct ways depending on their ethnic backgrounds. These structures have largely not changed even though we now have a democratic order: black children still attend schools that are little different to the Bantu Education system that was the cause of the Soweto uprising some forty years ago. South Africa now has a growing middle class of all races, but nearly half of our population is still excluded from stable livelihoods (Southall, 2016). Significant progress has been made in provision of housing and sanitation, but we still have statistics around maternal and child health that are completely out of kilter for a nation with this level of GDP. It is therefore not surprising that serious questions began to be asked by student activists in 2015, especially given that this was the point where the broader political order began to unravel. But the answers are not that straightforward. Yes, definitely, society needs to change. But how? And most crucially, what role should and could the university play in this regard?

Social Change and the Functions of the University

From a number of different positions there are compelling arguments that the university cannot be the central locus for social change. Herewith an extract from a recent piece by Robin Kelley, a UCLA professor and committed activist (Kelley, 2016). Reflecting on the recent student protests across US campuses, he writes of universities:

> As institutions they will never be engines of social transformation. Such a task is ultimately the work of political education and activism. By definition it takes place outside the university.

Coming from a completely different perspective, the somewhat iconoclastic Stanley Fish says in his rather provocative book *Save the World on Your Own Time* that university professors should leave their political commitments outside the classroom (Fish, 2008).

Whatever your political stripes, it is clear that the domain for societal change will be the political, whether in a system of democratic institutions or on the streets (or both). The university cannot be a representative body, it cannot make policy and it cannot dispense health and welfare. So what can it do?

Here we know the standard answer – research/teaching/administration/social engagement – but these are internal organizers for academic activity. What does the university do, and what should it do, from the perspective of society? A perspective is offered by Saleem Badat (2009), a former vice chancellor of a South African university, who says,

> The meaning of higher education and universities cannot be found in the content of their teaching and research, how they undertake these, or their admission policies. Instead, the core purposes of higher education and universities reside elsewhere. (p. 4)

From this, Badat identifies purposes and roles for the contemporary South African university slightly reorganized for purposes of this chapter:

1. Research and scholarship – production of new knowledge (Badat quite purposefully puts this last on his list but I am simply ordering to make clear the links with our research/teaching/and so on conceptualization of what we do)
2. Cultivation of highly educated and democratically minded people
3. Engaging with society both on development needs and challenges, and with its intellectual and cultural life

Here you can see the familiar themes peeping through, but framed now in terms of external purposes – what the university offers to society.

At this stage it is useful to take a step back and locate this contemporary framing within a broader perspective put forward by the historian and sociologist Manuel Castells (2001). Here Castells notes that universities at all times and places have served four different (and potentially contradictory) functions, but that the balance and form of these differs in particular periods. First, and contrary to a view that is often espoused, Castells points out that universities have always served an ideological function. This tends to represent the dominant ideologies in society, although in contexts of a repressive state the university tends more to foster challenges to this domination in the form of counter-hegemonic ideologies. Secondly, universities have always served as mechanisms of selection of dominant elites. This is even so in present massified and even universal systems, where stratification within the broader system preserves this function (as predicted by Trow, 1973). With regard to the third function, Castells notes – as is widely recognized – that research is a relative newcomer to the university, emerging in the nineteenth century and intensifying in our period not only due to the significance of knowledge in the globalized economy but also, I think, in the context of increasingly cash-strapped universities looking for third stream income. The fourth and final function which Castells argues, and probably currently the most significant one, is the training of the bureaucracy, going back to the early church schools and changing form but not function when industrialization required the production of engineers and other technically skilled personnel, and mass schooling and social welfare systems required armies of schoolteachers and social workers and so on.

This perspective on the functions of the university helps to tease out our contemporary position on higher education and social justice. Social justice is an ideology. It is a counter-hegemonic ideology to the neoliberal discourse that has become so prominent across much of the Anglophone world. The ideology of social justice is an important extension of the democratic commitment that Badat recognizes as a key function of the contemporary university. I need to clarify here my use of the term 'ideology' – this we can take to mean a normative view on how society should work and – in the context of the university – a view on what the roles of graduates will be in this regard. Ideology can function either to support a hegemonic order or to contest it.

As noted, Castells emphasizes that these functions of the university are often in contradiction and tension with each other. Most obviously, the ideological function will not always sit easily with the production of new knowledge. Ideology is the promotion (and expansion) of one viewpoint, while new knowledge in a university will often be about engaging in different and competing viewpoints. Furthermore, in a society in turmoil and competition over ideology, this tension will be seen in the university, most notably in the context of what we now term the 'global South'. The trick is for the university to meld these potentially contradictory functions together into some form that is reasonably compatible with the present times, and this challenge means a periodic remaking of the question: What is the university for? With regard to the risks if this is not accomplished, Castells is clear:

> The real issue ... is to create institutions solid enough and dynamic enough to stand the tensions that will necessarily trigger the simultaneous performance of somewhat contradictory functions. The ability to manage such contradictions, while emphasising the role of universities in the generation of knowledge and the training of labour in the context of the new requirements of the development process, will condition to a large extent the capacity of new countries and regions to become part of the dynamic system of the new world economy. (p. 212)

Returning then to a position on social justice and higher education, this is of course a key point for ideological contestation in our present society, and it is not surprising, as noted by Castells, that the university is a key site for protecting and expanding this counter-hegemonic discourse. And with Robin Kelley, and against Stanley Fish, it is entirely appropriate that students in their studies will be exposed to and expected to engage with what might be expected of our democratic societies and the degrees to which current arrangements are moving us forwards or backwards. These are powerful ideas, and we do well to produce graduates who are critical and dissatisfied with the societies in which they find themselves. However, as Kelley notes, the university cannot be the central locus for effecting this change. We need to produce graduates that will go into the streets and/or the boardrooms to act on the knowledge that they have taken in. Here it is worth noting another inherent contradiction in the functions of higher education as outlined by Castells – we frame what we give graduates as tremendously precious and important – yet we work within a system that by definition can only extend these privileges to a portion of society (as noted above this is true even for so-called 'universal' higher education systems where the resulting stratification means that only a small segment gets the truly elite version of higher education).

Contestation in the Postcolonial University

In the middle of one of our recent campus shutdowns at the University of Cape Town (UCT), I found myself asking the question: 'Can you run a functional university in a dysfunctional society?' Well of course you have to. Understanding the key functions outlined above that no other institution in society is placed to accomplish, we have to keep our universities going. But Castells, from a survey of postcolonial Africa, notes the severe challenges in this context – what tends to happen is that the ideological functions of the universities come to dominate at the expense of others, most notably at the expense of the production of knowledge and the necessary education of professionals for all domains in the modern society. With great irony, this situation means that these universities are not able to achieve what Castells calls their developmental function (the training of professionals), which of course will be centrally important if these societies are actually to accomplish the social changes that their ideological position might value – the building of strong and inclusive economies, the provision of services to the citizenry and so on.

Further analysis of the African post-independence context for higher education comes from the incisive work of Ugandan scholar Mahmood Mamdani. In a piece delivered to South African academics on the eve of the democracy, and noting early portents of what might come, Mamdani first urged the audience to abandon their idea of South African exceptionalism (Mamdani, 1993) – the idea held by many South Africans at that time that we would somehow be exempt from the social, political and economic difficulties that have plagued the postcolonial African context. Crucially, in running through the course of events as experienced in his home university, Makarere in the 1960s, he shows how the prominence of an Africanist ideological position in the post-independent university had severe and crippling consequences for its ability to ultimately function as a university. Once the now fully 'Africanized' university was fully subservient to the new nation state, it lost its autonomy and could no longer hold together its functions, most especially in the domain of production of knowledge. Makerere, once the global site for intellectual ferment, became a stagnant pool. Reflecting on these events, Mamdani asked the assembled South African academics:

> Are you condemned to suffer a replay of the old African script or are you in a position to learn from our experience? (p. 9–10)

At this point it is useful also to reference the key debate between Jakes Gerwels and Neville Alexander in 1987 at the University of the Western Cape

(UWC). Gerwels had famously declared UWC the 'intellectual home for the left'. Alexander, although most probably more radically left than most of the others in the room, stridently disagreed with this position, arguing that such a commitment would condemn the university to becoming a 'leftist bantustan', rather than being open to a broad set of ideas. Given the political mood of the time, it is perhaps not surprising that Gerwel won widespread support for his position. However, with the benefit of hindsight, Premesh Lalu comments of this move:

> It was a profound move, but it had some unforeseen consequences. The university continued to write itself into a marginal space. We were always lodged within a certain referentiality, always 'that', the other university of the left. It short-circuited other possibilities and gave rise to some dogmatic thinking. (Davis, 2012)

The Task for Education Researchers

If we are to retain a contemporary commitment to social justice (in the face of a narrow neoliberal hollowing out of higher education), alongside the other potentially contradictory functions of the university, what will this mean for us as higher education scholars and teachers? In order to take this forward, I have found productive the simple challenge posed in a recent keynote by Sharon Todd (2015), who challenged an audience of education researchers to be sure that they are asking educational questions. We cannot evade our own role in generating new knowledge to broaden our understanding of contemporary problems. Here I was struck by a recent comment of the higher education editor of a social media outlet, who noted how hard it was these days to get South African education academics to write about their research findings – in these heady times everyone wants to write op-eds but no one wants to make a contribution to the long haul. In order to expand on Todd's challenge, I would like to refer to Castells and the broader context for the work that I discussed earlier. In 2000, a series of seminars was arranged with South African academics to engage with Castells's emerging work on the contemporary condition of globalization, what he terms 'informationalism' and its implications for emerging economies such as South Africa, with an especial focus on education. Castells reportedly lamented that South African academics seemed stuck in the mode of asking 'how to' questions rather than the analytical focus that he deemed more important in research. Thus the questions were focused on 'how' we can resist the pernicious impacts of globalization, rather than an analytical understanding of the conditions – constraints and enablements – of the present context. Part of this can be related to an over-prioritizing of the ideological mode. Castells is quite frank in his assessment of this mode of academic work:

> What is to be done? Each time an intellectual has tried to answer this question, and seriously implement the answer, catastrophe has ensued. (Castells, 1998, cited in Muller, 2001, p. 273)

Therefore, we need to ask analytical education questions. In this regard our ideological commitment to social justice is a potentially rich and productive store, and a useful metric for a contemporary society in which it is often hard to find a moral compass – but we need to use this to frame educational questions rather than rhetorical statements or prescriptions for action. In a broader sense, the flagging of social justice also links with calls by Andrew Sayer and others for the bringing back in of normative concerns to social science (Flyvbjerg, 2001; Sayer, 2011). There is a rich emerging literature on the public good purposes of higher education, and here, I suggest, is a more nuanced framing of the normative that we need to guide our deliberations (see, for example, Lagemann & Lewis, 2011; Marginson, 2011; Nixon, 2011). An important point to make at this juncture is that any real discussion of social justice in society would need to centre on the full post-secondary education system, not just higher education. This is a serious concern in current South African discourse on the matter. Recent evidence from the OECD points again to the crucial (although complex) role of vocational education in advancing social equality in the long term (Busemeyer, 2014).

Currently there is a growing scholarship tracking the dramatic expansion of participation in higher education, particularly in Asia over recent times (Unterhalter & Carpentier, 2010). The trend seems unstoppable and driven mainly by aspirations of families rather than by government fiat (Carnoy et al., 2014; Marginson, 2016). These are times to make sure the questions we are asking of higher education are not trapped in thinking of the past. What are the particular dynamics of the expansion of higher education in South Africa – how is a system that massified early on for a small racially defined segment adjusting (or not) to the needs of broader massification across the population? How can we understand the protests of 2015–16 in this context, bearing in mind Trow's original analysis? What are the forms of capital that South African students from less privileged backgrounds are drawing on in order to succeed in South African higher education? What are the forms of pedagogy that are supporting the needs of these students? What do graduates make of the knowledge and dispositions that the university has fostered in them – how do these translate into their lives post university?

With regard to addressing the central educational questions of the day, I argue that the contribution of close-up research remains completely undervalued. Sadly this is a world that wants metrics, rankings and statistical correlations. In higher education I would be bold to say that yet another study which shows how students with high levels of motivation/self-efficacy/self-regulation tend to perform better academically is really a waste of everyone's time. There are important questions that are not being addressed, partly because these require an audience sophisticated enough to understand complex causality. Researchers need to be able to build explanatory accounts which draw on close-up data, but in analysis are able to locate it carefully in its historical and social context. We need to find ways to work with large sets of narrative data; to become more sophisticated in using observational and documentary data; to learn to work comparatively across contexts in a close-up mode. We need to listen closely to student voices; at the same time we need more than ever to avoid the 'epistemic fallacy' (Archer, 2007) which takes people's accounts of the way things seem to be the way they are. It is difficult to make sense easily of the challenging and fast moving times in which we are living. Crucially, there is much work to be done in interpreting findings and presenting these to multiple audiences. If the world out there has been raised on a diet of metrics and correlations, then the duty is going to fall to us as higher education scholars to raise the level of the conversation.

In closing, I want to end with something of a provocation. Readers will be aware that the UCT took the decision early in 2015 to remove the statue of Cecil John Rhodes from the campus. There was widespread agreement about this symbolic break, and only a few lone voices troubled the moment. A colleague Nicoli Nattrass[1] wrote the following:

> Removing the statue will provide the illusion that we have rid ourselves of Rhodes' legacy. It would cloak UCT in a false mantle of radicalism, hiding the embarrassing truth that we are an elite institution that reinforces social inequality on a daily basis. The statue should be moved – but let's keep it somewhere on campus to remind us that we are the living legacy of Rhodes' elitism, and have a corresponding debt to society.

This thoughtful challenge resonates with an earlier piece written in November 2013 by the then vice chancellor of the UCT, Prof Njabulo Ndebele. Aware of the long-standing debates about the location of the statue of Cecil John Rhodes on the UCT campus – these go back to the 1930s – he provides a provocative engagement with the perspective that the statue is designed to invoke:

> A concrete balustrade just below Rhodes allows you to stand there, your back to him. You too can assume his pose. ... For a while you might even experience the gaze of contentment: there, spread before you, is the world you had a hand in shaping.
>
> ...
>
> Although you and Rhodes command a view, the vista before you is too far and widespread to show its imperfections. At some time past you may have read about, heard about, or seen smoke rising from rampant fires in the informal settlements of KwaLanga along the highway to and from the airport; and from farther afield, in the townships of Gugulethu and Crossroads. You might have contemplated lives charred and belongings incinerated, families traumatised; and you might recall the clamours of tragedy in the newspapers, on radio and television, of political accusation and counter-accusation, and stories of poverty and wealth deposited on the deliberative tables of commissions of inquiry. (Ndebele, 2013)

What is the relationship between the university and the world that surrounds it? The deliberate colonial siting and architecture of UCT embodies the idea that the university is set apart, with an elevated view from which it can gaze upon and contemplate the world. Ndebele's inversion of Rhodes's gaze – to look closely at the misery that is also part of the colonial legacy and to avoid the comforts of an ideological blanket – is a useful reminder to higher education scholars of the important analytical work to be done if we are to make any progress in really alleviating the injustices of the past.

Note

1   https://www-uct-ac-za.ezproxy.uct.ac.za/mondaypaper/archives/?id=9992

References

Archer, M. S. (2007). Realism and the problem of agency. *Journal of Critical Realism*, 5(1), 11–20.

Badat, S. (2009). The role of higher education in society: Valuing higher education. *Paper Presented at the HERS-SA Academy 2009*, Cape Town.

Busemeyer, M. R. (2014). *Skills and Inequality: Partisan Politics and the Political Economy of Education Reforms in Western Welfare States*: Cambridge University Press.

Carnoy, M., Froumin, I., Loyalka, P. K., & Tilak, J. B. (2014). The concept of public goods, the state, and higher education finance: A view from the BRICs. *Higher Education, 68*, 359–378.

Castells, M. (2001). Universities as dynamic systems of contradictory functions. In J. Muller, N. Cloete, & S. Badat (Eds.), *Challenges of Globalisation: South African Debates with Manuel Castells*, 206–223. Cape Town: Maskew Miller Longman.

Cooper, D., & Subotzky, G. (2001). *The Skewed Revolution: Trends in South African Higher Education, 1988–1998*. Education Policy Unit, University of the Western Cape.

Davis, R. (2012). Remembering Jakes Gerwel. *Daily Maverick*. Retrieved from http://www.dailymaverick.co.za/article/2012-11-29-remembering-jakes-gerwel-.V0seq2DP6xI.

Fish, S. (2008). *Save the World on Your Own Time*. OUP USA.

Flyvbjerg, B. (2001). *Making Social Science Matter*. Cambridge: Cambridge University Press.

Hlalele, D., & Alexander, G. (2012). University access, inclusion and social justice. *South African Journal of Higher Education, 26*(3), 487–502.

Kelley, R. D. G. (2016). Black study, black struggle. *Boston Review*. Retrieved from https://bostonreview.net/forum/robin-d-g-kelley-black-study-black-struggle.

Lagemann, E. C., & Lewis, H. (Eds.). (2011). *What Is College For? The Public Purpose of Higher Education*. New York: Teachers College Press.

Leibowitz, B., & Bozalek, V. (2015). Foundation provision – a social justice perspective: Part 1: Leading article. *South African Journal of Higher Education, 29*(1), 8–25.

Mamdani, M. (1993). University crisis and reform: A reflection on the African experience. *Review of African Political Economy, 20*(58), 7–19.

Marginson, S. (2011). Higher education and public good. *Higher Education Quarterly, 65*(4), 411–433.

Marginson, S. (2016). High participation systems of higher education. *Journal of Higher Education, 87*(2), 243–271.

Muller, J. (2001). Concluding comments: Connectivity, capacity and knowledge. In J. Muller, N. Cloete, & S. Badat (Eds.), *Challenges of Globalisation: South African Debates with Manuel Castells*, 271–288. Cape Town: Maskew Miller Longman.

Ndebele, N. (2013). Introduction. In P. Weinberg (Ed.), *Viewpoints: The University of Cape Town and Its Treasures*. UCT Press.

Nixon, J. (2011). *Higher Education and the Public Good*. London: Continuum.

Rawls, J. (1971). *A Theory of Justice*. Cambridge, MA: Harvard University Press.

Reay, D., Davies, J., David, M., & Ball, S. J. (2001). Choices of degree or degrees of choice? Class, 'race' and the higher education choice process. *Sociology, 35*(4), 855–874.

Sayer, A. (2011). *Why Things Matter to People: Social Science, Values and Ethical Life*. Cambridge: Cambridge University Press.

Sen, A. (2011). *The Idea of Justice*. Cambridge, MA: Harvard University Press.

Southall, R. (2016). *The New Black Middle Class in South Africa*: Boydell & Brewer.

Todd, S. (2015). Facing Uncertainty in Education: Beyond the Harmonies of Eurovision Education. Paper Presented at the European Conference on Education Research (ECER), Budapest.

Trow, M. (1973). *Problems in the Transition from Elite to Mass Higher Education*. Berkeley: University of California.

Unterhalter, E., & Carpentier, V. (2010). *Global Inequalities and Higher Education: Whose Interests are We Serving?* London: Palgrave Macmillan.

Walke, M., & Unterhalter, E. (2007). *Amartya Sen's Capability Approach and Social Justice in Education*. Palgrave Macmillan.

Wilson-Strydom, M. (2011). University access for social justice: A capabilities perspective. *Education, 31*(3), 407–418.

Developing Socially Responsible Graduates through Global Citizenship Programme

Sarah Goodier, Carren Duffy and Suki Goodman

Introduction

Global citizenship programmes are flourishing around the world. The growing focus on developing a global perspective that is driving this increase has come about because of the rise of globalization, the increasing ease of world-wide interactions through international travel (Anderson et al., 2006; Caruana, 2010; Lagos, n.d.) and the development of information and communication technologies (ICTs) (Caruana, 2010; UNESCO, 2013). These factors have brought communities across the world virtually closer together, in terms of both social and business interactions. As a result, global issues have been recognized as having an increasingly significant impact on local issues and communities.

Schattle (2008) notes that discourse around global citizenship is most prominent in the education sector (compared to government, business or civil society). University graduates from around the world are said to lack knowledge relevant to this increasingly global, complex and diverse future (Petersen & Osman, 2013). Graduates entering the business world do not necessarily have this non-subject-specific knowledge at an appropriate level (Annette, 2002). The need for such knowledge has seen education institutions, particularly in higher education, incorporate internationalization and the development of civic-minded, socially responsible graduates into their strategic goals and as graduate attributes. As such these institutions have implemented global citizenship programmes into their curricula to fill the perceived gap in students' global knowledge and skills (Annette, 2002; Bourn, 2011; Bourn & Shiel, 2009; Brigham, 2011; Caruana, 2010; Dugan & Komives, 2007; Jorgenson & Shultz, 2012; Reade et al., 2013; UNESCO, 2013). The increase in such programmes has, therefore, resulted from the need to produce socially responsible graduates equipped to handle the increasingly global world. The availability of these programmes, in turn, adds to the student experience, providing them with offerings that have the potential to enhance their global perspective and sense of social responsibility.

While the increase in global citizenship programmes aimed to better prepare students for the global world of life and work is a laudable idea, a key question is this: Do we know what works in these kinds of programmes? The key assumptions underlying the approach that designers and implementers of global citizenship programmes take and the context in which they operate are both factors in shaping and determining programme success. Without a good understanding of these factors, programmes may fail to achieve their intended outcomes or be unable to demonstrate their successes (contribution of close-up research in Case, Chapter 8). Uncovering the basket of different approaches taken and the how these might affect student participation at university and on their leaving university and entering the world of work (participation and outcomes in McLean, Chapter 5) require further research. This chapter focuses on uncovering what forms global citizenship programmes take in different geographical contexts through a review of a set of discoverable programmes with publicly available information, research literature and published evaluations on global citizenship and these programmes.

South Africa's universities and the global citizenship programmes are of special interest as they are embedded in a unique context. The emphasis on social justice as a key element underlying the idea of citizenship is driven by the South African context of large inequalities across society (McMillan, 2013) that have persisted since 1994. Both basic (K-12) and HEIs have been historically divided along racial lines and with minimal resources being made available to historically black institutions (see Fisher, 1998 for an overview of the post-1994 restructuring of higher education in South Africa). In addition, the #feesmustfall movement, a student-led movement which gained prominence in 2015, has for the past few years highlighted social justice issues relating to high costs, lack of access and the slow pace of transformation in the higher education environment. Focusing on the contextual situation provides an opportunity to compare and contrast South Africa's global citizenship programmes with others around the globe. Are they using similar approaches? Can different approaches be linked to their different contexts? Is there evidence for success? These questions are explored in the rest of the chapter.

Method

An extensive literature review was conducted to identify research literature and published evaluations on global citizenship programmes as well as to ascertain the general state of global citizenship programmes globally. This review served to understand the broader context around these programmes in higher education and to allow for the South African global citizenship programmes to be located within this context. The review comprised three components:

1) A review of the literature, focused on the concept of global citizenship, programme context and assumptions: The review included peer-reviewed journal articles from 1990 to 2017.[1] Keywords used in various combinations in the literature search, which was conducted online, were the following: [global citizen], [program*], [service learning], [social justice], [higher education], [global citizenship], [pedagogy], [co-curricular], [co curricular], [enrichment program*], [blended learning] and [evaluation]. The databases searched were Google Scholar, EBSCOHost and JStor. Reference lists of relevant papers involving global citizenship programmes at HEIs were also investigated to identify other relevant sources. Specific searches for more information on the programmes identified were conducted using the programme name and the name of the associated university as search terms. The results from the review indicate that evaluation literature on global citizenship programmes is largely restricted to studies conducted as a part of social science research into such programmes.

2) A general Google search: In order to present a broad overview of global citizenship programmes currently available at HEIs around the globe for this study, a general Google search was conducted. The geographic region and the main characteristics of any global citizenship programmes run by HEIs that appeared within the top 250 search results were recorded. These characteristics were the following: country, target population, type of programme (study abroad, service learning and/or classroom base; classified by the categories identified in Goodier, Field and Goodman, 2018) and whether they were credit-bearing and/or non-credit bearing. The search term used for this search on Google was [global citizenship program*]. This phrase was used to keep the results broad, as using, for example, ['global citizenship' program*], would narrow the results to

only programmes that used the exact phrase contained in the quotation marks.

3) A specific Google search: The evaluator also conducted a focused online search to identify the global citizenship programmes at South African universities specifically. This search was conducted within each of the recognized South African universities' websites as listed on the Department of Higher Education and Training (DHET) site (DHET, 2017). The search was conducted either through the site search or, for sites that did not have search functionality, through Google using [site: www.website.com search term]. The search terms used were [citizenship], [global citizen] and [social engagement]. Search results that related to programmes that included elements of global citizenship, as the term is defined in the section 'an Overview of Global Citizenship' below, were recorded.

Results

An Overview of Global Citizenship

The concept of global citizenship refers broadly to a sense of identity, solidarity and belonging as part of humanity (UNESCO, 2013). This concept incorporates an awareness of a variety of cultural and geographic contexts as well as a moral responsibility to the global community (Hanson, 2010; UNESCO, 2013). This sense of responsibility can manifest in a number of ways, including volunteering in under-resourced communities (Bamber & Hankin, 2011), engaging in dialogue with people and groups who hold different perspectives (Keen & Hall, 2009) and gaining knowledge about global and local issues by participating in learning events (Lee et al., 2008). The concept of global citizenship, therefore, has inward and outward dimensions that are reflected in an individual's personal characteristics and social interactions (Hanson, 2010).

Due to the broad nature of the concept of global citizenship, there is little consensus in the literature on a generic definition of a global citizen or global citizenship (Caruana, 2014; Jorgenson & Shultz, 2012; Morais & Ogden, 2011; Myers, 2006; Oxley & Morris, 2013; Schattle, 2008; Sperandio, Grudzinski-Hall & Stewart-Gambino, 2010; UNESCO, 2014). Many articles reporting on this area of research either do not explicitly define the concept (Annette, 2002; Bamber & Hankin, 2011) or analyse ideas of what a global citizen should be

(Myers, 2009) or are perceived to be (Wilde et al., 2017). Where researchers offer definitions of global citizenship, these are varied, containing elements that are both ideologically and context-dependent (see Schattle (2008) for a review of different ideologies underlying such programmes). A few examples of such definitions are presented below (starting with the simpler definitions and leading up to more complicated descriptions):

- 'the idea that human beings are citizens of the world' (Dower & Williams, 2002, p. 1).
- 'knowledge and skills for social and environmental justice' (Andrzejewski & Alessio, 1999, p. 8).
- 'awareness, caring, and embracing cultural diversity while promoting social justice and sustainability, coupled with a sense of responsibility to act' (Reysen & Katzarska-Miller, 2013, p. 860).

In summary, global citizenship can be conceptual (centred on an idea) or practically oriented focusing on knowledge and skills acquisition. The scope of global citizenship reported in the literature, therefore, ranges from broad to narrow, while focusing on an area for action, for example, environmental justice.

More commonalities appear between definitions of a global citizen as such definitions largely refer to the knowledge, attitudes and values that such individuals are supposed to possess (Banks, 2008). These definitions include the following:

- Someone with a 'sophisticated understanding of the increasingly interconnected but unequal world, still plagued by violent conflicts, economic deprivation, and brutal inequities at home and abroad' (Association of American Colleges and Universities (AAC&U), 2002, p. 1).
- 'Someone who:
  - is aware of the wider world and has a sense of their own role as a world citizen
  - respects and values diversity
  - has an understanding of how the world works
  - is outraged by social injustice
  - participates in the community at a range of levels, from the local to the global
  - is willing to act to make the world a more equitable and sustainable place
  - takes responsibility for their actions' (Oxfam, 2008, p. 2).

- An individual with 'a sense of belonging to the global community and common humanity, with its presumed members experiencing solidarity and collective identity among themselves and collective responsibility at the global level' (UNESCO, 2013, p. 3).

Taking these definitions into account, a global citizen is someone who understands the interconnected nature of the today's world, understands that they have an active role as a member of the global community and that they are part of this community. Such an individual also has the skills to take responsible action and participate in this connected global community.

Despite the broad commonalities of the definitions of global citizenship shown above, there is no consensus as to what should form part of a global citizenship programme, either in terms of content or structure (UNESCO, 2014). Grudzinski-Hall (2007, p. 12) captures the ambiguity around the content of global citizenship programmes:

> Global Citizenship is a term used with increasing frequency to denote a wide range of educational and philosophical aims. The very trendy-ness of the term makes it difficult to pin down exactly what any institution – or even program or discipline – really intends to impart to students. Colleges and universities vary in not only how they understand the term, but also how its many definitions should be embedded in their curriculum.

This multiplicity of definitions, approaches and understandings presents a challenge for any investigation into what works for whom and in what contexts in these programmes. While there is, however, no clear best-practice approach in global citizenship programmes, the majority of universities aim to utilize global citizenship programmes in similar ways linked to desirable graduate attributes and enhancing the student experience. These include both to empower students to engage meaningfully and also, proactively, to enhance their global perspectives and enable them to better understand and serve their local communities and global society in both their work and social capacities (Caruana, 2010; Jorgenson & Shultz, 2012; UNESCO, 2013). For example, students who have participated in a global citizenship programme should be more socially responsible in businesses dealings, considering the implications of their decisions within a global context (Andrzejewski & Alessio, 1999) and better able to meaningfully engage with the communities where their companies do their work (Schwab, 2008). By implementing such programmes, it is hoped that graduates leave their institution with the necessary skills, knowledge and values required in today's diverse global work environment, as well as in their everyday lives (Jorgenson & Shultz, 2012; UNESCO, 2014).

The Rise of Global Citizenship Programmes

An increase in global citizenship programmes in the early to mid-2000s was noted by Schattle (2008), especially in the United States and the United Kingdom. Annual online literature searches by Jorgenson and Shultz (2012) between the years of 2007 and 2011 found an increase in the number of global citizenship programmes in the US, UK and Australian HEIs as well as evidence of such programmes starting up at universities across the globe. While online searches do not necessarily provide a comprehensive picture of all global citizenship programmes available, due to the nature of search engines and how webpages are sequenced in search results, they do enable a sub-sample of active programmes to be identified and their publicly available information to be analysed.

Of the sixty-four programmes which appeared in the general Google search results, the majority ($n = 35$) were run at US-based institutions, followed by institutions in both Australia and Canada (each with $n = 7$) and UK institutions ($n = 5$) (Table 9.1 and Figure 9.1). Except for the appearance of Canada, these locations mirror those identified by Jorgenson and Shultz (2012). Not all publicly available information for the programmes identified contained the details needed to classify their target population or approach. For those that did, most were targeted at all registered university students or undergraduate students. A few programmes targeted students taking a specific course or in a specific area of study. There was a relatively even mix of programmes that were either credit-bearing (curricular; $n = 17$) or non-credit bearing (co-curricular; $n = 22$), or contained elements of both ($n = 12$). The majority were partially classroom-based, with a period of study abroad ($n = 25$; 16 of which were US-based programmes) or service learning ($n = 16$). While it was rare, a few programmes included all three types of approaches (study abroad, service learning and classroom-based) ($n = 5$).

Global Citizenship Programmes in South Africa

While the majority of the programmes discovered through the general online search are based at universities in the United States, two South African programmes were also found: one based at the University of Cape Town (UCT) and one based at Stellenbosch University. These programmes were both classroom-based with elements of service learning and were available to either

Table 9.1 The Sixty-Four International Global Citizenship Programmes Identified

Country	Number of programmes	Primary approach: Study abroad (SA) Service learning (SL) Classroom-based (C) Unknown (?)	Target population (where specific student groups were named in the source, these have been specified)	Credit-bearing (CB)/ Non-credit bearing (NCB)
Australia	7	SA/C (2) SL/C (2) SA/SL/C (1) C (1)	University students (6) Undergraduates (1)	NCB (4) CB (2) NCB/CB (1)
Canada	7	C (3) SA (1) SA/SL/C (1) ? (1)	University students (2) Undergraduates (3) ? (1)	CB (4) NCB (1) NCB/CB (1) ? (1)
Hong Kong	2	C (1) SA (1)	Undergraduates (2)	NCB/CB (1) ? (1)
India	1	C (1)	Students on a specific programme (1)	NCB (1)
South Africa	2	SL/C (2)	University students (1) Postgraduates (1)	CB (1) NCB/CB (1)
The Netherlands	1	SA/SL/C (1)	? (1)	NCB/CB (1)
Turkey	1	C (1)	Third year students (1)	CB (1)
UK	5	C (3) SL (1) SL/C (1)	University students (2) Undergraduates (1) Postgraduates (1) First year students (1)	NCB (3) NCB/CB (1) ? (1)
US	35	C (13) SA/C (10) SA (4) SL/C (3) SA/SL/C (2) SL (2) ? (1)	University students (15) Undergraduates (13) Students on a specific programmes (3) First year students (1) Honours students (1) ? (2)	NCB (11) CB (9) NCB/CB (6) ? (9)
Various	2	C (2)	University students (2)	NCB (2)

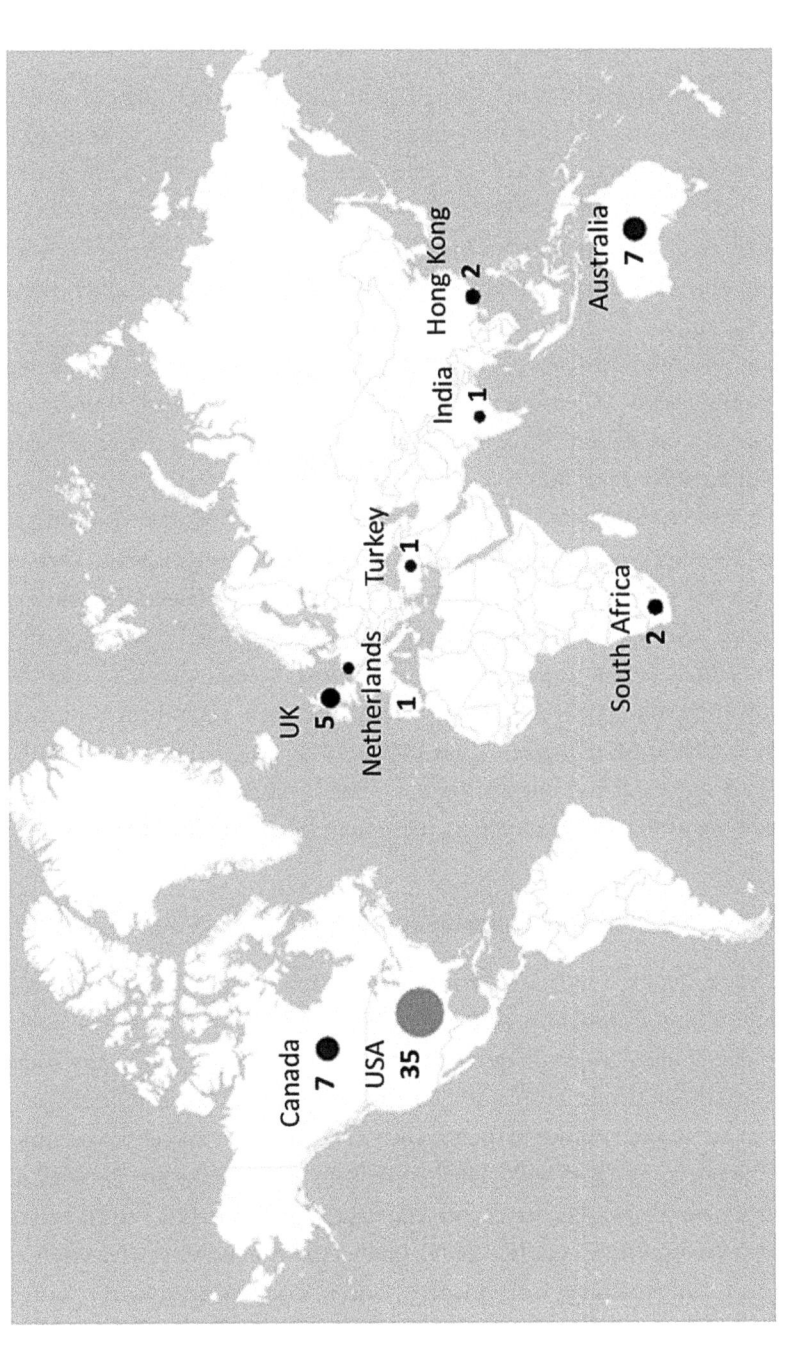

Figure 9.1 Map indicating the number and location of the sixty-four global citizenship programmes appearing in the top 250 Google search results. Various locations were specified for two of the programmes identified and these are not shown here. This map was created using Google Sheets.

all registered students (UCT) or to postgraduates (Stellenbosch). Stellenbosch took a credit-bearing approach in their course, while UCT had both credit-bearing and non-credit-bearing elements.

A further focused online search was conducted to explore the global citizenship programmes at South African universities specifically. This was to identify if any other of the universities had such programmes and to gather information around their approaches. Of the twenty-six universities and universities of technology in South Africa listed by DHET, five had such programmes, with two universities having two programmes each ($n = 7$) (see Table 9.2). Of these seven programmes, four of the programmes were co-curricular, while one was curricular and two had elements of both, with service learning and citizenship modules embedded in various degree programmes. There were twenty-one South African institutions for which no such programmes were discoverable online (*listed after Table 9.2).

While these seven South African programmes are listed on their institutions' websites together with some basic details about the programmes, further details are not publicly available for any except the UCT Global Citizenship Programme, which has a reasonably comprehensive course information site, including a breakdown of each of the programme's three modules. To date the only evaluation that has been published on any of these seven programmes is a theory evaluation looking at a global citizenship programme at one of the top-ranked South African universities (Goodier, Field & Goodman, 2018). No information is available on outcome achievement for any of these programmes.

How South African Programmes Compare

When comparing the South African programmes to the other global citizenship programmes from around the world, some interesting similarities and differences emerge. The South African programmes take a largely co-curricular approach, with most of the global citizenship programmes ($n = 6$) being run, in full or in part, as an extra activity and outside of the structure of the students' degree programme. Two of the five universities with global citizenship programmes are classified as fully or partially historically disadvantaged, namely the Universities of Fort Hare and Free State, respectively (DHET, 2013). Both of these universities have taken, at least in part, a curricular approach to global citizenship programming as opposed to the co-curricular approach taken by historically advantaged institutions. A combination of classroom-based and local service learning activities dominates the programmes' offerings. The service learning and volunteering components

Table 9.2 The Five South African Universities with Global Citizenship-like Programmes

University and province	Programme name	About the programme
University of Cape Town, Western Cape www.uct.ac.za	Global Citizenship Programme (GC)	• Co-curricular programme consisting of 3 short courses, usually run over a semester each; also 1 credit-bearing course available through the Faculty for Engineering and the Built Environment • Run through the Centre for Innovation in Learning and Teaching • Focuses on critical engagement (contemporary global and local debates, citizenship, service work, social justice) (University of Cape Town, 2017)
University of Fort Hare, Eastern Cape www.ufh.ac.za	Life Knowledge and Action	• Compulsory, credit-bearing first-year programme • Aims to produce well-rounded graduates who will be global citizens • Humanizing pedagogy, putting students at the centre • Outcomes: compassionate, socially engaged, critical and responsible citizens • Strong local focus; limited volunteering (University of Fort Hare, 2016)
University of Stellenbosch, Western Cape www.sun.ac.za	Global Citizenship Short Course	• Co-curricular 9-month short course run through the Postgraduate and International Office • Focuses on aspects of being a global citizen, community engagement and intercultural competence • Skills: Leadership, critical thinking and public reasoning; Adaptability; Teamwork (in a diverse environment); Problem-solving; Networking (Stellenbosch University Postgraduate and International Office, 2017)
University of the Free State, Free State www.ufs.ac.za	Community service learning and community service/ volunteering	• Credit-bearing and co-curricular options • Outcome: develop social responsibility and awareness among students (University of the Free State, 2017a)

(*Continued*)

Table 9.2 (Continued)

University and province	Programme name	About the programme
	Leadership for Change Programme	• Co-curricular opportunity to travel abroad to an international university for 2 weeks • Skills: contemplate, discuss and engage on issues of diversity, leadership and citizenship • Goal: need to acquire and enhance growth in knowledge and skills, to compare what they learn internationally with the situation at the UFS, initiate role as agents of change upon return (University of the Free State, 2017b)
University of the Witwatersrand, Gauteng www.wits.ac.za	Wits Peer Educator Programme	• Co-curricular peer education programme run through the Counselling and Careers Development Unit • Contributes to developing a global citizen as a confident leader, volunteering within the university community • Outcomes: Increased knowledge on various Social Justice issues; Interpersonal skills; Connecting and communicating with others; Events and project operational skills; Enhancing creativity and marketing ability; Group work skills; Self-confidence and leadership; Developing an ethos of volunteerism and citizenship (University of the Witwatersrand, 2017a)
	Global Citizens for Social Justice Programme	• Co-curricular volunteering and discussions and debate series • Skills: broaden knowledge of issues relating to global citizenship and social justice that go beyond the immediate requirements of degree; develop an awareness of yourself as a future citizen of the world (University of the Witwatersrand, 2017b)

*South African universities without global citizenship programmes: Cape Peninsula University of Technology (www.cput.ac.za), Central University of Technology (www.cut.ac.za), Durban Institute of Technology (www.dut.ac.za), Mangosuthu University of Technology (www.mantec.ac.za), Nelson Mandela Metropolitan University (www.nmmu.ac.za), North-West University (www.nwu.ac.za), Rhodes University (www.ru.ac.za), Sefako Makgatho Health Sciences University (www.smu.ac.za), Sol Plaatje University (www.spu.ac.za), Tshwane University of Technology (www.tut.ac.za), University of Johannesburg (www.uj.ac.za), University of KwaZulu-Natal (www.ukzn.ac.za), University of Limpopo (www.ul.ac.za), University of Mpumalanga (www.ump.ac.za), University of Pretoria (www.up.ac.za), University of South Africa (www.unisa.ac.za), University of Venda (www.univen.ac.za), University of the Western Cape (www.uwc.ac.za), University of Zululand (www.unizulu.ac.za), Vaal University of Technology (www.vut.ac.za), Walter Sisulu University (www.wsu.ac.za).

largely take place in poor communities close to the universities. All but one (14 per cent) of the seven South African programmes are locally focused with no study abroad or travel components. This is counter to the trend identified in the programmes from the general Google search, where 39 per cent had a study abroad or an international volunteering component, the latter usually in a developing country context. The only exception to this is the Leadership for Change Programme run at the University of the Free State which involves a two-week trip to an overseas university (University of the Free State, 2017b). This UFS programme has a specific goal involving the student participants comparing their learnings during this international trip with what is happening at UFS and using this a springboard to 'initiate role as agents of change upon return' (University of the Free State, 2017b, p. 1). Several of the other South African programmes aim to bring in elements of the global perspective through debating and discussing global issues and how global and local contexts relate to each other (e.g. University of Cape Town, 2017; University of the Witwatersrand, 2017b).

Key questions that arise from this more local approach are as follows: Can the outcomes relating to global citizenship knowledge and skills be achieved without an overseas experience? Can an understanding of how interconnected the world is today, active participation in the global community and being equipped to take responsible action be achieved without travelling beyond your countries borders? What are the social justice implications of where one is based, and how does local justice relate to global justice? Schattle (2007, p. 3) notes that 'you don't have to leave home to be a global citizen ... global citizenship now emerges frequently as a verb, a concept of action signifying ways of thinking and living', promoting the point of view that being a global citizen can be as much in the way you interact with the world on a local (or global) level. From an outcome-achievement point of view, however, a lack of publicly available research into and evaluations of various global citizenship programmes provides more questions than answers about what is necessary and does work in these programmes. What activities need to be in place to achieve the desired outcomes linked to travel are largely still waiting to be investigated. This presents an area where future evaluation work is needed to strengthen evidence for the best way forward for these programmes to maximally enrich the student experience.

In the case of the South African programmes financial resources of both the institutions and the students are limited, making travel abroad an additional expense and out of reach of many students. As such, if funding was not provided, programmes involving a travel component would exclude the majority of students from participating. Identifying outcomes linked to direct exposure to other places and cultures through travel and exploring innovative means of achieving these while instead remaining local would potentially strengthen what the South African programmes offer.

Conclusion

This chapter demonstrates how several different approaches inform the design of global citizenship programmes. As this South African group when contrasted to the global trend shows, some design characteristics are more common depending on the geographical location of the university where the programme is offered. While the small number of programmes and lack of publicly available information did not allow for a meaningful further analysis considering institutional differences, the difference in approaches by historically advantaged and disadvantaged South African institutions with regard to curricular and co-curricular programme design is an interesting finding. This points to the influence of both the past and present on the unique context of South Africa's universities in which these programmes currently operate, shaping how they are designed, implemented, and who they are being offered to and in what forms. With inequalities across South African society driving the emphasis on social justice as part of the concept of citizenship, these historical contextual and institutional differences merit further close-up research regarding their potential influence on programming, as well as whether similar differences are shaping programming in other countries' global citizenship programmes.

Regarding the lack of international components, the South African programmes tend to try and bridge the gap of access to global experiences through inclusive debate and discussion held locally, in order to make the programmes as accessible and inclusive as possible, given their available resources. As such, this strategy speaks to some of the social justice issues raised by #feesmustfall: costs and access. The lack of published literature on outcome achievement in global citizenship programmes means that, currently, there are more questions than answers about what works, both globally and in South Africa. Are these programmes achieving or are they able to achieve outcomes linked to global perspectives and knowledge? Do students carry what they have learnt in these programmes with them into their practices at work and in their communities? More information on the programmes being run, including results from evaluations considering outcome achievement would help to shed light on this. For many higher education programmes, considering their work through an evaluative lens has the potential to help to address these key questions and strengthen their offerings by promoting critical reflection on the programme within its context. Focusing on evidence-informed strategies is becoming increasingly important to programmes across the higher educationsector and, with reference to the South African focus of this chapter, within the resource-constrained South African higher educationenvironment (DHET, 2015). For example, if it was known that the outcomes relating to global citizenship knowledge and skills can be achieved, wholly or in part, without travelling beyond the country's borders, this would help to shape programme structure and inform which outcomes are achievable in a given programme's context. Explorations of the South African programmes and their successes have the potential to add valuable knowledge about what programme elements are critical to achieving global outcomes and whether this is possible through local programming alone.

Evaluation, by its nature, involves a close-up, applied research approach to the programme it focuses on. This helps to ensure that the evaluation process will produce data and results that are reliable, valid and useful given the context of the programme and what it should be achieving. Being able to demonstrate that a programme has a good theoretical grounding is implemented with fidelity and is producing the intended outcomes and impact can provide the evidence that funders and university management require to justify continued funding and support. As such, considering the work of the programme through this close-up evaluative lens at various points, such as in longitudinal studies (see McLean, Chapter 5), involving unravelling complex causalities (see Case, Chapter 8), has the potential to strengthen the offerings by providing timely, contextually informed information. This could strengthen the programmes to enable them to achieve the common goal of improving student success within the changing global context.

Note

1 The search was conducted in October 2017.

References

Anderson, P. H., Lawton, L., Rexeisen, R. J., & Hubbard, A. C. (2006). Short-term study abroad and intercultural sensitivity: A pilot study. *International Journal of Intercultural Relations, 30*(4), 457–469.

Andrzejewski, J., & Alessio, J. (1999). Education for global citizenship and social responsibility. *Progressive Perspectives, 1*(2), 2–17.

Annette, J. (2002). Service learning in an international context. *Frontiers: The Interdisciplinary Journal of Study Abroad, 8*(1), 83–93.

Association of American Colleges and Universities (AAC&U). (2002). *Liberal Education and Global Citizenship: The Arts of Democracy.* Washington, DC: Association of American Colleges and Universities.

Bamber, P., & Hankin, L. (2011). Transformative learning through service-learning: No passport required. *Education & Training, 53*(2/3), 190–206.

Banks, J. A. (2008). Diversity, group identity, and citizenship education in a global age. *Educational Researcher, 37*(3), 129–139.

Bourn, D. (2011). From internationalisation to global perspectives. *Higher Education Research & Development, 30*(5), 559–571.

Bourn, D., & Shiel, C. (2009) Global perspectives: Aligning agendas? *Environmental Education Research, 15*(6), 661–677.

Brigham, M. (2011). Creating a global citizen and assessing outcomes. *Journal of Global Citizenship & Equity Education, 1*(1), 15–43.

Caruana, V. (2010). Global Citizenship For All: Putting the 'higher' back into UK Higher Education. In F. Maringe, & N. Foskett (Eds.), *Globalization and Internationalization in Higher Education*, 5164. London: Continuum.

Caruana, V. (2014). Re-thinking global citizenship in higher education: From cosmopolitanism and international mobility to cosmopolitanisation, resilience and resilient thinking. *Higher Education Quarterly, 68*(1), 85–104.

Department of Higher Education and Training (DHET). (2013). Report of the Ministerial Committee for the Review of the Funding of Universities. Retrieved from http://www.dhet.gov.za/Financial%20and%20Physical%20Planning/Report%20of%20the%20Ministerial%20Committee%20for%20the%20Review%20of%20the%20Funding%20of%20Universities.pdf. Accessed 1 June 2016.

Department of Higher Education and Training (DHET). (2015). Speech by the Minister of Higher Education and Training, DR BE Nzimande, to parliament, 27 October 2015. Retrieved from http://www.dhet.gov.za/SiteAssets/Fees%20Must%20Fall/BEN%20speech%20Fees%20Debate,%2027%20Oct%202015.pdf. Accessed 1 June 2016.

Department of Higher Education and Training (DHET). (2017). *Universities.* Retrieved from http://www.dhet.gov.za/SitePages/InstUniversities.aspx.

Dower, N., & Williams, J. (2002). *Global Citizenship: A Critical Introduction.* New York: Routledge.

Dugan, J. P., & Komives, S. R. (2007). *Developing Leadership Capacity in College Students: Findings From a National Study.* College Park, MD: National Clearinghouse for Leadership Programs.

Fisher, G. (1998). Policy, governance and the reconstruction of higher education in South Africa. *Higher Education Policy, 11*, 121–140.

Goodier, S., Field, C., & Goodman, S. (2018). The need for theory evaluation in global citizenship programmes: The case of the GCSA programme. *Evaluation and Program Planning*, 66, 7–19.

Grudzinski-Hall, M. (2007). *How Do College and University Undergraduate-level Global Citizenship Programs Advance the Development and Experiences of Global Competencies?* Pennsylvania: Drexel University.

Hanson, L. (2010). Global citizenship, global health, and the internationalization of curriculum: A study of transformative potential. *Journal of Studies in International Education*, 14(1), 70–88.

Jorgenson, S., & Shultz, L. (2012). Global citizenship education (GCE) in post-secondary institutions: What is protected and what is hidden under the umbrella of GCE? *Journal of Global Citizenship & Equity Education*, 2(1), 1–22.

Keen, C., & Hall, K. (2009). Engaging with difference matters: Longitudinal student outcomes of co-curricular service-learning programs. *The Journal of Higher Education*, 80(1), 59–79.

Lagos, T. G. (No date). Global citizenship – Towards a definition. Retrieved from: https ://depts. washington.edu/gcp/pdf/globalcitizenship.pdf.

Lee, S. Y., Olszewski-Kubilius, P., Donahue, R., & Weimholt, K. (2008). The Civic Leadership Institute: A service-learning program for academically gifted youth. *Journal of Advanced Academics*, 19(2), 272–308.

McMillan, J. (2013). 'Service learning' or 'learning service'?. In R. Osman, & N. Petersen (Eds.), *Service Learning in South Africa*, 33–58. Cape Town, South Africa: Oxford University Press.

Morais, D. B., & Ogden, A. C. (2011). Initial development and validation of the global citizenship scale. *Journal of Studies in International Education*, 15(5), 445–466.

Myers, J. P. (2006). Rethinking the social studies curriculum in the context of globalization: Education for global citizenship in the U.S. *Theory and Research in Social Education*, 34(3), 370–394.

Myers, J. P. (2009). 'To benefit the world by whatever means possible': Adolescents' constructions of global citizenship. *Educational Research Journal*, 36(3), 483–502.

Oxfam. (2008). *Getting Started with Global Citizenship: A Guide for New Teachers*. Oxford: Oxfam.

Oxley, L., & Morris, P. (2013). Global citizenship: A typology for distinguishing its multiple conceptions. *British Journal of Educational Studies*, 61(3), 301–325.

Petersen, N., & Osman, R. (2013). An Introduction to Service Learning in South Africa. In R. Osman, & N. Petersen (Eds.), *Service Learning in South Africa*, 2–32. Cape Town, South Africa: Oxford University Press.

Reade, C., Reckmeyer, W. J., Cabot, M., Jaehne, D., & Novak, M. (2013). Educating global citizens for the 21st century. *Journal of Corporate Citizenship*, 49, 100–116.

Reysen, S., & Katzarska-Miller, I. (2013). A model of global citizenship: Antecedents and outcomes. *International Journal of Psychology*, 48(5), 858–870.

Schattle, H. (2007). *The Practices of Global Citizenship*. New York: Rowman & Littlefield.

Schattle, H. (2008). Education for global citizenship: Illustrations of ideological pluralism and adaptation. *Journal of Political Ideologies, 13*(1), 73–94.

Schwab, K. (2008). Global corporate citizenship: Working with governments and civil society. *Foreign Affairs, 87*(1), 107–118.

Sperandio, J., Grudzinski-Hall, M., & Stewart-Gambino, H. (2010). Developing an undergraduate global citizenship program: Challenges of definition and assessment. *International Journal of Teaching and Learning in Higher Education, 22*(1), 12–22.

Stellenbosch University Postgraduate and International Office. (2017). Global Citizenship Short Course. Retrieved from https://www0.sun.ac.za/international/current-students/international-opportunities-for-su-students/internationalisation-home/global-citizenship-short-course.html.

UNESCO. (2013). *Global Citizenship Education: An Emerging Perspective*. Paris: UNESCO. Retrieved from http://unesdoc.unesco.org/images/0022/002241/224115E.pdf.

UNESCO. (2014). *Global Citizenship Education: Preparing Learners for the Challenges of the Twenty-First Century*. Paris: UNESCO. Retrieved from http://unesdoc.unesco.org/images/0022/002277/227729E.pdf.

University of Cape Town. (2017). *UCT Global Citizenship: Leading for Social Justice*. Retrieved from http://www.globalcitizen.uct.ac.za/.

University of Fort Hare. (2016). *Student Guide 2017*. Fort Hare: University of Fort Hare.

University of the Free State. (2017a). *Community Engagement*. Retrieved from http://supportservices.ufs.ac.za/content.aspx?dcode=451.

University of the Free State. (2017b). *Leadership for Change Programme Home*. Retrieved from https://www.ufs.ac.za/supportservices/departments/student-affairs-home/leadership-for-change/leadership-for-change-programme-home/about/about-the-programme.

University of the Witwatersrand. (2017a). *Peer Educator Service*. Retrieved from http://www.wits.ac.za/prospective/studentservices/ccdu/11487/peer_educator_programme.html.

University of the Witwatersrand. (2017b). *Wits Citizenship and Community Outreach (WCCO)*. Retrieved from https://www.wits.ac.za/students/development-and-leadership-unit/wits-citizenship-and-community-outreach/.

Wilde, R., Bentall, C., Blum, N., & Bourn, D. (2017). Student volunteering and global citizenship at UCL. Development Education Research Centre Discussion Paper, University College London.

10

Developing Critical Citizens by Changing the Higher Education Curriculum

Langutani M. Masehela

Introduction

The two-decade old democratic government of South Africa brought unexpected realities that citizens have to face and deal with. As a consequence, the eventualities of this century should create an enabling environment that can allow teachers and students in all levels of education to become not only critical citizens but creative and innovative more than ever before as they prepare for the world of work. Therefore, the purpose of higher education in general and of the university in particular needs to be revisited. I argue in this chapter that addressing challenges of social injustice, unemployment in particular, should not be solely a government responsibility but the higher education sector should also share this responsibility. The knowledge question in this study is the question of what can we teach our students so that they can build a sense of independence by the time they leave the four walls of their Alma Matar? What should be included in the curriculum to enable students not to wait for government or private sector employment but be driven by a desire to be self-employed? Case (Chapter 8) asks the question: 'To what degree can institutions formulated to produce an elite be reformed to meet the needs of a different world?' These are relevant questions in the South African higher education context where massification became real through admission of students from all socio-economic backgrounds such as first generation, poor, rural, urban and rich. Among these diverse groups of students one finds academically gifted and less gifted, creative and less creative, socially exposed and less exposed students under a single study programme. As a result, the kind of graduate produced by the higher education sector varies dramatically. I will use ideas of Martha Nussbaum's capability approach to argue how rethinking of the curriculum could unfold in higher education, especially in rural-based universities that attract students from low economic backgrounds which also feature earlier generations that possess less formal education. Nussbaum's framework of cultivating humanity can be a great starting point to reimaging the desired curriculum meant for addressing the current challenges in the South Africa.

I argue, in this chapter, that it is academic institutions' responsibility to build into the existing curriculum a sense of 'independent-standing', thinking out of the box, by building into the curriculum a culture of creativity, innovation and a desire for entrepreneurial ability. In essence, my argument is centred around the thought that university students of today should find the curriculum as something that promotes critical citizenry, entrepreneurial thinking and of course life skills, especially to students from historically disadvantaged backgrounds. My concern is that universities tend to focus on their graduation numbers because they are held account for these but do not tend to focus on the employment opportunities of their graduates. According to a study conducted by Statistics South Africa (2016), the official unemployment in South Africa was 25.2 per cent and it had increased to 26.4 per cent in 2015. The South African government has established the National Youth Development Agency (NYDA) with the aim of addressing a myriad of challenges that the youth face in the country, including unemployment (NYDA Strategy, 2015).

Currently in my institution, students are increasingly enrolling for teaching qualifications because this is one sector that still has high employment opportunities. Therefore, students who regard a university qualification to be a path to improved socio-economic standing are more likely to consider teaching as a safe option to minimize chances of unemployment. This behaviour is worrisome because it defeats the purpose of becoming a teacher. The profession no longer attracts those who have a calling for it but stranded youth resort to teaching. However, falling back to teaching does not fully address the challenge of unemployment of graduates from historically disadvantaged universities. Graduates from these universities are generally considered ill-equipped for the job market compared to their counterparts from traditionally advantaged institutions in South Africa. Pauw, Bhorat and Goga (2006) argue that many of the graduates who lack the relevant skills critical for the workplace come from historically black institutions where they were not granted an opportunity to develop these skills or acquire work experience.

In this chapter, I address this challenge by drawing on the ideas of Martha Nussbaum to redesign the university curriculum for students from historically disadvantaged institutions. It is important to note that I do not see Nussbaum as providing solutions to South Africa's problems but rather see her capability approach as a useful tool to think about how to develop responses to higher education curriculum.

Nussbaum and the Capability Approach

Martha Nussbaum is a contemporary American philosopher with a joint appointment as a distinguished professor of Law and Ethics at the University of Chicago (National Endowment for the Humanities, 2017). South African educationists such as Melanie Walker and others have extensively used Nussbaum's work to address some of the education challenges in the country. In her argument challenging university education, Nussbaum asks, 'What contribution can a university education make to building a more just society with human dignity (Nussbaum, 2000) and well-being for all (Sen, 1999), and, how are graduates being educated in universities to be the responsible and critical citizens?' Nussbaum (2010) argues that universities not only have the responsibility of producing knowledge but should also contribute to sustainable democratic societies by educating socially critical and concerned citizens, who will also contribute to economic development for themselves and for others with fewer advantages. She further argues that income and wealth frequently play a central role in the measurement of who has an economically viable life.

Nussbaum (1997a,b) produced a list of central human capabilities which are separate and indispensable. This implies each item in the list is independent of the other and therefore needs to be satisfied independently. According to Nussbaum these capabilities support human powers of practical reason and choice. The list consists of the following items:

1. Life
2. Bodily health
3. Bodily integrity
4. Senses, imagination and thought
5. Emotions
6. Practical reason
7. Affiliation (friendship and respect)
8. Other species (relationship with other animals, plants, etc.)
9. Play
10. Control over one's environment (political and material)

Nussbaum (1997b, p. 85) characterizes the significance of this list in these terms: 'My claim is that a life that lacks any one of these capabilities, no matter what else it has, will fall short of being a good human life.' Applying these ideas to the South African context, Melanie Walker (2013) posed questions about what universities should try to address in their quest to cultivating graduates with capabilities that will make their lives better. She asks,

> What picture would emerge if we used human capabilities – the opportunities to choose many valuable ways of being and doing for our well-being – as the yardstick to evaluate higher education? What policies would be designed and implemented? What would curriculum and pedagogy, governance, research, and relationships with publics look like? What would students have reason to value doing and being, and how would this be shaped by their education and experiences at university? How would graduates use their knowledge and skills to make good lives for themselves while also contributing to sustainable human development? (Walker, 2013, p. 1)

While all these capabilities remain relevant to a student studying in a historically disadvantaged institution in South Africa, some of them are more critical in the process of cultivating a well-rounded graduate. Nussbaum (2000) asks the question: 'What contribution can a university education make to building a more just society with human dignity?' A graduate who is not fearful (number 5 emotions), a graduate who has control over her environment (number 10), that is a graduate who has a say in what should form part of the curriculum in their study programme and a student who can envision her future beyond being just an employee (number 4). This is a student who knows why they are at university and studying towards that particular qualification. In so doing universities will be empowering their students.

Current Reality

In Chapter 8, Case argues that while the participation rate in higher education has remarkably increased, there still remains unresolved questions about how class continues to impact on educational experiences and life opportunities. This is evident in the differentiated HEIs in South Africa. According to Greyling (2015) historically disadvantaged institutions enrol students in fields of study with low employment prospects while historically advantaged institutions ensure large enrolments in programmes with high employment prospects. On the contrary, historically disadvantaged institutions are commonly known to have high enrolments of students from disadvantaged backgrounds. Similarly, in the UK, Reay et al. (2001) observed that social class continues to impact on the experiences of higher education with elite institutions attracting more students from middle and upper social classes. This means that historically disadvantaged institutions have students with different needs because their students tend to be from different backgrounds as those of the elite.

As an educational development practitioner in this historically disadvantaged institution, I got inspired to challenge myself to rethink, re-imagine and re-enact the curriculum in order to increase my students' life chances for success, capabilities and functionings in society; especially as historically disadvantaged institutions continue to attract students from disadvantaged backgrounds. Therefore, in essence, the students require a different form of pedagogies to assist them achieve what an average student from an elite university who comes from an elite socio-economic background would receive.

The persistence of these inequalities meant that academics and curriculum designers from historically disadvantaged institutions have a double responsibility. First, these institutions have a responsibility to expose students to the world, possibilities and opportunities that easily present themselves to students from elite institutions. Second, students who fall within the bracket of low achievers need extra attention to help them gain confidence, thinking and intellectual capabilities. Curriculum for such students should be able to address these challenges in order to improve their experiences at university and their life chances after graduation.

Government alone is not solely responsible for addressing the challenges of social injustice, such as unemployment. Higher education also has an important role to play. The current debates around decolonizing the curriculum would only be relevant if more emphasis is also on the quality of graduates the current curriculum produces. Quality in the sense that the graduates should have spontaneous functionings and capabilities that enable them to think creatively about how to become active economic contributors in the country. This challenge not only is confronted by government and institutions of higher learning but involves all other key stakeholders of the sector. In South Africa, the CHE should be directly involved in addressing the matter. CHE is the national council responsible for assuring the quality of HEIs in general. It appoints a permanent body called the Higher Education Quality Committee (HEQC, 2014) which is responsible for

- promoting quality in higher education,
- auditing the quality assurance mechanisms of institutions of higher education,

- accrediting programmes of higher education and
- capacity development.

With its powers to influence what and how HEIs should offer, the CHE is better positioned to influence what could be contained in the curriculum of various qualifications of higher education as it attempts to influence the building of a curriculum that aims to produce graduates who can make a significant and meaningful contribution to South African society. Therefore, among other things, I propose that academic institutions should take the responsibility of building into the existing curriculum a sense of 'independent-standing', by building into the curriculum a culture of creativity, innovation and a desire for self-employment, that is, entrepreneurial abilities. The challenge that higher education curriculum designers have to face is not just cultivating innovative graduates, but more importantly, it is about how that could be achieved in historically disadvantaged institutions that attract mainly students from rural communities who have had less life opportunities in their early years of life.

Rethinking the Curriculum: Thinking Out of the Box

Nussbaum argues that for social justice, citizens have the right to be on the same level of educational attainment (1997a). However, it is common knowledge that not all citizens receive the same level of educational attainment. In South Africa during the apartheid regime it was common knowledge that graduates from historically disadvantaged universities were offered inferior qualifications than their counterparts from historically advantaged institutions. This has had a damning effect on graduates from historically disadvantaged institutions because high unemployment rate mostly affects graduates from there. Greyling (2015) found that employers prefer to recruit graduates from privileged institutions because they assume these graduates acquire the right skills for the work place. She further noted that graduates from historically disadvantaged institutions are said to receive less career guidance and life skills than their privileged counterparts. I provide an analysis of a one year postgraduate certificate in education (PGCE) offered at a historically disadvantaged university in South Africa. I have provided mostly the prominent weaknesses that lead to graduates not meeting all Nussbaum's central human capabilities.

In view of the PGCE curriculum of the historically disadvantaged institution in question in this chapter, it is evident that the focus of the curriculum is more on providing pedagogical skills in the teaching of subject matter at school level than anything else. The curriculum has methodology modules that students choose from according to their prospective teaching subjects. In addition they have two modules that they enrol for to address psychological, sociological and philosophical understanding of their profession. The two modules, Foundations of Education: Educational Psychology and History of Education (EPH 4541) and Education Foundations: Educational Philosophy and Educational Sociology (EPS 4541), only focus on assisting student teachers to gain understanding of the learners they will engage with at school level. There is no provision for aspects that could address life skills and entrepreneurial skills to candidate teachers.

I, therefore, advocate for the inclusion of life skills and entrepreneurial skills in a postgraduate certificate of this nature. According to Suminar et al. (2016) life skills scope should cover cognitive, social and personal skills. Cognitive skills include critical thinking, taking decisions and accepting a risk. Social skills include communication skills, collaboration, empathy and negotiation. Personal skills include managing emotions, self and self-control. On the other hand, there are aspects of entrepreneurship that are seen to be of value in any university study programme. Entrepreneurship, as well, is highly recommended in the PGCE programme. According to Yimamu (2018) entrepreneurship is not only about starting your own business but about innovation and creativity in what one does. He further says that planning and creating a strategy is critical in entrepreneurship. These are aspects that are not covered explicitly in the certificate curriculum. Instead, the most salient features of the curriculum are pedagogical matters.

In essence, student teachers are provided more information on how they could best understand their learners at school. Though that is an important aspect of the programme itself, there is more to it than only understanding prospective learners especially in this era that is marked by high levels of unemployment.

Another challenge that could be presented in the PGCE programme could be that course work is offered in less than five months since classes begin in February and end in May when exams begin for semester 1. Then in semester 2 practical work runs until October. During this period, student teachers are placed in schools across the country. They are then allocated mentors, who are comprised of retired teachers, to monitor how they apply the theory they were taught in the past few months. In the process they are compiling a portfolio of evidence which they submit to the faculty at the end of the year in November. Therefore, given the tight schedule that the postgraduate certificate has, there is an indication that there is too little room to adjust the programme in order to fit in new topics for inclusion into the programme.

Reimagining the Curriculum

In reimagining the curriculum, I therefore suggest two alternatives to addressing the issue of broadening the scope of the PGCE programme to include life and entrepreneurial skills. One alternative could be that the two skills courses be embedded into the two modules that focus on psychology and history of education as well as the other that covers sociology and philosophy. The rationale behind this suggestion is that psychology in its nature details learning theories. Therefore, not only learning theories of understanding school learners should be studied here but learning theories that suggest novel ways of looking at the teaching profession as an independent teacher or as a teacher outside of formal employment. Suminar et al. (2016) developed a model of learning in life skills education. This model can be embedded not only in the teacher certificate course but across the mainstream curriculum in the institution. It is imperative to train student teachers not only how they should deal with school learners but also they should set up a school especially in needy communities. The second alternative could be that the institution develops a skills course that should be done by all students across the institution. This could be done during the second or final year of study. The course should cover life and entrepreneurial skills customized to a specific programme of study.

The re-imagined curriculum should take into account the views of development theorists such as Nussbaum, Sen, Walker and related others. In addition to this, it would be beneficial to also take into account the critical role played by all stakeholders involved such as academics, academic developers, student counsellors in career development, professionals in the profession and students during the process of designing the curriculum. Should there be a team engagement that involves discipline experts, development activities (human and academic developers) in a curriculum design process there is likely to be an outcome that could change the status quo. It should be important for them to ask questions such as what will the programme do to change the life of those who study it. The programme should in one way or the other enable a student to satisfy all of the ten points. Should graduates lack any of the listed capabilities, then the programme is short of important characteristics of an effective curriculum. In reimagining the curriculum, curriculum designers could ask central question of what *should* a graduate be capable of doing with an Education qualification provided they never find employment? Nussbaum on the other hand could ask the question this way: Do the newly qualified teachers satisfy all the central human capabilities? However, this could be challenged, for instance, capability number 1: life. It argues that every human being should live life to the fullest without danger of dying immaturely. This could be challenged because as human beings it is not always easy to have control over our lives. One may meet an untimely death as a result of a road accident or any other kind of accident. Similarly, capability number 2: healthy body. Although this can be challenged because human beings should take responsibility for eating the kind of food that is right for their bodies, they also should develop a habit of conducting general check-up so as to enable early diagnosis of illnesses in their bodies.

All this might sound irrelevant to curriculum development. However, there is some wisdom in considering life skills courses to be embedded in qualification courses in higher education. Currently in some institutions the life skills course, which is housed in the student counselling services of an institution, is offered to specific students such as peer helpers, mentors, tutors and student representative council on request. And this is a once off two-day training session. As we re-imagine a curriculum that could produce graduates with entrepreneurial abilities across disciplines, we should also have cultivated in the same graduate a sense of taking responsibility of their body, private, social life and environment.

Re-Enacting the Curriculum

What has been shared in this chapter thus far confirms that the current curriculum programmes do not necessarily produce the desired graduates especially those from historically disadvantaged institutions. In view of that misnomer, university teachers (academics and academic and educational developers) are rightfully placed to re-enact the curriculum to a level that could produce a much more critical citizenry. The newly sworn in president of South Africa, Cyril Ramaphosa (2018), announced during his debut state of the nation address that youth unemployment is the most grave and pressing challenge that the country is facing. This is in line with the national youth accord that states that social partners and government recognize the urgent attention that unemployment crises requires in this country (Youth Employment Accord, 2014, p. 3). Ramaphosa has since put in place structures that should see to improved employment. This might be a strategy to grow youth and total employment. Interestingly, none of these structures include universities or the higher education sector except for politicians encouraging the youth to study technical courses in technical and vocational training institutions across the country. Nonetheless, the opposite is happening. Unemployment in South Africa is growing by the day. I therefore argue that academics and academic developers should not be left in the periphery in this development initiative. There has to be a structured relationship between universities youth organizations as well as professional organizations to reconstruct university curriculum to come up with something that will not only help produce mass graduates but graduates that are ready to tackle local societal challenges. Ramaphosa (2018) further talked about setting up a youth working group that will ensure that policies and programmes advance their programmes.

What would our PGCE graduates have been exposed to if they were to become creative and innovative citizens ready for the world of self-employment and independence? Nussbaum (1997b, p. 8) argues for the cultivation of humanity. She argues for a critical citizen, one who embraces diversity and sees himself as part of the bigger whole (not a local but a global citizen) and one who is sensitive to other people who are different from her. I would also add a citizen who is responsible in his dealings with others around him. Furthermore, the citizen should be able to think out of the box and challenge the status core responsibly and with respect. This, I consider, is an approach that could be viewed as a decolonized form of engaging students of higher learning because it will encourage engagement between academic programme designers and special government organizations, in particular, the NYDA. I suggest developing a much stronger relationship between universities and the NYDA, as a starting point. This should not mean that other development agencies should not form relationships with institutions of higher learning.

In building the relationship it is imperative for both parties to have a shared understanding of who they are starting from the self or personal, the social and the professional. Students who understand where they come from and where they want to go easily transform themselves in the social environment in order to fit in or to change the status quo. As a result when it comes to the professional, they get to understand where their contribution could make an impact as they re-enact their educational gains.

The National Youth Development Agency and Its Strategy

The approach of the National Development Plan is to develop people's capabilities so that they are able to improve their lives through education, skills development, health care, access to better health care, access to public transport and so on (NYDA 5 Year Strategic Plan, 2015). Therefore this strategic plan opens up an opportunity for academic institutions with particular reference to academics and academic developers to directly engage with the NYDA as a development agency. The NYDA envisions itself as a credible and capable development agency for the Youths of South Africa. However, I argue that for the NYDA to see itself as a credible and capable development agency there has to be a mutual relationship between itself and post-schools institutions. Their relationship will lead to fruition in instances where there will be a contract between the two entities.

Not only youth agencies should be involved in the curriculum development process of higher education, prospective employers can play a vital role in influencing what should be contained in the curriculum package in order to produce a work ready graduate. It is important to note that prospective employees in this regard are not necessarily involved in the design process in order to produce graduates who should serve them at the end of the day, but to produce graduates who should become strong competitors in the field.

I further suggest that a professional qualification programme should have a module located in the final year that not only focuses on research, as most do, but in addition to research it should provide a practical opportunity to set up a small business that would address societal needs of a specific community. It is critical to understand that these students come from communities that are faced with numerous challenges that cannot only be solved by government.

Suggested Relationship between Youth Organizations (e.g. NYDA) and Higher Education

In addressing issues of social justice in higher education, especially for students studying in historically disadvantaged institutions who come from low-income families with little exposure to socio-economic opportunities, it is imperative to offer them opportunities that they missed at some point in their lives. Having considered the NYDA's strategy as well as Nussbaum's capability approach, I now propose a socially just strategy aimed at addressing Nussbaum's central human capabilities shared above.

Conclusion

I have argued in this chapter that if we could re-Think, re-Imagine and re-Enact (TIE) the curriculum in historically disadvantaged institutions, we could succeed in building a citizenry that is responsible, innovative, critical and entrepreneurial for justice to prevail to the less fortunate citizens. Once we understand our students as individuals, it becomes easier to work with them and help bring out the best in them.

Nussbaum's capability approach, though crafted from an American perspective, remains relevant to the African context. This is an indication that as human beings, there is a common thread that binds us together despite the context in which we are placed. I therefore conclude by pointing that Nussbaum's capability approach is relevant for the African context; hence, it is noticeable that she has influenced a number of African philosophers as well.

References

Greyling, L. (2015). Graduate unemployment in South Africa: Perspectives from the banking sector. *SA Journal of Human Resource Management, 13*(1), 1–9.

National Endowment for the Humanities. (2017), https://www.neh.gov/news/press-release/2017-01-18.

National Youth Development Agency. (2015). *Strategic Plan 2015-2020*. Midrand, South Africa.

Nussbaum, M. (1997a). Capabilities and human rights. *Fordham Law Review, 66*, 273. Retrieved from http://ir.lawnet.fordham.edu/flr/vol66/iss2/2.

Nussbaum, M. (1997b). *Cultivating Humanity*. Cambridge, MA: Harvard University Press.

Nussbaum, M. (2000). *Women and Human Development*. Cambridge: Cambridge University Press.

Nussbaum, M. (2010). *Not For Profit*. Princeton: Princeton University Press.

Pauw, K., Bhorat, H., & Goga, S. (2006). Graduate unemployment in the context of skills shortages, education and training: Findings from a survey. Retrieved from http://papers.ssrn.com/sol3/papers.cfm?abstract_id=961353. Accessed 26 June 2014.

Ramaphosa, M. C. (2018). South African State of the Nation Address. South African National Youth Development Agency. 2015 Strategy.

Reay, D., Davies, J., David, M., & Ball, S. J. (2001). Choices of degree or degrees of choice? Class, 'race' and the higher education choice process. *Sociology, 35*(4), 855–874. Printed in the United Kingdom © 2001 BSA Publications Limited.

Sen, A. (1999). *Development as Freedom*. New York: Anchor Books.

South African Youth Employment Accord. (2014). Signed at Hector Pieterson Memorial, Orlando, Soweto.

South African Council on Higher Education. (2001). HEQC Founding Document. Pretoria. Council on Higher Education.

Statistics South Africa. (2016). Labour Force Survey. Statistical Release: P0211. Pretoria, South Africa.

Suminar, T., Prihatin, T., & Syarif, M. I. (2016). Model of learning development on program life skills education for rural communities. *International Journal of Information and Education Technology*, 6(6), 496–499.

Walker, M. (2013). *Universities, Development and Social Justice: A Human Capabilities Perspective*. keynote for VI Congreso Universidad y Cooperación al Desarrollo, Valencia, 24 April 20.

Yimamu, N. (2018). Entrepreneurship and Entrepreneurial Motivation. Central University of Applied Sciences. Thesis for degree programme.

11

Human Flourishing and Child Protection in Teacher Education

Angela Fenton

In Chapter 8, we are prompted by Jennifer Case to examine how we might forward the notion of social justice into our engagements with higher education. If, as Case suggests, with reference to Nussbaum (2003), Sen (2011) and Walker and Unterhalter (2007), we start with a conception of human flourishing of social justice, then higher education organizations have clear social justice responsibilities linked to an inherent role in the advancement of society. Indeed, I write as an academic from a university (Charles Sturt University) that has its origins as an experimental farm and combined vocational colleges and whose motto is proudly portrayed as 'for the public good' (CSU, 2018a). Case, however, prompts us to examine more deeply the connections higher education has with society and social justice and to explore the tensions and inherited inequities in our own nuanced contexts. It is pertinent to note therefore that the context for my research is also from a higher education institution that, like many universities in Australia, is named after a colonial explorer. The tension of this connection – with a namesake who, despite 'having an earnest desire to promote the public good', was a historical figure at a colonizing time of undeniable social injustice against the Indigenous people of Australia – has not been lost.

Most recently, leaders at our university have returned to foundational issues of social justice to re-examine with Aboriginal elders what 'for the public good' has meant historically and what it may might mean for the future of our university. It is a meaningful step that has encouraged us to examine how we might manage 'such contradictions' (Castells, 2001) in our work and decide 'what is to be done?' (Case, Chapter 8) about social justice questions. To this extent, CSU academics have been challenged to reconsider and enact, the ethos of their higher education work according to 'yindyamarra winhanganha' an Aboriginal (Wiradjuri) phrase meaning 'the wisdom of respectfully knowing how to live well in a world worth living in' (CSU, 2018b). It is from this changing higher education context that I present below a 'close-up' (Trowler, 2012) research project that was funded by the university under the auspices of a newly formed 'Uimagine' grant initiative.

Close-Up Research

The rationale for obtaining funding for the research aligned with a question asked by Todd (2015) and Case in Chapter 8 – 'What are the educational questions that need attention?' Applicants were asked to design and implement projects in answer to the question: 'Imagine if you could make a difference in your work. What would you do?' As such, we were challenged to engage with Case's question of what we should do from the perspective of society and to examine how our research could make a difference with societal need or challenge (Badat, 2009). Trowler (2012) claims that to make a difference in society we need to engage with complex, 'wicked issues' in close-up research. In Chapter 8 Case suggests that to do this, a reframing of our work to an 'external purpose' is also essential if we are to genuinely address social justice issues in higher education. The research project was therefore anchored in a significant worldwide societal need for child protection amid the social injustice of child abuse and neglect.

Higher education organizations have clear social justice responsibilities for child protection, delivering a range of cross-discipline courses to students who will encounter child abuse in their roles, including social workers, health and medical professionals. The specific urgent educational question the project sought to study, however, was limited to improving the minimal preparation in child protection that Australian universities currently offer pre-service teachers. Current teacher preparation has long been criticized as inadequate and is generally limited to an adjunct, obligatory-reporting workshop or online module of a few hours within a three- to four-year teaching degree (Arnold & Maoi-Taddeo, 2007). Yet, child abuse continually raises itself as a most important factor influencing young children's ability to thrive, and pre-service teachers expressed that they feel most underprepared in their higher education courses to take action to protect children (Fenton, 2013). The research project, therefore, aimed to address the educational question of 'how do we better prepare our teachers for their vital child protection roles?' Foundational to the project was the goal of making a positive difference for families and children at risk of, or experiencing, the social injustice of child abuse and neglect.

Locating Social Justice Responsibilities in Higher Education

Child abuse and neglect is a complex societal issue that crosses many physical and moral borders and prevents human flourishing. There is wholehearted agreement that physical, sexual, verbal, emotional and spiritual abuse is a social justice issue that detrimentally affects children and families, locally, nationally and internationally (Bone & Fenton, 2015; Abused Child Trust, 2014; Australian Institute of Health & Welfare, 2017; International Society for Prevention of Child Abuse and Neglect, 2014; Pinheiro, 2006). This would seem reason enough to conclude that the role and standing of teachers in maintaining child safety in Australia is a timely issue of great public concern. Case (Chapter 8), however, encourages us to dig deeper into the history and context of our work and warns us to move beyond a purely ideological focus in our work – to ask the important question – 'What is the relationship between the university and the world that surrounds it?'

The Australian Institute of Health and Welfare (AIHW, 2017) states that the most recent figures for Australia indicate that during 2015–16, there were 225,487 Australian children suspected of being harmed or at risk of harm from abuse and/or neglect. Within these figures, over 30,000 cases of substantiated child abuse or neglect are identified annually in CSU's footprint of New South Wales. There is a national framework for child protection (Council of Australian Governments, 2009), though each state and territory has separate definitions and statutory responsibilities for child protection. Reports of abuse and neglect are often 'missed', and formal notifications of abuse are deemed to be the 'tip of the iceberg' (Sedlak, 2001). Regardless, one in thirty-three children receive formal child protection services in Australia, meaning the likelihood of graduate teachers at our university encountering a child at risk in their career is undeniable. Of additional concern, the Royal Commission into Institutional Responses to Child Abuse (Commonwealth Government of Australia, 2017) recently revealed further grave and extended suffering of victims of child abuse in educational systems. Although educators are mandated to report abuse and protect children (Australian Institute of Family Studies [AIFS], 2016), the commission reported that, paradoxically, many of the perpetrators of such abuse were educators in positions of power (Commonwealth Government of Australia, 2016).

Case again urges us to look even further though – to consider closely 'the misery that is also part of the colonial legacy and to avoid the comforts of an ideological blanket'. This, states Case, is 'the important analytical work to be done if we are to make any progress in really alleviating the injustices of the past'. For example, in Australia's child protection figures, '12,903 Aboriginal and Torres Strait Islander children were the subject of a substantiation,' and these children are almost seven times more likely to be the subject of substantiated reports than non-Indigenous children (AIHW, 2017). This is consistent with poor Indigenous health outcomes across multiple indicators compared to the non-Indigenous population in Australia. The reasons for this are complex and intrinsically connected to past government policies and the legacy of colonization:

> Poverty, assimilation policies, intergenerational trauma and discrimination and forced child removals have all contributed to the over-representation of Aboriginal and Torres Strait Islander children in care, as have cultural differences in childrearing practices and family structure. (Human Rights and Equal Opportunity Commission [HREOC], 1997; SNAICC, 2016; Titterton, 2017 as cited in AIFS, 2019)

Since 2006, the Close the Gap Campaign (Australian Human Rights Commission, 2018) has enlisted Australia's peak Indigenous and non-Indigenous health bodies to seek to improve health and life expectation equality for Australia's Aboriginal and Torres Strait Islander peoples. While progress has been made in some areas, such as infant mortality rates – child protection remains a 'wicked issue' (Trowler, 2012).

Strengths approaches, emanating from the United States (Saleebey, 2009), have been found to assist social workers to prepare for complex social justice issues such as child protection, family violence and drug and alcohol addiction. Strengths approaches are often described as methods for supporting individuals, families, groups, organizations and communities (O'Neil, 2005; Scott & O'Neil, 2003). In an Australian version of the approach, McCashen (2005) describes the strengths approach as a collaborative and solutions-based 'philosophy for working with people to bring about change … [that] acknowledges and addresses power imbalances between people working in human services' (p. v). The approach involves exploring issues with stakeholders, identifying strengths and resources to assist with developing strategies for solutions to issues. Although the successful application of this approach in the social services field is evident (St. Lukes Anglicare, 2016), the approach has not been widely used in educational contexts and is not a common focus in Australian teacher education courses (Education Services Australia, 2011).

In higher education, increased preparation for child protection in teacher education programmes has been recommended for well over three decades (Baginsky, 2003; Levin, 1983; Watts, 1997). Despite this, little has changed in the format of teaching preparation for child safety in this time. A medical, deficits-based reporting model has been the standard format for decades (Arnold & Maoi-Taddeo, 2007). Both practising and student teachers continue to report feeling underprepared and lacking confidence in their child protection roles (Laskey, 2005; Singh, 2005). Yet, educators, in contact with children on an extended and regular basis, are ideally placed for implementing protection strategies and making a difference in child well-being (Briggs & Hawkins, 1997; MacIntyre & Carr, 2000). I have found that pre-service teachers fully understood child abuse as a most important factor influencing young children's ability to thrive. However, they also expressed that they feel most underprepared in their higher education courses to take action in child protection (Fenton, 2013).

Strengths-Based Model of Child Protection

Within the higher education context outlined above, the aim of the university project was to develop and evaluate a strengths-based model of child protection preparation within a teacher education degree. This aim implicitly recognized the inherent responsibility of a university in preparing students for social justice issues that they are likely to encounter in their future practice. In this case, an interactive child protection website was designed and embedded into an initial teacher education course at the university. The site was organized as a resource repository (not an assessable subject site) which students can access throughout their three- to four-year degree course. The research participants had access to the pilot site, and the final site will be accessible to students from their first enrolment through to graduation in their teaching course.

The site contained digital media training resources, including videos, discussion boards, links to child protection organizations' websites, newly developed learning modules and interactive, real-life, scenario-based simulations. Videos included interviews with practising teachers, principals, social workers and child protection professionals. The learning modules contained content from traditional mandatory reporting workshops (such as indicators of abuse and neglect and processes for reporting suspected cases) but additional factors were incorporated. Students examined their 'duty of care', for example, and obligations under the United Nations Rights of the Child (Alston & Brennan, 1991). Statistics were presented and then dissected so that participants had a fuller understanding of both the occurrence of different abuse categories and the increased risks for different groups of children. For example, the possible reasons for the over-representation of Indigenous children in child protection figures were critically examined.

The interactive scenarios were designed to guide and support students to work through complex child abuse situations and protection decisions that they are likely to encounter in their careers as teachers. Participants were encouraged to examine the contextual and cultural factors influencing the scenarios. For instance, students received an audio visual scenario through the site (a possible physical abuse situation with a young child) and were given the role of the early childhood teacher. Students were posed decision-making questions from the scenario, were prompted to make choices about responses to the situation and were then given guidance from child protection specialists, dependant on their choices as they worked through the situation.

Through a module and resources on the site the participants were also explicitly introduced to a strengths approach (McCashen, 2005; Glicken, 2004; Saleebey, 2009). For example, they are guided that the strengths approach is based upon principles of 'respect, self-determination, empowerment, social justice and the sharing of power' (McCashen, 2005, p. 2). In essence the students were introduced to a philosophy for working with people to bring about change, requiring positive attitudes about dignity, capacities, rights, uniqueness and commonalities (McCashen, 2005, p. 2). A core principle of the approach is working from values, beliefs and actions that share 'power-with', rather than exerting 'power-over' others (McCashen, 2005, p. 19).

Participants were given integrated opportunities to practice using the approach as well as opportunities for deep reflexivity, in an aim to increase student awareness and confidence in child protection. In the site design, for instance,

Table 11.1 The Column Approach

Issue	Vision	Strengths	Resources	Plan
What is happening? What have you observed or been told? Category of abuse or protection need	What do you want to be happening instead? What will be different when the issues are addressed?	What strengths do you (child or family) have that might be helpful? What do you do well?	Who else might be able to help? What other skills, organizations or resources might be useful?	What steps can be taken? Strengths and resources used? Who will do what? When? How? By when?

Source: Adapted from The Strengths Approach (p. 48), by McCashen, 2005, Bendigo: Innovative Resources. Copyright 2005 by the St. Lukes Innovative Resources. Reprinted with permission.

the interactive scenario appeared after completing a strengths approach learning module. Participants were introduced to a five-step guide for implementing a strengths approach to child protection – known as the Column Approach – as shown in Table 11.1.

Method

A case study model (Yin, 2009) was used for the close-up research to describe and evaluate stakeholder (pre-service teachers') engagement with a pilot site. Ethics approval was granted from the University Ethics Committee (protocol 2016/023) to allow student teachers to give feedback on the pilot site and resources. Care was taken to ensure that participants had access to counselling services should the sensitive nature of the child protection materials cause distress, and they were made aware that involvement in the research was not linked with their course marks.

The research participants were a small group of (forty) Bachelor of Education (birth to five) teacher education students who gave voluntary consent to access the site for one week and give responses to the site organization and resources. The participants were all completing their studies part-time by distance education while they worked in early childhood education and care services. They included a mix of mature students and recent school-leavers. Participants ranged from students who were just beginning their course to those who were ready to graduate. Only two of the participants identified as male, which is representative of the female dominated enrolments for this course overall.

Student responses were gathered (pre and post to their access of the pilot site), using a brief online survey (Survey Monkey) comprising of ten questions. Further in-depth email interviews (EViews, Fenton, 2013) were also used for gathering additional qualitative data. This collection technique, termed an EView, is a strengths-based email letter containing prompts to individual research participants inviting them to share perspectives on key research terms. Each email letter was personalized (typed in an informal conversational style) and was different for each research participant but guided by a standard structure asking participants to give feedback on the project.

EViews contain personalized comments and variations depending on the previous interactions with participants – in this case – through either the site discussion board or the participant's previous survey responses. This method of data collection aimed to capture the context and individual circumstances of the participants involved to give a more nuanced findings. Case argues that 'researchers need to be able to build explanatory accounts which draw on close-up data, but in analysis are able to locate it carefully in its historical and social context'. While this qualitative data technique aimed to capture important 'student voices' in this research, it was important to also acknowledge the risk of 'epistemic fallacy' (Archer, 2007) when interpreting the context-specific data for wider audiences.

Additional quantitative descriptive statistics were gained using a Blackboard Learning Analytics computer program that gathered data about student access and engagement to the site resources. The statistics indicated which sections and tools of the pilot site were activated and the duration and frequency of usage. Analysis of the participants' responses is applied to identify the particular elements of site that might contribute most to enhanced confidence in child protection. Thematic analysis (Aronson, 1994) was applied to all participant data collected in order to sieve the combined data for meaning and clues and to be attuned to solutions and different stakeholder perspectives as they emerge (Denzin & Lincoln, 2005; Patton, 2002).

Results

Survey and EView responses from the participants prior to accessing the child protection site revealed different individual perspectives on child protection. Many of the student responses indicated a lack of confidence and some reflected on their own personal experiences. All responses indicated the need for more teacher preparation in this area of practice. Typical general responses at this stage were the following:

> I realise it is a serious issue and needs to be addressed. Circumstances surrounding possible abuse or neglect can be confronting and make me feel like I shouldn't overstep boundaries, however I know it is for the child's benefit and that is what helps me to feel confident and follow my suspicions and addressing any potential abuse/neglect issue. (Participant 27, 2016)

> In theory I feel confident however, when it comes to a real life situation I feel that confidence would decrease. (Participant 29, 2016)

> After 30 years of working in the early Childhood sector I have had to address cases of child abuse and neglect several times. It's never easy but knowing its helping a child makes it easier. (Participant 12, 2016)

> I've never had first-hand experience with addresses issues of this magnitude and so only have my prior knowledge and research on which I can draw. (Participant 32, 2016)

Survey and EView responses from participants following the site access overall expressed an increase in perceived confidence, and all responses demonstrated a commitment to action in child protection responsibilities. For instance, typical general responses at this stage included

> I'm clear on my legal obligations moral and ethical obligations. The information on neglect was also very helpful and I feel much more confident with regard to this aspect of child protection having visited the site, worked through the workshop and completed the scenario questions. (Participant 14, 2016)
>
> Every time as a pre-service or qualified teacher we come into contact with reminders about child protection we become more equipped to handle a situation we may find ourselves in. (Participant 4, 2016)
>
> I found this an easy to use site. This approach was much easier to understand and follow than previous training I have done. (Participant 1, 2016)
>
> I was very interested and excited to find new ideas there about the concerns and resolutions for issues like these [child abuse and protection] within early childhood. (Participant 3, 2016)

Blackboard Learning Analytic figures revealed many linear 'hits' from participants when initially accessing all sections of the pilot site. A wave-like usage pattern was recorded – with access dropping away after initial heavy exploring of different sections. The interactive scenario was rated as the most useful section in the site, with 80 per cent of participants rating this tool as 'extremely useful'. Participants accessed this section of the site most frequently and participants engaged for extended blocks of time (fifteen to thirty minutes): 'I liked the scenario section the most as it helped to test our knowledge and gain confidence in our role' (Participant 34, 2016). Many participants returned to the scenario and the strengths approach module on multiple occasions: 'I particularly like using the strengths approach and the five column suggestion. It works well for me to think through a problem this way, plus it breaks it up into manageable chunks' (Participant 6, 2016).

Links to discussion boards, resources and child protection organizations through the site were also heavily utilized. All participants downloaded a Column Approach template, for example. The resources section showed a cluster pattern of usage of multiple hits with short periods of access. This section was accessed most frequently for short periods (two to five minutes) and demonstrates a pattern of use, expressed by one participant as 'easy to dip in and out – to find what you might need to help with a particular child or category of abuse quickly – download – or just to find out where to get help with reporting' (Participant 18, 2016). Participants contributed to the online discussion forums frequently, contributing multiple postings (more than in average subject forums).

Discussion and Early Findings

The responses prior to accessing the site confirmed that the pre-service teachers understood the complexity and significant ethical duty for teachers in child protection, as identified in the literature. For many participants their responses at this stage focused on previous experiences and expressions of lack of confidence in child protection as potential teachers. All participants affirmed the need for more preparation and tools to assist in protecting children, and they perceived existing teacher preparation as lacking in this area.

Interest in the pilot site was evident from the participants' initial responses. They appeared to welcome and value the opportunity to explore the site and were evaluating the potential of the site to assist teachers more broadly: 'It would be valuable if this site could be made available to the wider sector. Free quality resources such as this are much needed and would assist in minimising the amount of misinformation and misunderstanding among early childhood practitioners' (Participant 20). The qualitative responses indicated that the positive framing of the opportunities for child protection, as well as clear links to support and multiple resource/organizations available to assist teachers in their child protection roles, were appreciated by the pre-service teachers. The participants commented on abuse and neglect statistics and the urgent need to make a difference in protecting children and preventing child abuse. Case (Chapter 8) argues that our work needs to cover such 'powerful ideas' and that 'we do well to produce graduates who are critical and dissatisfied with the societies in which they find themselves'. The participants in the study expressed discontent with the 'unacceptable' (Participant 18) high numbers of children experiencing child abuse and neglect and discussed how as future teachers they should be advocates for children's rights and influential in preventing child abuse and in assisting children in need of protection.

The first rush of heavy access to the site may have been due to the compressed nature of the pilot site and is possibly the main reason for intensified early activity followed by a 'drop away'. This wave pattern could be mirrored in the final site 'roll out', however, and if so it will be important to give students 'cues to nudge' and encourage further access and return usage of the site throughout the duration of their course. Particular sections of the site showed clusters of use – the resources section, for example. This cluster indicates the participants accessed this section quickly to find out what resources were available and often saved the web links for future use. The scenario section was most accessed and for extended periods of time. When answering the early childhood (physical abuse) scenario questions, all participants were able to identify strengths and give practical resources to assist with developing strategies for the child and parent in that particular scenario. In essence, participants used a strengths approach and found clear solutions to a complex issue (Hodges & Clifton, 2004).

The results overall suggested that the use of Learning Analytics paired with analysis of the participant qualitative comments were a useful way of monitoring engagement with the online resources. Learning analytics provided additional 'measurement, collection, analysis and reporting' of the ways that the participants navigated and used the online site 'for purposes of understanding and optimising learning and the environments in which it occurs' (as cited in Long & Siemens, 2011, p. 34). General responses to the pilot site confirmed that participants accessed all sections of the site and found the interactive elements of the site engaging in comparison to the 'one off departmental presentation' (Participant 28, 2016) typically offered. Participants' comments seemed to support the intentional design elements that Biggs and Tang (2007) describe as vital to rich teaching and learning contexts in higher education. These features include a motivational context, formative feedback and reflective practice (p. 92). Participant 8 reflected that while initially she was unsure of a teacher's role in reporting child abuse, after engaging in the interactive scenario the need for teachers to be involved with child protection was clear – 'It is definitely something that I am now very passionate about.'

Positive student engagement (Hoskins, 2012; Kahn, 2014; Leach & Zepke, 2011) to the site and resources appeared to be a key element in the early responses of the participants, encouragingly evident in both the 'numbers and words' (McArthur, Chapter 1). Engagement was evident from the Learning Analytics gathered for each site section and across the range of responses from participants regardless of age or gender. For example, one participant stated, 'This is so useful. I am a pre-service teacher although I am in my 30th year of working with children and their families with Family Day Care' (Participant 12, 2016) while another commented, 'I am a new student this is my first session and as a male it is reassuring to have this information as I worry about stories of teachers being wrongly accused of child abuse' (Participant 11, 2016). However, student engagement is a complex, multifaceted construct (Axelson & Flick, 2010; Kahu, 2014; Zepke, 2014), and further analysis will be required to identify if particular elements of this project in higher education contribute to enhanced preparation for child protection. The participants' interest in child protection at the very least, however, appears to point towards agreeance with Case's proposition in Chapter 8 that 'we cannot evade our own role in generating new knowledge to broaden our understanding of contemporary problems'.

Responses to the project support earlier research that found strengths approaches (McCashen, 2005) contributed to increased awareness and confidence in child protection education (Fenton, 2013). Participants described the strengths approach as a 'practical process' (Participant 6, 2016) and a 'positive way of dealing with possible abuse' (Participant 11, 2016) with steps that were 'easy to follow and implement in practice' (Participant 34, 2016). The learning module on the strengths approach appeared to allow students to explore abuse definitions and protection issues from different stakeholder perspectives (this section often experienced multiple return 'visits'): 'A strengths approach really works well for me. I like to break things down … appeals to me visually as a learner (Participant 29, 2016).'

The *actualization* of a strengths approach to child protection preparation in the project was a complex feat, involving both theory and practice elements in the design process and a need 'to breach these separations' (McArthur, Chapter 1). Case (Chapter 8) examines how ideal definitions of social justice centred on fairness are often of 'limited utility when faced with real world contexts [such as child protection], where ideals are seldom attained but the necessity for moral judgements is important'. To this extent, although traditional child protection workshops include definitions of child abuse and the mandatory reporting (social justice) requirements for teachers, they do not typically include features that examine the complex moral judgements required in authentic child abuse cases. They do not reveal to students, for example, how child protection cases might happen in practice and how they might be able to make a positive impact with their actions as teachers. In this regard, findings suggest that the interactive scenario tool was the most useful tool for all of the participants. Qualitative feedback suggests that they found the scenario (and accompanying guiding responses) both engaging and challenging as it offered 'a real life situation' for which participants felt they needed preparation. Participants indicated they (typically) felt more prepared for the 'type of situation if it ever happened to a child in my class' (Participant 7, 2016). A student (about to graduate) commented:

> Child protection was barely touched when I started my teaching degree. I actually don't remember much at all. It's a HUGE part of teaching and sometimes teachers are the very first point of call for getting some of these kids the help that they need. They have the rapport with the kiddies and sometimes they feel safe enough to disclose to them what's going on at home. Teachers need to know what to do and how to go about it including what to say to the children to ensure that they have an obligation to tell and that the child won't be in trouble. This type of preparation is so important.

For the next stage of the project, the pilot site will be refined based on the student feedback and a revised site and resources offered to all teacher education students (approximately 8,000) at the university (Charles Sturt University, 2016). An important implication that arose from the pilot study was the recognition that when locating social justice issues in higher education contexts, there is a need to continually reflect and refine programmes according to stakeholders' experiences and evaluations to ensure that content is contextualized and relevant for each offering.

Conclusion

Through the articulation of a current child protection research project, this chapter examined how we might 'forward the notion of social justice into our engagements with higher education' (Case, Chapter 8). If, as Case suggests, we start with a conception of human flourishing of social justice, then it has been argued that HEIs, and teacher preparation programmes in particular, have clear social justice responsibilities for child protection. Early findings seem to suggest that the strengths-based interactive child protection site tools not only were engaging, practical and informative for the participants but also may assist in raising their child protection confidence. Participants reported an increase in knowledge and understanding of their important child protection roles as future teachers as a result of using the pilot site. 'The content of this approach is really powerful – from power over to power with. Intrinsic motivation is just so, so (well …) powerful for everyone' (Participant 29, 2016). When Case states that 'human flourishing feels so close to an intrinsic understanding of the purposes of education', the imperative to actualize this statement remains. For this case study, it is the explicit conclusion to continue preparing teachers to enable children to thrive.

References

Abused Child Trust [ACT for Kids]. (2014). *What Is Child Abuse and Neglect?* Retrieved from http://www.actforkids.com.au/what-is-child-abuse-and-neglect.html.

Alston, P., & Brennan, G. (Eds.). (1991). *The UN Children's Convention and Australia.* Canberra: Human Rights and Equal Opportunity Commission, ANU Centre for International and Public Law & Australian Council of Social Service.

Archer, M. S. (2007). Realism and the problem of agency. *Journal of Critical Realism*, 5(1), 11–20.

Arnold, L., & Maio-Taddeo, C. (2007). *Professionals Protecting Children: Child Protection and Teacher Education in Australia* [Monograph]. Adelaide, SA: Australian Centre for Child Protection.

Aronson, J. (1994). A pragmatic view of thematic analysis. *The Qualitative Report*, 2(1). Retrieved from http://www.nova.edu/ssss/QR/BackIssues/QR2-1/aronson.html.

Australian Human Rights Commission. (2018). *Close the Gap: Indigenous Health Campaign.* Retrieved from https://www.humanrights.gov.au/our-work/aboriginal-and-torres-strait-islander-social-justice/projects/close-gap-indigenous-health.

Australian Institute of Family Studies. (2016). *National Framework for Protecting Australia's Children 2009–2020.* Retrieved from https://www.dss.gov.au/our-responsibilities/families-and-children/publications-articles/protecting-children-is-everyones-business.

Australian Institute of Family Studies. (2019). *Child Protection and Aboriginal and Torres Strait Islander Children.* Retrieved from https://aifs.gov.au/cfca/publications/child-protection-and-aboriginal-and-torres-strait-islander-children.

Australian Institute of Health and Welfare. (2017). *Child Protection Australia 2015–16.* Child Welfare Series No. 66 Cat. No. CWS 60). Retrieved from http://www.aihw.gov.au.

Axelson, R., & Flick, A. (2010). Defining student engagement. *Change: The Magazine of Higher Learning*, 43(1), 38–43.

Badat, S. (2009). The role of higher education in society: Valuing higher education. *Paper Presented at the HERS-SA Academy 2009*, Cape Town.

Baginsky, M. (2003). Newly qualified teachers and child protection: A survey of their views, training and experiences. *Child Abuse Review*, 12(2), 119–127. doi: 10.1002/car.783.

Biggs, J., & Tang, C. (2007). *Teaching for Quality Learning at University* (3rd ed.). Maidenhead, UK: Open University Press.

Bone, J., & Fenton, A. (2015). Spirituality and child protection: A strengths based approach. *International Journal of Children's Spirituality*, 20(2), 86–99. doi:

10.1080/1364436X.2015.1030594. Retrieved from http://www.tandfonline.com/doi/abs/10.1080/1364436X.2015.1030594.

Briggs, F., & Hawkins, R. (1997). *Child Protection: A Guide for Teachers and Child Care Professionals*. Crows Nest, NSW: Allen & Unwin.

Castells, M. (2001). Universities as Dynamic Systems of Contradictory Functions. In J. Muller, N. Cloete, & S. Badat (Eds.), *Challenges of Globalisation: South African Debates with Manuel Castells*, 206–223. Cape Town: Maskew Miller Longman.

Charles Sturt University. (2016). *Statistical Profile*. Retrieved from https://www.csu.edu.au/__data/assets/pdf_file/0018/1413504/CSU-Statistical-Profile-2014.pdf.

Charles Sturt University. (2018a). *History*. Retrieved from http://www.csu.edu.au/about/history.

Charles Sturt University. (2018b). *Yindyamarra Winhanganha*. Retrieved from https://www.csu.edu.au/csu-live/csu-live/category/my-csu-experience/videos/yindyamarra-winhanganha.

Commonwealth Government of Australia. (2017). *Royal Commission into Institutional Responses to Child Sexual Abuse*. Retrieved from http://www.childabuseroyalcommission.gov.au/.

Council of Australian Governments. (2009). *National Framework For Protecting Australia's Children 2009–2020*. Retrieved from https://www.dss.gov.au/our-responsibilities/families-and-children/publications-articles/protecting-children-is-everyones-business.

Denzin, N., & Lincoln, Y. (2005). Introduction: The discipline and practice of qualitative research. In N. K. Denzin & Y. S. Lincoln (Eds.), *The SAGE Handbook of Qualitative Research* (3rd ed.), 1–32. Thousand Oaks, CA: Sage.

Education Services Australia. (2011). *Accreditation of Initial Teacher Education Programs in Australia: Standards and Procedures*. Carlton, VIC: Ministerial Council for Education, Early Childhood Development and Youth Affairs.

Fenton, A. (2013). *A Strengths Approach to Child Protection Education* (Doctoral dissertation). Retrieved from http://eprints.jcu.edu.au/24044/.

Glicken, M. D. (2004). *Using the Strengths Perspective*. Boston, MA: Pearson.

Hodges, T., & Clifton, D. O. (2004). Strengths-based development in practice. In P. Linley & S. Joseph (Eds.), *International Handbook of Positive Psychology in Practice: From Research to Application*, 256–269. Hoboken, NY: Wiley.

Hoskins, B. (2012). Connections, engagement and presence. *The Journal of Continuing Higher Education, 60*, 51–53.

Human Rights and Equal Opportunity Commission [HREOC]. (1997). Bringing them Home Report, *1997*. Retrieved from https://www.humanrights.gov.au/publications/bringing-them-home-report-1997.

International Society for Prevention of Child Abuse and Neglect [ISPCAN]. (2014). *World Perspectives on Child Abuse* (11th ed.). Carol Stream, IL: Author. Retrieved from http://c.ymcdn.com/sites/www.ispcan.org/resource/resmgr/World_Perspectives/WP14_Exec_Summary_FINAL.pdf.

Kahn, P. (2014), Theorising student engagement in higher education. *British Educational Research Journal, 40*, 1005–1018. doi: 10.1002/berj.3121.

Kahu, E. (2014). Increasing the emotional engagement of first year mature-aged distance students: Interest and belonging. *The International Journal of the First Year in Higher Education, 5*(2), 45–55. doi: 10.5204/intjfyhe.v5i2.231.

Laskey, L. (2005). Making a difference in child protection: Towards an effective education for teachers. In M. Cooper (Ed.), *Teacher Education: Local and Global; Australian Teacher Education Association 33rd Annual Conference, Surfers Paradise,* Conference Proceedings, 265–273. Retrieved from http://atea.edu.au/index.php?option=com_jdownloads&Itemi d=132&task=viewcategory&catid=58.

Leach, L., & Zepke, N. (2011). Engaging students in learning: A review of a conceptual organiser. *Higher Education Research & Development, 30*(2), 193–204. Retrieved fromhttp://www.tandfonline.com/doi/abs/10.1080/07294360.2010.509761.

Levin, P. G. (1983). Teacher perceptions, attitudes and reporting of child abuse and neglect. *Child Welfare, 62*(1), 14–20.

Long, P., & Siemens, G. (2011). Penetrating the fog: Analytics in Higher Education. *Educause Review*, September/October 2011, 31–40. Retrieved from http://www.educause.edu/ero/article/penetrating-fog-analytics-learning-and-education.

MacIntyre, D., & Carr, A. (2000). Prevention of child sexual abuse: Implications of programme evaluation research. *Child Abuse Review, 9*(3), 183–199. doi: 10.1002/1099-0852(200005/06) 9:3<183::AID-CAR595>3.0.CO;2-I.

McCashen, W. (2005). *The Strengths Approach*. Bendigo, VIC: St. Luke's Innovative Resources.

Nussbaum, M. C. (2003). Capabilities as fundamental entitlements: Sen and social justice. *Feminist Economics, 9*(2–3), 33–59.

O'Neil, D. (2005). How can a strengths approach increase safety in a child protection context? *Children Australia, 30*(4), 28–32.

Patton, M. (2002). *Qualitative Research and Evaluation Methods* (3rd ed.). London, UK: Sage.

Pinheiro, P. S. (2006). *Violence Against Children: United Nations Secretary General's Study.* Retrieved from the United Nations Children's fund website http://www.unicef.org/violence study/reports.html.

Saleebey, D. (Ed.). (2009). *The Strengths Perspective in Social Work Practice* (5th ed.). Boston, MA: Pearson.

Scott, D. A., & O'Neil, D. (2003). *Beyond Child Rescue Developing Family-Centred Practice at St. Luke's*. Bendigo, VIC: Solutions Press.

Sedlak, A. J. (2001). *A History of the National Incidence Study of Child Abuse and Neglect.* Retrieved from the Children's Bureau, Administration of Children and Families, U.S. Department of Health and Human Services website. https://www.nis4.org/NIS_History.pdf.

Sen, A. (2011). *The Idea of Justice*. Cambridge, MA: Harvard University Press.

Singh, P. (2005). Risk management vs risk retreat. In P.L. Jeffrey (Ed.), *AARE 2004 Conference Papers* [Conference of the Australian Association for Research in Education, 28 November–2 December 2004], pp. 1–17. AARE.

SNAICC. (2016). *The Family Matters Report: Measuring Trends to Turn the Tide on Aboriginal and Torres Strait Islander Child Safety and Removal.* Melbourne: SNAICC, the University of Melbourne, Save the Children Australia and the Centre for Evidence and Implementation.

St. Lukes Anglicare. (2016). *Innovative Resources.* Retrieved from http://innovativeresources.org/.

Titterton, A. (2017). Indigenous access to family law in Australia and caring for Indigenous children. *University of New South Wales Law Journal, 40*(1), 146–185.

Todd, S. (2015). Facing Uncertainty in Education: Beyond the Harmonies of Eurovision Education. Paper Presented at the European Conference on Education Research (ECER), Budapest.

Trowler, P. (2012). Wicked issues in situating theory in close-up research. *Higher Education Research and Development, 31*(3), 273–284. doi: 10.1080/07294360.2011.631515.

Walker, M., & Unterhalter, E. (2007). *Amartya Sen's Capability Approach and Social Justice in Education.* London: Palgrave Macmillan.

Watts, V. (1997). *Responding to Child Abuse: A Handbook for Teachers.* Rockhampton, Australia: Central Queensland University Press.

Yin, R. K. (2009). *Case Study Research: Design and Methods* (4th ed.). Los Angeles: Sage.

Zepke, N. (2014). Student engagement research in higher education: Questioning an academic orthodoxy. *Teaching in Higher Education, 19*(6), 697–708. doi: 10.1080/13562517.2014.901956.

Part Four

Conclusions

12

What Is Different about Socially Just Higher Education Research?

Paul Ashwin and Jan McArthur

Introduction

In this chapter we explore what this book offers as a whole to our understanding of social justice and higher education. We consider how the book provides different ways of locating social justice in higher education by returning to the question of what we do differently when social justice is at the fore of what and how we research higher education. In the introductory chapter we explored this in terms of the spatial, temporal, philosophical and methodological senses of locating social justice. Now we want to highlight the educational role of universities, specifically their role in providing students with access to powerful knowledge that transforms their sense of who they are, what they can achieve in the world and what they can contribute to society. Put simply, there is a fundamental connection between knowledge and social justice (McArthur, 2013, 2018). Bringing knowledge to the fore, we use Bernstein's (2000) notion of the 'pedagogic device' to structure the rest of the chapter. We explore what the book as a whole tells us about how issues of social justice are implicated in: the production of knowledge through higher education research; the transformation of knowledge into higher education curricula; and who students become through their engagement with the knowledge that higher education offers. We conclude by considering what is highlighted by locating social justice in higher education research.

Ways of Locating Social Justice in Higher Education Research

The central question underpinning this book is 'how do we engage with higher education research differently if we are committed to social justice?' As Jan

McArthur explores in Chapter 1, theories play a key role in shaping how we understand and engage with our research and the social world. This highlights the need to consider the role of theories in our research practices. One way of understanding the role of theories within this is to see theories as simplifying the social world so that we can engage with it (Ashwin, 2009). This suggests that taking a social justice perspective involves attending to simplifications that foreground issues of fairness, equity, human flourishing and living fulfilling lives. Each of these issues are, however, complex and so this simplification is necessarily nuanced. We should not confuse this process with homogenization or harmonization, but instead understand it as a process of making sense of messy realities. On the one hand, simplification is necessary otherwise it is impossible to make sense of the multiple and intersecting lived realities that make up the social world. On the other hand, we do not want to lose the richness of that social world and its necessarily messy character (Law, 2004). Indeed, coping with messy reality is a social justice issue as it embraces the stories and experiences of those most affected by injustices, such as people who are marginalized, displaced or ignored (McArthur, 2012).

A number of such theoretical perspectives are explored in this book, including those informed by the work of Basil Bernstein (2000), Miranda Fricker (2007), and Martha Nussbaum (2006) and Amartya Sen (2010). These perspectives are brought together and articulated in different ways in the chapters but what unites these approaches is a concern with the educational role of higher education. All of the chapters focus on the ways in which higher education provides people and society with knowledge that increases their understanding of the world and can help to improve their experiences of that world. However, they do this in different ways. For example, some chapters focus more on higher education's role in knowledge production and dissemination (e.g. Teresa Carvalho in Chapter 2 and Sharon McCulloch and Karin Tusting in Chapter 4), while other chapters, such as those by Carolin Kreber (Chapter 6), Langutani Masehela (Chapter 10) and Angela Fenton (Chapter 11), examine the role of higher education in developing professionals that can make a positive contribution to their societies.

Thinking about the educational role of higher education highlights the importance of knowledge in our research and teaching practices. Knowledge is key because it is what we seek to generate when we research, it is what we seek to give students access to when we teach and it is what students seek to gain through their engagement with higher education. These different ways of thinking about knowledge are usefully captured in Bernstein's (1990, 2000) notion of the 'pedagogic device', which brings together the contexts in which knowledge is produced through research, transformed into the curriculum of particular courses, and then changed again as students develop their own understanding of that knowledge. In separating the ways in which knowledge is produced, transformed into curriculum and understood by students, the pedagogic device can be seen as highlighting three different forms of knowledge: knowledge-as-research, knowledge-as-curriculum and knowledge-as-student-understanding (Ashwin, 2014). What Bernstein makes clear is that the transformation of knowledge as it moves from each of these contexts is not simply based on the logic of knowledge itself. Rather, these transformations are the sites of struggle in which different voices seek to impose particular versions of legitimate knowledge, curriculum and student understanding.

If we use Bernstein's (2000) perspective to consider the contribution of the chapters in this book then it also highlights questions about our expertise as researchers and educators. This is because we need to be clear about how we can draw on our understanding of powerful knowledge in order to address issues of social justice. Without such knowledge and expertise, it is not clear why we should be in a position to research and teach about these issues.

It is important to note that, as with any approach, examining the contributions to the book in terms of different forms of knowledge highlights some aspects of the relationships between higher education and social justice but also puts other important aspects of these relationships into the background. In particular, focusing on knowledge in this way gives less of a sense of the identities of academics and students in educational interactions. This means that in the following discussions the intersections of age, disabilities, ethnicities, genders, sexualities and social class are less prominent than in many examinations of higher education and social justice. However, this should not be taken as an indication that they are not significant, and as we identified in the introductory chapter, there is important work being undertaken on these intersections (e.g. see Waller, Ingram & Ward, 2017; Arday & Mizra, 2018; Howell, 2018; Ngabaza, Shefer & Clowes, 2018; Walker, 2018). Working to ensure that individuals' backgrounds and identities do not define their life chances is central to any approach to social justice, and the following examination of the location of social justice in different forms of knowledge is predicated on this commitment.

Locating Social Justice in Knowledge-as-Research

Focusing on knowledge-as-research draws our attention to the production of knowledge through our research endeavours. If we are motivated by issues of social justice in our research, we need to have a sense of why our research is important and powerful in relation to these issues. The chapters in this book highlight three aspects of this. First, there is the question of how we attend to issues of social justice in our research processes and ensure that our practices as researchers are aligned with the commitment to social justice that we pursue in our research. Second, there is the issue of the kinds of knowledge that we seek to produce through our research and how we try to ensure that this has the power to contribute meaningfully to issues of social justice. Third, there is the issue of the ways in which we ensure that this power is realized through the impact of our research.

In relation to the process of research, both Teresa Carvalho (Chapter 2) and Vicki Trowler (Chapter 3) highlight the need to consider carefully why we are conducting research. Carvalho highlights the need to consider whether we are focused on developing knowledge for its own sake or to meet external demands of policy makers. A key element of this is to consider who will have access to the knowledge that is produced through this research. Trowler argues that we need to pay close attention to how we position the participants who are the focus of our research: Are we conducting research on these participants or conducting research for these participants? Trowler highlights a tension for researchers in working with marginalized groups: Is the primary intention to contribute to existing bodies of knowledge or is it to respect the categories of those who are researched? Jan McArthur (Chapter 1) offers one way of addressing this tension by considering the dichotomy of student and teacher. McArthur argues that rather than denying the differences between students and teachers, we need to respect their different perspectives and consider how they interrelate. The same can be argued in relation to the knowledge of the participants and existing bodies of knowledge about their practices, so that, rather than denying the different accounts offered by the body of knowledge and the experiences of participants, we explore the relations between these different accounts. One approach to this is offered in two of the elements of Monica McLean's account of powerful knowledge (Chapter 5): the production of knowledge that respects participants' everyday experiences but also enables them to see beyond them and the acceptance that such knowledge should always be open to challenge. This involves the tireless questioning that McArthur highlights in Chapter 1.

The importance of such tireless questioning in our research is also highlighted in Vicki Trowler's response to Jan McArthur's call to move beyond dichotomies. Trowler argues that we need to interrogate the relations between insider and outsider perspectives. Trowler suggests that whether one is an insider or an outsider is a matter of degree. As a result, we need to develop reflexive strategies that can help us to understand what we have in common and how we differ from the participants in our research. This involves both recognizing how we are complicit in the inequalities we are researching and recognizing how our research can contribute to addressing these inequalities. Carolin Kreber (Chapter 6) explores how involving students in research with their communities offers one way of doing this. However, in Chapter 2, Teresa Carvalho's examination of the impact of NPM on higher education's contribution to social justice highlights that this reflexivity needs to go beyond our engagement in particular research projects. We also need to consider how we contribute to the maintenance or challenging of inequalities in our fields of research and universities. This can be seen to relate to the distribution rules that structure knowledge-as-research, which Bernstein (1990, p. 183) argues govern 'who can transmit what to whom, and under what conditions'. This highlights the need to consider who is able to gain access to the field of research, what can be legitimately taught in universities, who can be seen as a legitimate teacher and student and what are the conditions in which these practices take place (see Ashwin, 2009 for a fuller discussion of the distribution rules in relation to higher education).

In terms of the kinds of knowledge that we seek to produce through our research, the chapters in this book emphasize that this knowledge needs to provide reliable explanations, offer a close-up view of higher education on a large scale, be sensitive to the differences between higher education contexts and be based on a sustained engagement with particular higher education contexts. In Chapter 5, Monica McLean highlights the ways in which powerful knowledge needs to provide reliable explanations and offer the basis for changing the way things are. In order to support such change, in Chapter 8, Jenni Case argues that close-up research needs to take account of the way in which public discourse is dominated by university rankings. To have credibility in these contexts, we need to consider how to develop convincing explanatory accounts that are based on large-scale close-up research and are carefully situated in their historical and social context. The chapters by Case, McArthur, McLean and Trowler, all highlight that these accounts need be based on a long-term engagement with our research sites rather than simply based on a snapshot of participants' experiences. We need to demonstrate a long-term commitment to engaging with our participants' ways of understanding the world as this is essential to the success of socially just research, both in terms of the process and outcomes of the research.

These views of the kinds of knowledge that we need to produce can be seen to relate to Jan McArthur's argument in Chapter 1 that we need to avoid the dichotomization of quantitative and qualitative research and instead build explanatory accounts that incorporate both kinds of evidence. As a whole, this involves an argument that goes way beyond the standard call for mixed methods studies. It is an argument for a collective effort to bring related studies together that are based on different perspectives of the people and practices that we are researching, both near and far, in order to develop multi-perspectival explanations of issues of social justice in higher education. This is what we referred to in the introductory chapter as genuinely collaborative research in the broadest sense. In this view of knowledge, our understanding comes from our engagement with the body of knowledge as a whole rather than from simply engaging with single projects or sets of projects. It also emphasizes our responsibility as researchers to be stewards of these bodies of knowledge and find ways of making them accessible to all of those who will benefit from engaging with them.

This latter point highlights the need to think carefully about how we make the outcomes of our research accessible to a range of audiences. In Chapter 8, Jenni Case emphasizes the need to translate our explanatory accounts for a range of audiences, while Sharon McCulloch and Karin Tusting (Chapter 4) highlight the challenges of this process in their exploration of how academics have responded to the impact agenda. They show how the links to social justice are more obvious in relation to some research but that there is also a tension between whether academics engage with the impact agenda in order to contribute to social justice or to advance their individual careers. This again highlights the importance of how we understand the nature of the knowledge we produce in our research. The individual career perspective highlights this knowledge and its impact as the property of the individual researcher whereas, as we discussed earlier, it is the collective body of knowledge, rather than the individual project or research, that is important in developing a powerful understanding of the world that contributes to greater social justice. Our research builds on the research of others and is based on the insights of those involved in our research, which means that we need to recognize knowledge and its impact as collective. This recognition of the collective production of knowledge again highlights the importance of, as Teresa Carvalho does in Chapter 2, considering the working conditions of those who work in our fields and how these are structured in terms of age, disabilities, ethnicities, genders, sexualities and social class.

However, as Jan McArthur emphasizes in Chapter 1, we should not get drawn into the dichotomy of simply dismissing the individual contribution to the development of knowledge. We should appreciate the individual contribution but recognize that this is in the service of the wider body of collective knowledge rather than knowledge simply being produced in order to serve the career of the individual. We also need to consider, in line with Teresa Carvalho's examination of the impact of NPM in Chapter 2, how our engagement in practices that seek to emphasize the individual contribution rather than the collective achievement impacts on others in our research fields and institutions.

Overall, locating social justice in knowledge-as-research involves thinking about how we position ourselves as researchers in relation to our research participants, to the collective body of knowledge that our research contributes to, to other contributors to that body of knowledge and to those who can benefit from the insights that are gained through this research.

Locating Social Justice in Knowledge-as-Curriculum

Focusing on how knowledge is recontextualized into curriculum highlights the ways in which we use our knowledge of higher education and social justice in order to develop programmes of education for students. Two aspects of this process are highlighted by the chapters in this book: how a consideration of social justice issues might inform the overall aims of curricula and how it might inform the forms of curricula that we develop.

In Chapter 5, Monica McLean examines how epistemic justice can be served through the education that universities offer. She argues that while universities can be complicit in reproducing social inequalities this does not always need to be the case and that universities have an important role in opening up the space for change. Such spaces will not be perfect, but it is important to do what we can to put a break on injustice. To do this we need to have a clear sense of what constitutes epistemic injustice and the ways in which we might challenge and reduce it. From this we can gain a sense that the overall aims of a socially just curriculum need to be developed in response to a clear sense of the nature of injustice.

In terms of particular approaches to curriculum, the chapters in the book offer a variety of approaches. Carolin Kreber (Chapter 6) offers a whole curriculum approach in which a programme is designed to inform the development of a professional identity that ensures a commitment to public service. Kreber focuses on four capabilities (a) senses, imagination, and thought, (b) practical reasoning, (c) affiliation and (d) having control over one's political (and material) environment, which she argues are essential for individuals to participate in decision-making or public deliberation on issues affecting their lives. In Chapter 10, Langutani Masehela also takes a capability approach and has a similar concern with developing students who can be part of a critical citizenry. She explores this concern through her reimagining of a curriculum of a PGCE at a historically disadvantaged South African university. Masehela highlights the importance that such curricula take seriously the situation that students will face when they graduate. She also highlights the need to link such curricula to government policies.

In Chapter 9, Sarah Goodier, Carren Duffy and Suki Goodman examine another way of developing a commitment to social justice in graduates in the form of global citizenship modules rather than the development of a whole programme. Through their systematic literature review they find that there is a lack of consensus around what these modules involve although there is a broad sense that it is about students developing a sense of identity and solidarity as members of the global community. More than this, students need to be able to participate actively in positively developing this community. While Goodier, Duffy and Goodman focus on whether these modules are credit bearing or not, another important question is how they relate to students' wider programmes of study. Regardless of whether students receive academic credit, if these modules are not meaningfully integrated into students' overall programme of study, then they will not have the opportunity to refine and develop their commitment to social justice in a sustained way that allows them to understand it from different perspectives and gain a rich sense of what this commitment involves. Without this sustained engagement, it seems unlikely that students will develop a lasting commitment to social justice that continues to evolve through their lives after graduation.

In Chapter 11, Angela Fenton gives a sense of how such modules can be integrated in her exploration of how an interactive child protection website was designed and embedded into an initial teacher education course. The students had access to this site throughout their degree programme and were introduced to the strengths approach to child protection that informed the resources. An interesting question arising from this chapter is whether and how the students continue to draw on the strengths approach after graduation when they are teaching. This concern with how students engage with the world beyond higher education informs Natasa Lackovic's consideration of how students can be prepared to critically engage with social media in Chapter 7. She highlights the ways in which students seem to see social media as primarily a medium for entertainment and business rather than as a something through which they can critically engage with the world. She argues that social media are perceived as supporting both liberating social change (techno optimism) and social control and oppression (techno pessimism). In order to counteract techno pessimism, Lackovic argues students should be supported to create or curate alternative social media platforms.

It is important to note that these different approaches can be seen to contradict each other. For example, the whole programme approach that Carolin Kreber advocates in Chapter 6 can be seen as being in opposition to the single module approach of global citizenship programmes explored by Sarah Goodier, Carren Duffy and Suki Goodman in Chapter 9. By contrast, Natasa Lackovic's argument for helping students to develop critical approaches to social media in Chapter 7 could be seen to align to a number of the other approaches to knowledge-as-curriculum. However, in line with Jan McArthur's argument in Chapter 1, to dichotomize approaches in this way would be a mistake. What is needed is a variety of approaches to developing knowledge-as-curriculum that respond to the particular forms of knowledge, the particular students who will engage with them, and who those students will become based on their engagement with that knowledge (Ashwin, 2019). As Monica McLean argues in Chapter 5, drawing on Sen (2010), no approach will be perfect and we need to engage with the messy educational reality of attempting to give students access to powerful knowledge.

Locating social justice in knowledge-as-curriculum has highlighted a number of different approaches to offering students access to powerful knowledge that can change their understanding of the world and themselves. None of these approaches offer recipes that can be simply transferred to any context. Rather, they offer a possibility that can be considered by higher education teachers, based on their understanding of the particular knowledge they are seeking to offer students access to, the particular students they are teaching, and the particular context in which they are teaching. In arguing for an approach that takes account of who students are and who they expect to become in the future, we need to be aware of the potential of reinforcing a separation between elite and mass higher education. The worst of all possible worlds would be a situation in which privileged students study traditional curricula in elite institutions while disadvantaged students engage with socially just curricula in mass institutions. However, our awareness of this danger should not stop us from being bold in developing alternative ways of bringing students into relation with powerful knowledge.

Locating Social Justice in Knowledge-as-Student-Understanding

A focus on locating social justice in knowledge-as-student-understanding highlights who students will become through their engagement with powerful knowledge. The chapters in this book give a sense of a variety of futures that attending to social justice in higher education research can help to support.

The chapters by Carolin Kreber (Chapter 6) Sarah Goodier, Carren Duffy and Suki Goodman (Chapter 9), Langutani Masehela (Chapter 10) and Angela Fenton (Chapter 11), all give a clear sense of the kinds of graduates and professionals they are trying to develop through educational interventions. They hold in common a commitment to developing graduates who are aware of social challenges and seek to engage with finding positive ways of addressing these challenges. For example, Kreber emphasizes how rather than learning that professions simply do things *for* the public, students learn that society may be served better if professionals do things *with* the public.

In Chapter 8, Jenni Case argues that we need to consider the relationship between universities and the world. Part of this requires us to think carefully about how graduates are supported in their engagement with the world. Is there an ongoing role for universities in supporting graduates to make a positive contribution to society? Or should universities support their graduates in making links to other institutions and networks that can provide this kind of help? This concern resonates with Natasa Lackovic highlighting of the importance of scaffolding students' engagement with social media so that they can engage with it in a critical and thoughtful way in Chapter 7.

In her discussion of dichotomies in Chapter 1, Jan McArthur highlights the ways in which the future is shaped by the past and present but is not predetermined by them and is open to change. She emphasizes that we need to be open to a range of relationships between the past, present and future. We can use this to think about students' relationship with higher education. We need to be open to different ways of understanding who our students are when they enter higher education, of understanding how they are engaging with their education and of understanding who they will become through their education. What we need to be clear about is what expertise we have to support them in this process, as our educational relationship with our students is founded on this expertise. Being clear about our expertise is also an essential element of challenging the deprofessionalization of higher education that Teresa Carvalho highlights in Chapter 2 because this expertise is central to the claim that being an academic is a professional vocation.

Considering how social justice is located in relation to knowledge-as-student-understanding highlights the need to consider who students will become through their engagement in higher education and how universities can support them beyond their time as students. This is not a fixed view; it is something that we need to discuss with our students and has to be open to change.

Conclusion

In conclusion we can consider the overarching question of this book: What do we do differently when social justice is at the fore of what and how we research?

We have seen how this involves being aware of how we generate knowledge, the relationships we have with our research participants, the kinds of knowledge we are interested in, how we generate curriculum with an awareness of who our students are and who they will become, and a constant questioning of how we are supporting them to develop these futures.

Four elements come to the fore in considering what we do differently when our research has social justice at its core. First that in foregrounding questions of social justice, we tend to focus on higher education as an educational enterprise rather than as an enterprise that is focused on prestige and esteem. This highlights the ways in which higher education can offer access to knowledge that can transform people's sense of themselves and the world rather than the ways in which the gaining of a degree can increase people's social standing.

Second, we need to encourage a variety of visions of what social justice can look like. There is no single vision of what social justice looks like at all times and in all situations. Instead, by seeing the world from a variety of perspectives, it can allow us to see what different perspectives offer us in particular situations. We cannot combine all of these perspectives into a single view but rather need to examine which view is the most promising in a particular setting. This examination needs to involve a range of voices and perspectives rather than being offered by a single researcher or educator. This needs to involve the perspectives of those we research and teach with and to be undertaken in dialogue with the collective body of knowledge about our areas of research. Socially just research, in the twin senses of being about social justice and for social justice, cannot occur in isolation and is instead inherently collaborative. In this dialogue and collaboration, it is important that we recognize our expertise as researchers and educators, the expertise our research participants and students bring with them, and the similarities and differences between these different forms of expertise.

Third, a key responsibility of higher education that is motivated by considerations of social justice is to consider how things could be other than how they are now. There is, therefore, a fundamental commitment to change. In doing so, as Sen (2010) argues, we must not be seduced by the perfection of utopian thinking but rather seek to make an imperfect situation a little better. This involves recognizing that any progress or setbacks are temporary and the key is to continue to work for social justice however bleak or promising the situation appears to be.

Fourth, we need to think beyond our individual positions as researchers and teachers and consider how we contribute to the structuring of our research fields and institutions. In what ways do our day-to-day practices contribute to the maintenance and challenging of inequalities in the disciplines and universities in which we work? This is again a matter of how we can contribute to improving things rather than expecting perfection, but it is still an important element of our commitment to social justice. There is something particularly hollow about an academic career forged on researching issues of social justice, which does not also seek to address inequalities within the institutions in which this work is undertaken.

The chapters in this book all seek to make a contribution to developing a socially just higher education that is built on a multi-perspectival view of the potential of higher education to change society for the better. However, more work is needed so that we have a greater number of ways of locating social justice in higher education research. The strength of social justice research, and higher education itself, lies in its nurturing and embrace of diverse perspectives, mediated by our shared humanity.

References

Arday, J., & Mirza, H. (Eds.). (2018). *Dismantling Race in Higher Education: Racism, Whiteness and Decolonising the Academy*. Cham, Switzerland: Palgrave Macmillan.

Ashwin, P. (2009). *Analysing Teaching-Learning Interactions in Higher Education: Accounting for Structure and Agency*. London: Continuum.

Ashwin, P. (2014). Knowledge, curriculum and student understanding. *Higher Education, 67*, 123–126.

Ashwin, P. (2019). *Transforming University Teaching*. Centre for Global Higher Education Working Paper 49. Retrieved from https://www.researchcghe.org/perch/resources/publications/to-publish-wp49.pdf.

Bernstein, B. (1990). *The Structuring of Pedagogic Discourse: Volume IV Class, Codes and Control*. London: Routledge.

Bernstein, B. (2000). *Pedagogy, Symbolic Control and Identity: Theory, Research and Critique* (Rev. edn). Oxford: Rowman and Littlefield Publishers.

Fricker, M. (2007). *Epistemic Injustice*. Oxford: Oxford University Press.

Howell, C. (2018). Participation of Students with Disabilities in South African Higher Education: Contesting the Uncontested. In N. Singal, P. Lynch, & S. T. Johansson (Eds.), *Education and Disability in the Global South: New Perspectives from Africa and Asia*, 127–143. London: Bloomsbury.

Law, J. (2004). *After Method: Mess in Social Science Research*. Abingdon: Routledge.

McArthur, J. (2012). Virtuous mess and wicked clarity: Struggle in Higher Education Research. *Higher Education Research and Development*, 31(3), 419–430.

McArthur, J. (2013). *Rethinking Knowledge in Higher Education: Adorno and Social Justice*. London: Bloomsbury.

McArthur, J. (2018). When Thought Gets Left Alone: Thinking, Recognition and Social Justice. In S. S. E. Bengsten & R. Barnett (Eds.), *The Thinking University*, 155–166. Cham: Springer.

Ngabaza, S., Shefer, T., & Clowes, L. (2018). Students' narratives on gender and sexuality in the project of social justice and belonging in higher education. *South African Journal of Higher Education*, 32(3), 139–153.

Nussbaum, M. C. (2006). *Frontiers of Justice*. Cambridge, MA: Belknap Press of Harvard University Press.

Sen, A. (2010). *The Idea of Justice*. London: Penguin.

Walker, M. (2018). Aspirations and equality in higher education: Gender in a South African University. *Cambridge Journal of Education*, 48(1), 123–139.

Waller, R., Ingram, N., & Ward, M. R. (Eds.). (2017). *Higher Education and Social Inequalities: University Admissions, Experiences, and Outcomes*. London: Routledge.

Index

Abbas, Andrea   12
academics, social justice research
    impact on
    as collective/individual
        responsibility   79–80
    discipline with perspectives on   77–80
    higher education, marketized
        perspective on   71–2
    knowledge-power relations   129
    marketization affects   72–3
    national and institutional priorities
        80–3
    perspectives on social justice   70–84
    and social justice, relationship between
        74
    study   74–5
    understandings of   75–7
action   107, 112–13
    Arendt's theory of   16, 110–11
    in critical media literacy   129–30
    disciplinary   65
    informed   129
    natality   111
    plurality   111
Adorno, Theodor   5, 7, 14–15, 27
    approach to dialecticism   30–2
    critical theory   5, 27–35
    negative dialectics   31
    non-identity, understanding of   30–1, 32
Alexander, Neville   144–5
'Arab spring'   131
Arendt, Hannah   16, 110
Aristotle   5
Ashwin, Paul   12, 201–12
Atkins, L.   4, 13
Australia   184–6
Australian Institute of Health and Welfare
    (AIHW)   184

Badat, Saleem   141
Balkans   122

Ball, Stephen   39, 44, 95
Bantu Education system   140
Barnes, Caroline   97
Bathmaker, Ann-Marie   95
Berk, R.   124
Bernstein, B.   18, 92–8, 201–3, 205
Bhorat, H.   170
Biesta, G. J.   112
Biggs, J.   192
Blackboard Learning Analytics, computer
    program   189, 190
Booth, Charles   26, 29
Bourdieu, Pierre   94
Brennan, J.   41
Bringing Knowledge Back In (Young)   93
Brookfield, S.   29, 31
Burbules, N. C.   124
Butler, J.   53

capabilities   90, 106–7, 115
    in decision-making/public
        deliberation   106–7
    expansion as professional ideal
        107–9
Carvalho, Teresa   9, 10, 12, 15, 204, 205, 207
Case, Jennifer   7, 13, 16, 96, 169, 182, 183, 191, 205, 210
Castells, Manuel   142–3, 144, 146
child abuse/neglect   184–6, 187, 189–93
child protection, strengths-based
    model of   186–94
    findings on   191–4
    method   188–9
    perspectives on   189–91
    principle   187
    strengths approach   187–8
Chubb, J.   78, 79
citizens
    critical   169–80
    global   9, 151–65

civic media literacies   119–20, 124, 125, 129–30
Clegg, S.   55–6, 59
cognitive skills   175
communication   64
community-based research, for social justice through higher education   9–10, 14, 16, 104–15
    capabilities in   90, 106–9
    democracy in   109–11
    freedom in   110–11
    as pedagogy   111–13
    reconsiderations   113–15
    students involvement in   107
conceptual knowledge   93
consumer culture   33
contextual knowledge   93
Council of Higher Education (CHE)   56, 173–4
critical theory   5
    dialecticism   27–32
    implications of   32–5
Crozier, Gill   95
CUDOS (Community, Universalism, Disinterestedness, Originality, Scepticism)   43
cultural capitals   62, 94
curriculum, higher education   169–80
    current reality   172–4
    Nussbaum and capability approach   171–2
    NYDA and   178–9
        and higher education   179
        strategic plan of   178–9
    PGCE   174–5
    re-enacting   177–9
    reimagining   176–7
    rethinking of   174–5
'cyber utopia' tools of oppression. *See* Twitter

David, Miriam   95
democracy   109–11
democratic professionalism   109–11, 112, 113
dialecticism   14–15
    Adorno's approach to   30–2
    critical theory   27–32
    in higher education research   24–5, 27–32

implications of critical theory   32–5
    individual *vs.* social   34–5
    optimism *vs.* pessimism   31
    student identity, approach to   33–5
dichotomization   25–6
    higher education research   24–7
    of student identity   33–5
    theory *vs.* practice   26–7
digital whiteness   122
disciplinary knowledge   94
Diversity   97
Duckworth, V.   4, 13
Duffy, Carren   9, 17, 208, 210
Dzur, A.   109–11, 113

educational attainment   174
Educational Research for Social Justice (Griffiths)   4
education researchers, task for   145–8
Ellsworth, E.   125
entrepreneurial skills   175, 176
entrepreneurship   175
epistemic in/justice   89–90
    defining of   90–2
    research   94–9
    university, epistemological access at   92–4
Epistemic Injustice: Power and the Ethics of Knowing (Fricker)   90
epistemological access   92–4
epistemology   5–6, 7, 14
    endogenous   64
    exogenous   64
EViews   188–9, 190

Fenton, Angela   7, 17, 208, 210
fields   16, 94–6
Fish, Stanley   141, 143
Foucault, M.   66
Frankfurt School   14, 24, 28
Fraser, Nancy   6, 32, 53
freedom   110–11
Fricker, Miranda   5, 7, 14, 16, 90–101
Fuchs, Christian   120, 121, 131

Gajjala, R.   122
Gerwels, Jakes   144–5
Gibbons, M.   43
Giroux, H. A.   124

global citizenship programmes 9, 17, 151–65, 208
  definitions 155–6
  literature, review of 153
  map 159
  methods 153–4
  overview of 154–7
  rise of 157
  South Africa's universities and 152–4, 157–64
  in United Kingdom 157
  in United States 157
Goga, S. 170
Goodier, Sarah 9, 17, 208, 210
Goodman, Suki 9, 17, 208, 210
graduates
  PGCE 178
  socially responsible 151–65, 170
Greyling, L. 172, 174
Griffiths, Morwenna 2, 3, 4, 6, 14

Habermas, J. 97
habitus 16, 94–6
Hammersley, M. 14
Hart, Caroline 95
Hartley, M. 110
hermeneutic injustice 91
hermeneutic justice 91–2
hidden transcripts 57, 64
Higher Education Close-Up (HECU) conference 3
higher education institutions (HEIs) 39–40
  subordinate estate of 61–3
Higher Education Quality Committee (HEQC) 173–4
higher education research
  community-based research 9–10, 14, 16, 104–15
  curriculum 169–80
  dialecticism in 24–5, 27–35
  dichotomies 24–7, 33–5
  economic relevance of 42
  education researchers, task for 145–8
  as ethnography 55–7
  injustice within 13, 89–101
  internationalization of 11
  managerialism in 38–41, 46–8
  marketization perspective on 71–3
  near and far perspectives in 23–36

neoliberal management practices in 10
new public management in 15, 38–47
politicization of 14
purpose of 72
sector, differentiation within 12
sector and economic interests, relationship between 11–12
social change and 141–3
social justice in 1–14, 24, 38, 40–1, 53–67
  impacts 70–84, 140–8
  insider and outsider perspectives 53–67
  locating, ways of 201–3
  responsibilities 184–6
  social media as critical media pedagogy tools in 123–6
  within society 9
  in South African context 12–13, 96, 140–1, 144–6, 157–64, 169–79
  student-teacher relationship 15, 34
  understanding of 201–12
universities
  functions of 141–3
  postcolonial, contestation in 144–5
  working-class students and 95
Hobson, J. 122
Honneth, Axel 5, 7
Horkheimer, M. 28, 31, 32
human flourishing, of social justice 140, 182–4, 194

ideology 142–3
Illich, Ivan 110
impact 71–2, 74, 76
information and communication technologies (ICTs) 151
informed consent 59
injustices of higher education 89–90. See also social injustice
insider-outsider research 9
insiders 55–7
  case studies 57–63
  dimensions
    location 56
    subjectivities 56
    time 56
  hidden transcripts and 57
invisible pedagogies 98

James, David   95–6
Jenkins, Celia   97
Jones, D.   63, 66, 67
Jorgenson, S.   157

Kelley, Robin   141, 143
knowledge
   conceptual   93
   contextual   93
   social justice in   43, 202–3
      as curriculum   207–9
      as research   203–7
      as student understanding   210–11
      transformation of   203
Kolsaker, A.   44
Kreber, Carolin   9, 13, 16, 205, 207–8, 210

Lackovic, Natasa   6, 9, 16, 208–9
Lawrence, Stephen   91
learning analytics   189, 190, 192
Legitimation Code Theory   96
life skills   175, 176–7
Luckett, Kathy   96

The Making of the English Working Class (Thompson)   26
Mamdani, Mahmood   144
managerialism, in higher education   38–41, 46–8
Maruyama, M.   64–5, 66–7
Masehela, Langutani   9, 17, 208, 210
Maton, Karl   96
McArthur, Jan   6–10, 14–17, 23–36, 40, 53, 61, 120, 121, 132, 201–12
McCashen, W.   185
McCulloch, Sharon   9, 15, 206
McLean, Monica   12, 13, 14, 16, 79, 106, 204, 205, 207
media   124
middle-class children   93, 95
Mihailidis, Paul   120, 121, 124, 125, 127–9, 132
mis/recognition   54–5, 96
modernity, dual potential of   97
morality   81
Morrow, Wally   92
Muller, J.   99, 100
Murthy, D.   120
Musselin, C.   45–6

Naidoo, R.   41
National Youth Development Agency (NYDA)   170, 179–80
Nattrass, Nicoli   147
Ndebele, Njabulo   147
neoliberalism   15, 39
new public management (NPM)   15
   on academic professions   46–7
   entrepreneurialism and   39, 42–3
   on gender composition of academic career   46
   in higher education   38–47
   managerialism and   39–41
   neoliberalism and   39
   reforms in higher education   39–40
non-identity, understanding of   30–1, 32
non-neutrality, in social media   121–3
non-traditional higher education students, case study   57–9, 64–5
   comparative study on   60–1
Nussbaum, M. C.   5, 6, 7, 106–9, 122, 169–70
   and capability approach   5, 6, 16, 106–9, 114–15, 171–2, 180
   framework of cultivating humanity   170, 178
   on universality   106

Oancea, A.   79
oppression, cyber utopia tools of. *See* Twitter
othering
   conduit for   127–30
   in social media   122–3

paleonomy   32
Pauw, K.   170
pedagogic device   202–3
pedagogy   91, 96–8
   community-based research as   111–13
   higher education   105
   professional programmes as   114
   public   112
   and research, integration of   105
   with social media   123–6
   tools in higher education   119–33
people-as-knowers   90–1
Pereira, Mar   47
personal skills   175

PLACE (Proprietary, Local, Authoritarian, Commissioned and Expert)   43
political liberalism   107
polyocular anthropology   64
postgraduate certificate in education (PGCE)   174-6
power   15
Presley, Woodrow   115
procedural knowledge   93
profession   105, 107-9, 112
professional action   110
professional programmes   105, 112-13, 115
professional responsibility   106
propositional knowledge   93
public pedagogy   112
public transcripts   64

qualification, education   170, 176
'Quality and Inequality in First Degrees' project   93, 97

Ramaphosa, Cyril   177-8
Rashomon effect   56
Rawls, J.   5, 7, 140
Reay, D.   173
Reay, Diane   95
recontextualization   93-4
Reed, M.   78, 79
REF, UK's   70-1, 73, 74, 79, 80-2
reflexivity   63
The Republic (Plato)   5
Research Excellence Framework (REF)   15
Research Methods for Social Justice and Equity in Education (Atkins & Duckworth)   4
Richter, G.   32
Robinson, Tom   90
Rowland, S.   33
Rowntree, Seebhom   26, 29

Sagan, Carl   23
Saltmarsh, J.   110
San Code of Research Ethics   54, 59
Save the World on Your Own Time (Fish)   141
Sayer, Andrew   146
Schattle, H.   151, 157, 163
Schultze, U.   55

Scott, J. C.   57, 64
self-awareness   14
Sen, Amartya   5, 6, 7, 72, 97, 106, 140, 212
Shalem, Y.   96
Shay, Suellen   96
Shultz, L.   157
Slonimsky, L.   96
social change   141-3
social inequalities   41, 105, 121, 207
social injustice
    of distribution   53-5
    locating moments of   11-13
    mis/recognition   54-5
    recognition   23-4, 53-5
    and social media   121-6
social justice
    commitment to   4, 23-9, 32-3, 35-6
    epistemic   5-6, 7, 14
    in higher education research   1-14, 24, 38, 40-1
        community-based research   104-15
        impacts   70-84, 140-8
        insider and outsider perspectives   53-67
        locating, ways of   201-3
        responsibilities   184-6
    human flourishing of   140, 182-4, 194
    imperfect understanding of   7-8
    implications of   9
    knowledge and   201
    in knowledge-as-curriculum   207-9
    in knowledge-as-research   203-7
    in knowledge-as-student-understanding   210-11
    locating moments of   11-13, 16, 184-6
    locations of   8-11, 15
    meanings of   5-8
    methodological challenges of locating   13-14
    morality and   81
    outcomes-based understanding of   6-7
    pedagogies   16
    people, relationships between   7
    philosophical perspectives   5-8
    social contract approaches to   6-7
    in South Africa   8, 139, 140-1, 144-6
    understandings of   6, 201-12

in United Kingdom   16, 139–40, 157
in United States   16, 139–40, 157
social media   9, 16
  civic media literacy   129–30
  as conduit for othering   127–30
  as critical media pedagogy tools in
      higher education   123–6
  implications   130–2
  non-neutrality and othering in   121–3
  and social (in)justice   121–6
  as spectacle entertainment   127–30
  spectatorship   128
  for students   119–20
  Twitter   120, 126–30
Social Media: A Critical Introduction
      (Fuchs)   121
social responsibility   81
social skills   175
social trustee professionalism   109–11
South Africa
  exceptionalism   144
  global citizenship programmes
      152–4, 157–64
  higher education in   12–13, 17, 96,
      140–1, 144–6, 157–64, 169–79
  NYDA in   170
  post-independence context for higher
      education in   144–5
  social justice in   8, 139, 140–1, 144–6
  unemployment in   170, 177–8
  urban *vs.* rural   9
spectatorship   128
Spivak, Gayatri C.   62
Stevenson, J.   55–6, 59
student-teacher relationship   15, 34
subjectivities   17, 56, 57–9, 60
Suoranta, J.   125–6

Tang, C.   192
Teelken, C.   82
testimonial injustice   90–1
testimonial justice   91
A Theory of Justice (Rawls)   5
Thompson, E. P.   26
Todd, Sharon   145, 183
To Kill a Mocking Bird   90
Trowler, Vicki   2, 7, 9, 10, 13, 15, 183, 203
Tusting, Karin   9, 15, 206
Twitter   16, 64, 120, 121, 126–30
  as conduit for othering   127–30
  as spectacle entertainment   127–30

unemployment, in South Africa   170,
      177–8
United Kingdom
  global citizenship programmes in
      157
  social justice in   16, 139–40, 157
United States
  global citizenship programmes in
      157
  social justice in   16, 139–40, 157
universities   72–3
  curriculum for students   169–80
  education   89, 91, 95, 171, 172, 201
  education researchers, task for
      145–8
  epistemological access at   92–4
  functions of   141–3
  graduates   151–65
  postcolonial, contestation in   144–5
  professional programmes in   105,
      112–13, 115
  qualification   170
  rural-based   170
  social change and   141–3
  South African   141–2, 144–6
University of Cape Town (UCT)   144,
      147–8, 157, 160
University of Western Cape (UWC)
      144–5
Unterhalter, Elaine   140

Vadén, T.   125–6
Van Maanen, J.   53

Walker, Melanie   79, 106, 140, 172
Watkins, S.   122
WhatsApp groups   64
whiteness   122
Wilsdon, J.   82
women
  career, neoliberal management
      approaches to   9
  in teaching   46
working-class children   93, 95

Yimamu, N.   175
Young, Michael   93

Zajda, J.   41
Zhang, Y.   122
Ziman, J.   43